Prevention
Psychology

Prevention Psychology

ENHANCING PERSONAL AND SOCIAL WELL-BEING

JOHN L. ROMANO

AMERICAN PSYCHOLOGICAL ASSOCIATION
WASHINGTON, DC

Published by
American Psychological Association
750 First Street, NE
Washington, DC 20002
www.apa.org

To order
APA Order Department
P.O. Box 92984
Washington, DC 20090-2984
Tel: (800) 374-2721; Direct: (202) 336-5510
Fax: (202) 336-5502; TDD/TTY: (202) 336-6123
Online: www.apa.org/pubs/books
E-mail: order@apa.org

In the U.K., Europe, Africa, and the Middle East, copies may be ordered from
American Psychological Association
3 Henrietta Street
Covent Garden, London
WC2E 8LU England

Typeset in Goudy by Circle Graphics, Inc., Columbia, MD

Printer: Maple Press, York, PA
Cover Designer: Berg Design, Albany, NY

The opinions and statements published are the responsibility of the authors, and such opinions and statements do not necessarily represent the policies of the American Psychological Association.

Library of Congress Cataloging-in-Publication Data

Romano, John L.
  Prevention psychology : enhancing personal and social well-being / by John L. Romano.
    page cm
  Includes bibliographical references and index.
  ISBN 978-1-4338-1791-5 — ISBN 1-4338-1791-8 1. Stress (Psychology)—Prevention.
2. Developmental psychology. 3. School violence—Prevention. I. Title.
  RC455.4.S87R66 2014
  616.89'05—dc23
                    2014006057

British Library Cataloguing-in-Publication Data
A CIP record is available from the British Library.

Printed in the United States of America
First Edition

http://dx.doi.org/10.1037/14442-000

Dedicated to my children—Michelle, Christopher, and Jacqueline—and grandchildren—Elena, Danny, Joey, and Cecilia.

May their lives be enriched through innovations in prevention.

CONTENTS

Acknowledgments .... *ix*

Chapter 1.   Introduction 3

Chapter 2.   History of Prevention 11

Chapter 3.   Prevention Theories for Behavior Change 23

Chapter 4.   Protective Factors: Promoting Strengths
              and Building Positive Behaviors 47

Chapter 5.   Social Justice and Public Policy Advocacy 65

Chapter 6.   Prevention Applications in Educational Settings 83

Chapter 7.   Prevention Applications in Community
              and Medical Settings....................................... 107

Chapter 8.   Recommendations for Developing, Implementing,
              and Evaluating Prevention Interventions...................... 131

Chapter 9.   Prevention Ethics, Education, and Funding 143

Chapter 10.   Mapping an Agenda for the Future
               of Prevention Psychology 157

Appendix A: American Psychological Association Guidelines
               for Prevention in Psychology 161

Appendix B: Prevention Resources 163

References 171

Index 207

About the Author 221

ACKNOWLEDGMENTS

I am very grateful to many individuals who contributed to the development of this book, and I want to acknowledge their contributions. The APA Books publications staff and editors, including Ann Butler, Beth Hatch, Susan Reynolds, Nikki Seifert, and Ron Teeter, provided guidance, technical assistance, and support at different stages during the development and writing of this book. A draft of the book was reviewed by anonymous reviewers and I am grateful for the valuable feedback they provided. I also acknowledge Mary Hardiman, APA staff for the Committee on Professional Practice and Standards and the Board of Professional Affairs. Mary provided invaluable assistance to colleagues and myself who developed the APA "Guidelines for Prevention in Psychology," an important milestone in prevention psychology.

Professional colleagues and students helped shaped my views and vision for prevention. Specifically, my wonderful colleagues (too numerous to list here) in the Prevention Section of the Society of Counseling Psychology whose dedication and commitment to prevention are extraordinary. They provided motivation and encouragement for this book. At the University of Minnesota I am fortunate to interact with wonderful colleagues and students. Several students, most of whom have graduated and gone on to professional careers in counseling and psychology, contributed directly to parts of this book. They are Juliet Ross-Hatcher, Jian-Ming Hou, Hyun Kyung Lee, Ziqiu Li, Jason Netland, Arunya Tuicomepee, Erin VandenLangenberg, and KyuJin Yon. Dr. Tom Skovholt has been an invaluable colleague and friend at the University of Minnesota. He offered much guidance, support, and friendship throughout the development of this book.

My family has provided much joy and support. My siblings, Robert, a highly respected psychologist and educator in the Boston area, and my sister, Sister Geraldine, teacher, counselor, and spiritual adviser, gave invaluable support and encouragement not only for this project, but in many areas of my life. We were fortunate that our parents provided a solid foundation on which to build our lives. My partner, Mary Kay Metz, a clinical social worker, offered conversation and insight about prevention through the eyes of her profession; however, most importantly, gave unwavering support, encouragement, and love throughout the process of developing and writing this book. My adult children and grandchildren, to whom I dedicate this book, live nearby, and for them I am eternally grateful. They provide countless hours of support, fun, and distractions from the rigors and labor of academic writing.

Prevention Psychology

1

INTRODUCTION

Few would argue about the benefits of prevention. We all receive messages daily about the importance of a maintaining a healthy diet and body weight, getting enough sleep, practicing safe sex, avoiding the dangers of tobacco, and using alcohol responsibly, to list just a few. All of these efforts are made to ward off physical and psychological ills and to promote personal well-being by maintaining healthy lifestyles now and in the future. Some people will strictly adhere to prevention and health promotion practices, others will ignore them, and most will attempt to follow some of them with varying degrees of success.

Prevention science as a professional specialty has goals similar to those of individual, self-directed efforts to promote health. However, prevention science seeks to prevent psychological and physical ills and promote overall health and well-being through evidence-based practices at individual and systemic levels. Therefore, prevention is important because the professional specialty addresses health promotion at individual levels of intervention, as

DOI: 10.1037/14442-001
Prevention Psychology: Enhancing Personal and Social Well-Being, by J. L. Romano

well as through larger social levels of intervention to improve and strengthen health and well-being across society. Prevention is an interdisciplinary specialty that requires conceptual sophistication, research, and policy actions from multiple disciplines, including psychology, counseling, social work, education, health sciences, economics, and public affairs. Given the major advances in prevention in recent years, a major goal of this book is to present in one volume prevention as a specialty in psychology with applicability to other mental health professions.

The book is designed to close a gap in the education and training of students, psychologists, other mental health professionals, and those in other professions who desire increased knowledge and training in prevention. The book is a broad-based and resource-rich introduction to prevention, giving attention to interventions and research in different settings across the life span. The content is appropriate for advanced undergraduate and graduate students desiring an introduction to prevention history, theory, research, and applications, and also for professionals who have received little, if any, education and training in prevention.

PREVENTION PSYCHOLOGY DEFINED

Prevention psychology is a term introduced in this book to highlight the importance of prevention in psychology and other mental health disciplines. Unlike other specialty areas within psychology, such as abnormal psychology, which have more prominence, prevention psychology has received much less attention in the training and activities of psychologists and other mental health professionals. Also, unlike some other fields of study, prevention psychology emphasizes evidence-based practices that use psychological theory to advance health and well-being at individual and systemic levels. Using relevant data to inform policymakers, prevention psychology also advocates for policies that promote institutional and societal change to enhance the health and well-being of a population. Examples of policy changes may include funding for early childhood education, school-based alcohol and drug prevention programs, and laws that empower disenfranchised members of society.

Prevention psychology, in partnership with other disciplines and specialties, contributes to evidence-based interventions designed to prevent problems and to strengthen individual and community protections from personal and psychological distress. Therefore, prevention psychology offers theoretical perspectives and empirically based research that can support prevention interventions to keep schools, workplaces, and neighborhoods healthy.

PREVENTION DEFINED

Although the word *prevention* has a common meaning among laypersons, there has been much discussion and debate among professionals about its full meaning. For many years, Caplan's (1964) definition of *prevention* was cited almost exclusively by professionals, and it is still widely used today. Caplan delineated three types of prevention: primary, secondary, and tertiary prevention.

- *Primary prevention* refers to interventions designed to prevent problems from ever occurring across the population or within a subgroup or system. For example, comprehensive school-based programs delivered to the entire school to prevent school violence and bullying are considered primary prevention, as are school-based programs to prevent substance use among all youth. Recommendations that all infants receive a polio vaccine or all adults receive a yearly seasonal flu vaccination are other examples of primary prevention.
- *Secondary prevention* targets groups that are at risk for developing a problem. For example, recommending early mammograms for women with a family history of breast cancer or recommending suicide screenings for depressed adolescents are considered secondary prevention interventions. Head Start programs that provide pre- and early school education for low-income children who are identified to be at risk for poor school achievement are examples of secondary prevention programs.
- *Tertiary prevention* focuses on limiting the impact of a problem that has already occurred. Examples of tertiary prevention include Alcoholics Anonymous programs, exercise programs for people recovering from a heart attack, and support groups for women who have left their home due to domestic violence.

Although Caplan's definition of *prevention* provided an early and important framework for prevention in the mental health fields, Cowen (1983) argued that the tertiary component is more aligned with treatment rather than prevention. To address some of the controversy about Caplan's (1964) definition, Gordon (1987) offered three alternative prevention classifications: universal, selective, and indicated.

- In Gordon's classification, *universal prevention* refers to prevention interventions that offer value to an entire group or population, and thus they are similar to primary prevention interventions. For example, mass media messages that remind people to use seat belts are examples of universal prevention.

- *Selective prevention* refers to interventions that are most beneficial to individuals or subgroups that are at above-average risk for developing a disorder and that may even be experiencing a few symptoms. The Head Start program is an example of a selective prevention intervention. Another example is a summer academic curriculum for incoming college freshmen who did not meet traditional admission requirements. The enriched summer curriculum strengthens student academic skills to prevent poor grades or premature dropout.
- *Indicated prevention* interventions are for individuals or groups who are at high risk for an illness or problem behavior and who may already be showing some symptoms of a problem (National Research Council and Institute of Medicine, 2009). However, symptoms are at a subclinical level of a problem or disorder. An example of an indicated prevention intervention is one that addresses alcohol use for high school students who have been cited for underage drinking. Another example might be a support group for seniors who have recently lost their spouses or partners and are experiencing loneliness and symptoms of depression.

As the examples show, it may be difficult to distinguish between selective and indicated prevention; under Caplan's classification, selective and indicated would be considered secondary prevention. Although Conyne (2004) noted that the historical classifications of prevention may have lost their usefulness, the Institute of Medicine's Committee on Prevention of Mental Disorders (Mrazek & Haggerty, 1994) in its classic volume adopted Gordon's prevention framework. The committee considered only interventions that occur before the onset of a problem or illness as preventive. Thus, the Committee on Prevention of Mental Disorders did not consider tertiary prevention interventions to be within the prevention spectrum.

The Caplan (1964) and Gordon (1987) prevention classifications were originally proposed for the prevention of physical health disorders within a public health model and not the prevention of mental health and behavioral problems. Therefore, the classifications have limitations when applied to mental health and behavioral problems. For example, in mental health preventive work, primary and universal prevention (i.e., prevent a problem from ever occurring) have limitations, and are not realistic. For example, depression and anxiety may occur at different life stages, and mental health professionals would not presume to prevent them from ever occurring, especially in the same way as vaccines inoculate infants against disease. The traditional classifications are also problematic because in some settings and with some ages, it is difficult to determine who is at risk and would benefit most from secondary, selective, or indicated prevention interventions. Therefore, many school-based programs are often delivered to an entire grade level or school, although not all students are equally at risk for engaging in problem behaviors. Similarly, universal and primary prevention media messages to discourage people from engaging in unhealthy and risk behaviors are delivered to all, without consideration of risk levels. It is assumed that all will benefit from universal prevention messages, which may be true for some messages (e.g., "buckle up") but not others (e.g., "practice safe sex").

The historical definitions of prevention as discussed above have limitations. Therefore, to expand the definition and conceptualization of *prevention*, Romano and Hage (2000b) developed a five-part definition: (a) stop a problem from ever occurring (similar to primary and universal prevention); (b) delay the onset of an age-related problem (e.g., teen pregnancy) or intervene with those at risk for a problem (similar to secondary, selective, and indicated prevention); (c) reduce the impact of an existing problem (similar to tertiary prevention); (d) strengthen knowledge, attitudes, behaviors, and skills of individuals or groups to enhance protections against problems and disorders (e.g., adolescent safe-sex education to protect against sexually transmitted infections and unwanted pregnancy, health and wellness education programs for middle-age men and women to prevent health problems as they age); and (e) support and advocate for institutional, community, and government policies that promote physical and emotional health and well-being (e.g., endorsing legislation that prohibits cigarette smoking in public places, using relevant data about a prevention topic to inform decision makers about the policy's potential impact of the policy on a community, collaborating with community partners and government agencies to seek funding for a community program to prevent problems and promote physical and emotional health).

The definition of prevention has evolved since the conceptualizations of prevention were made popular by Caplan (1964) and Gordon (1987). Topics and perspectives that are included under the prevention umbrella have broadened (Conyne, 2004; Romano & Hage, 2000b). The National Research Council and the Institute of Medicine's (2009) Committee on the Prevention of Mental Disorders and Substance Abuse Among Children, Youth, and Young Adults defined *prevention interventions* as those that occur before the onset of a problem. The committee also addressed the importance of risk and protective factors in preventing or reducing problem behaviors. The volume of research about risks and protections in prevention work has increased tremendously since the earlier volume distributed by the Institute of Medicine's Committee on Prevention of Mental Disorders (Mrazek & Haggerty, 1994).

In addition, advocacy and social justice efforts to promote equality, empowerment, and opportunity are recognized as important prevention strategies to enhance lives and prevent disorders through systemic and institutional change (Albee, 1996, 2000; Kenny, Horne, Orpinas, & Reese, 2009a; Vera & Kenny, 2013). Therefore, in this volume, prevention is conceptualized broadly to include the prevention and reduction of problems and behaviors of individuals and groups by reducing variables that place them at risk for problems and by promoting variables that protect against problems. In addition, activities that promote systemic and institutional changes that enhance health and well-being are also considered and promoted as very important to an overall prevention strategy. Throughout the chapters of this book, examples addressing this conceptual definition of prevention are discussed.

PROMISE OF PREVENTION IN THE 21ST CENTURY

The history of prevention in the mental health professions as presented in the Chapter 2 of this volume shows how the specialty has advanced during the 20th and 21st centuries, highlighting major developments. Prevention in the mental health field has faced several barriers historically, including emphasis on remedial and crisis care interventions, lack of funding for prevention research and practice, limited education about prevention in graduate training programs, and the absence of requirements for prevention knowledge and supervised skills training in professional accreditation and license guidelines. However, as is summarized in succeeding chapters, the time is right for an increased and renewed emphasis on prevention research, applications, and training as called for by several scholars during this century (Albee, 2000; Conyne, 2004; Kenny et al., 2009a; Romano & Hage, 2000a).

It is fortunate that prevention psychology applications have increased in popularity in recent years. For example, the 2010 U.S. Patient Protection and Affordable Care Act provides for prevention services at different ages to promote health and well-being and prevent disease in several areas, including the prevention of depression, sexually transmitted infections, and interpersonal violence. In addition, the U.S. government's comprehensive National Prevention Strategy (National Prevention Council, 2011) addresses the importance of prevention across the life cycle with a holistic focus on the individual and systems across society (see Figure 1.1). Finally, the American Psychological Association (APA) approved in 2013 the first document of its kind, titled "Guidelines for Prevention in Psychology" (see Appendix A). These "Prevention Guidelines" were adapted from an earlier article on best practices in prevention (Hage et al., 2007).

Although there is recognition that problems can be prevented and protections strengthened, how best to do so will continue to be a challenge in the 21st century. Advances in neuroscience, genetics, and technological sophistication

CS223388-A

Figure 1.1. U.S. National Prevention Strategy: America's plan for better health and wellness. From *National Prevention Strategy,* by the National Prevention Council, U.S. Department of Health and Human Services, Office of the Surgeon General, 2011. Washington, DC: Author. In the public domain.

will significantly add to the repertoire of knowledge and skills available to prevention specialists as they develop prevention interventions across the life span.

THIS BOOK

This book presents an overview of prevention and practical guidance for those who wish to increase their knowledge and understanding of prevention, and design and implement prevention programs. The book summarizes prevention history, theories, and research important to the specialty. In addition, the chapters describe numerous examples of prevention applications in different settings and age groups. Also highlighted are prevention ethics, professional training, and funding challenges and opportunities. Although the book is intended to appeal primarily to mental health professionals and students-in-training, prevention is a multidisciplinary specialty, and therefore, the book should also appeal to professionals and students in other fields that contribute to the prevention specialty, including education, nursing, public health, and public policy.

Chapter 2 provides a historical context for prevention in the physical and behavioral sciences. Chapter 3 summarizes major behavioral change theories that have been prominently used to guide prevention interventions. Chapter 4 identifies protective factors to promote emotional health and well-being in prevention. Chapter 5 advocates for increased attention to policy initiatives that promote institutional and societal changes that enhance the health and well-being of the population. Such policies are often consistent with social justice issues related to empowerment of disenfranchised groups and reductions in educational and health disparities across the population. Chapters 6 and 7 present examples of prevention interventions in educational and community and medical settings. Chapter 8 provides practical recommendations for designing and implementing prevention programs. Chapter 9 discusses the professional issues of ethics, training, and funding as they relate to the science and practice of prevention. Finally, Chapter 10 considers future directions for prevention. Appendix A presents the American Psychological Association "Prevention Guidelines," and Appendix B provides an annotated list of resources for the prevention specialist.

2

HISTORY OF PREVENTION

Several authors have written detailed histories of the evolution of prevention as applied to the field of mental health during the 20th century (e.g., Conyne, 2013; Duncan, 1994; Mrazek & Haggerty, 1994; Romano & Hage, 2000b; Spaulding & Balch, 1983). Kenny and Romano (2009) even traced the concept of prevention back to antiquity and into the 21st century. Although I do not repeat such a detailed history here, I do highlight important prevention events in psychology and other mental health professions during the past 100 years, especially events and movements that were omitted in some earlier histories. As can be seen, social movements, political actions, and the development of the mental health professions all intersect across the history of prevention.

DOI: 10.1037/14442-002
Prevention Psychology: Enhancing Personal and Social Well-Being, by J. L. Romano
Copyright © 2015 by the American Psychological Association. All rights reserved.

THE EARLY 20TH CENTURY AND
MENTAL HEALTH PROMOTION

Most authors begin the modern history of the prevention of mental illness with the mental hygiene movement founded by Clifford Beers in the early 20th century. Yale educated, and with his own history of mental illness, Beers (1908) wrote his autobiography, *A Mind That Found Itself*, about his harrowing experiences as a patient in institutions for the mentally disturbed. In this classic work, Beers described the physical and emotional abuse that he and other patients experienced in several institutions for the insane, a term used at that time to describe mental illness. As a result of his classic autobiographical work, he and other social reformers formed the National Committee for Mental Hygiene (now called Mental Health America) in 1909. Long (1989) wrote a fascinating history of the mental hygiene and mental health movement in the United States. She described the first public meeting of the National Committee for Mental Hygiene held in New York City in 1910 on "Prevention of Insanity." About 100 attendees at this meeting of professionals and laypeople were concerned about the rapid increase of insanity in New York State and the drain on the state budget as a result of caring for those afflicted. Opinions expressed at the meeting about mental illness and how to prevent it are enlightening as they reflect thinking at the time, as well as ideas that continue to this day. Long selected passages from the proceedings of the meeting (State Charities Aid Association, 1910) to give a flavor of the participants' thinking: "The prevention of insanity . . . involved not only the prevention of the entrance of germs and poisonous substances into the body but also such matters as heredity and the control of complex social relations" (p. 9). Long noted that participants spoke of alcohol and drug addiction, syphilis, and the influence of fatigue and stress as some of the causal factors. Participants emphasized that stress and strain are often "due to improper environment, including housing, clothing, occupation, recreation, food, and habits of thought" (p. 9). Prevention was optimistically endorsed at the meeting by Dr. Stark, a noted Columbia University professor of neurology, who commented that with proper treatment and care, insanity could be prevented "if taken early enough in life . . . there is a chance of preventing 35% of cases of insanity" (p. 10).

In 1913, the first outpatient mental hygiene clinic was established in Connecticut. The interdisciplinary journal *Mental Hygiene*, whose early editorial boards were dominated by psychiatrists, was first published in 1917 by the National Committee for Mental Hygiene. All of these efforts greatly increased public awareness about mental disorders and mental illness, and leaders strongly advocated for humane and improved treatments for people with mental disorders. Scholars also began to give attention to the importance of mental health (as reflected in the term *mental hygiene*) and the prevention of mental illness.

In the 1920s, the National Committee for Mental Hygiene assisted in the establishment of child guidance clinics, and these efforts were influenced by theories of European-born psychiatrists Adolf Meyer and Alfred Adler. Meyer recommended treating the whole patient and understanding the patient's environment. Adler's theories of personality have a strong emphasis on prevention and health promotion, including advocacy for parent education and community service. The psychological testing movement gained popularity in the 1920s, especially through the aptitude and intelligence testing of World War I armed services personnel.

About the time of the start of the mental hygiene movement, Frank Parsons (1909) wrote the now classic book *Choosing a Vocation*. Thus, the specialty of vocational guidance was born, and at about the same time, the first Vocational Guidance Bureau was established in Boston. The vocational guidance movement gave voice to the importance of helping people find suitable employment, as the United States was rapidly becoming industrialized and people were flocking to the cities from small towns and rural areas, seeking employment opportunities. In 1913, the National Vocational Guidance Association was formed, and high schools across the country began to offer vocational guidance classes to help students make decisions about postsecondary employment (Schmidt, 2008). The vocational guidance movement gave rise to the counseling and psychology professions, which include prevention as an important component of their missions. These professions are currently supported by several organizations, including the American Counseling Association, the National Career Development Association, the American School Counseling Association, and the Society of Counseling Psychology (Division 17 of the American Psychological Association [APA]).

During the 1930s, the White House Conference on Child Health and Protection recommended expanding the focus of care to address social and environmental factors that affect the health and well-being of children (Mrazek & Haggerty, 1994). However, Mrazek and Haggerty (1994) also indicated that the commitment to prevention in the United States decreased during the same decade as an illness-treatment orientation began to dominate and was reinforced by insurance companies. It is unfortunate that the emphasis on remedial and crisis intervention as primary ways to deliver psychological and physical health care with corresponding insurance reimbursements has continued into the 21st century.

The 1930s also witnessed an expansion of the eugenics movement in the United States, which advocated for sterilization and prohibited procreation among the physically and emotionally disabled as ways to prevent future mental and physical disorders. Many states enacted laws that supported eugenics, one of the most dishonorable movements promoted in the interest of prevention. Gallagher (1999) detailed the history of the eugenics movement in the state of Vermont from the late 19th century to the mid-20th century in her book *Breeding Better Vermonters: The Eugenics Project in the Green Mountain State*. The book is instructive in many ways, but especially for its historical perspectives on the relationships among science, social mores, race, culture, and the ethics of social movements. A study of the eugenics movement may be instructive in the 21st century, with the increases in research and applications of human genetics and the ethical issues that they present. Fortunately, eugenics practices did not prevail in the United States, although eugenics was the basis of Nazi Germany's horrific plan to exterminate the Jewish population and other groups.

U.S. GOVERNMENT: HEALTH PROMOTION AND DISEASE PREVENTION

The 1940s and 1950s saw a reemergence of the focus on mental health in the United States. In 1946 the National Mental Health Act was passed by the U.S. Congress and signed by President Truman. The law created the National Institute of Mental Health (NIMH), whose mission was to study the causes and treatment of mental illness. The hope was that NIMH would promote and advance mental health research, which would eventually lead to the prevention of mental illness. The Mental Health Act was the first of its kind to focus on the mental health of U.S. citizens, and the Act came about, at least partially, because of the high incidence of mental health problems in soldiers returning home from World War II combat duty.

In addition to NIMH, another federal agency, the Communicable Disease Center, was established in 1946, with offices in Atlanta, Georgia. The Communicable Disease Center was created from several wartime agencies that were fighting the spread of diseases such as malaria and typhoid fever during World War II. During its early years, the Communicable Disease Center focused on combating malaria, but in 1957 added the prevention of other communicable diseases to its portfolio, specifically sexually transmitted diseases, and in 1960 the control of tuberculosis was added. In 1967 the agency was renamed the National Communicable Disease Center, and in 1980 the name was changed again to the Centers for Disease Control (CDC). In 1992, through an act of Congress, the agency was renamed the Centers for Disease Control and Prevention, its current name. Congress directed that the acronym CDC remain for recognition purposes, and the agency is widely recognized today as the CDC. The CDC is under the U.S. Department of Health and Human Services, and it is charged with promoting the health and well-being of U.S. citizens through activities across the spectrum of physical, psychological, and social conditions. The mission of the CDC has broadened considerably since its creation in 1946, to include major societal issues and health problems. For example, the range of health issues addressed by the CDC includes health emergencies (e.g., the H1N1 flu pandemic), national disaster preparedness, healthy work environments, and the impact of health promotion and prevention beyond the U.S. borders. The CDC also supports empirical investigations to promote health and well-being, to prevent physical disease and psychological distress, and to ameliorate harmful social conditions. Examples of these research areas are youth violence prevention, prevention of sexually transmitted diseases, smoking cessation, and child maltreatment.

Another important U.S. government agency that addresses prevention is the U.S. Public Health Service, headed by the Surgeon General of the United States. The Public Health Service traces its history back to 1798, and in 1870 the position of U.S. Surgeon General was created. Although initially formed as an independent government agency, the Public Health Service became part of the U.S. Department of Health, Education, and Welfare in 1953, and is currently under the U.S. Department of Health and Human Services.

The Office of the Surgeon General strongly advocates for health promotion and prevention of unhealthy lifestyle behaviors. The landmark 1964 Surgeon General's report on smoking and health was the first widely published work to demonstrate links between cigarette smoking and cancer and other diseases. Over the past 50 years, this document has been the foundation for many policies and programs aimed at cigarette smoking prevention and cessation. Relevant activities have included cigarette package warning labels about the dangers of smoking, prohibitions on cigarette advertising and marketing to youth and young adults, and bans on smoking in public buildings. To prevent the harmful effects of secondhand smoke to workers and customers, California became the first state to ban cigarette smoking in bars and restaurants in 2000. Since then, several cities and states have passed similar legislation, although not without much controversy and political debate.

The U.S. Surgeon General's Office published the first report on the health of the nation in 1979. This report, called *Healthy People: The Surgeon General's Report on Health Promotion and Disease Prevention*, set national health goals and recommendations to improve the health of the nation across the life span, from infancy through older adulthood. The 1979 report stressed the importance of preventive health services (e.g., prenatal care) and the promotion of personal health (e.g., eating nutritiously, refraining from smoking). Since 1979, *Healthy People* reports have been published every 10 years in 1990, 2000, and 2010 (U.S. Department of Health and Human Services, 2011). One of the goals listed in the 2010 *Healthy People* is to eliminate health disparities across the United States so that citizens have equal access to physical and psychological health care, regardless of race, culture, age, gender, or economic standing. The U.S. Department of Health and Human Services (2010b) published *Healthy People 2020*, articulating a 10-year agenda to improve the nation's health.

The Office of the U.S. Surgeon General's first comprehensive report on mental health in the United States was published in 1999 (U.S. Department of Health and Human Services, 1999). The report increased public awareness of the importance of mental health and well-being and their relationship to improving the overall health of the nation. The report used a scientific and empirical approach to address the full spectrum of mental health issues: mental health promotion, prevention of mental illness, and treatment of mental health problems across the life span. The document discussed five overarching themes.

- First, mental health promotion and mental illness prevention require a public health approach. Such an approach entails not only diagnosis and treatment of illness but also epidemiological studies of the population to prevent disorders, and it promotes health and well-being and increases access to services and evaluates those services (Last & Wallace, 1992).
- Second, mental disorders are disabling, and the burdens they impose on individuals and entire countries have been greatly underestimated.
- Third, the concepts of mental health and mental illness are to be viewed on a continuum of functioning. *Mental health* refers to successfully performing tasks of living, such as being productive, forming healthy relationships, and being able to cope with change and adversity. *Mental illness* refers to all diagnosable mental disorders that are identified by changes in mood, thoughts, and behaviors that create impaired functioning.
- Fourth, the mind and body are integral to each other and to physical and mental well-being. The integration of mental and physical health is critically important to one's overall health and the health of the nation.
- Fifth, stigma continues to exert a major influence on several dimensions of mental health care. The stigma and lack of understanding of mental health disorders can prevent people from seeking psychological help and lead to reduced funding for mental health treatment and prevention services. Further, stigma and misunderstanding can result in the ostracism of individuals with mental health disorders from their families and communities.

The theme of stigma and misunderstanding was further detailed in a follow-up supplemental report that focused on mental health and culture, race, and ethnicity (U.S. Department of Health and Human Services, 2001). Among the major themes of the report were the role of these factors in the promotion of mental health and the treatment of mental illness, and disparities in mental health care and services among populations of color within the United States.

MID- TO LATE 20TH CENTURY AND PREVENTION

The history of prevention also includes major political and social movements of the later 20th century. President Kennedy's signing of the Community Mental Health Act in 1963 funded community mental health centers and targeted prevention as important to an overall mental health policy agenda, although the prevention objective received much less attention during implementation. President Johnson declared a "War on Poverty" in the United States during his administration, and federal legislation created programs such as Head Start and Upward Bound to strengthen the educational preparedness and well-being of children and adolescents. Both programs have continued to receive federal funding into the 21st century.

The 1960s and 1970s also brought about social reforms and federal legislation that promoted racial and women's equality in all areas of life in the United States, most notably in voting rights, in the workplace, in education, and at home. The civil rights and women's social movements set the stage for federal legislation such as the Civil Rights Act of 1964; Title IX Education Amendments of 1972, which provided equal educational opportunities for men and women in all activities (e.g., academic, athletics, nonsport activities); the Americans With Disabilities Act of 1990; the Mental Health Parity Act of 1996; and the Mental Health Parity and Addiction Equity Act of 2008. The latter was finally passed by Congress and signed by President George W. Bush after more than 10 years of effort (the bill was eventually passed as part of a federal economic stimulus bill to revitalize the U.S. economy). The two mental health parity acts mandated that individuals must receive health insurance coverage for mental health services similar to that offered for physical health care.

The social and political movements and legislation during the latter part of the 20th century facilitated the development of physical and psychological well-being for many groups throughout the United States. Although the promotion of mental health and the prevention of psychological distress may not be obvious to the casual observer in legislative actions, the laws opened up opportunities to previously disempowered groups and gave large segments of the population improved access to career and educational opportunities, as well as the political strength to work to remove barriers to their pursuit and enjoyment of personal health and well-being.

Community Psychology and Prevention

The social activism during the 1960s in the United States led to a historic meeting of social-minded psychologists in Swampscott, Massachusetts, in 1965. Now referred to as the Swampscott Conference, the meeting is considered the beginning of the specialty of community psychology, with its very strong emphasis on social activism and prevention. Reflecting on the Swampscott meeting, Rickel (1987) wrote that community psychologists were asked to solve problems of society and serve as social change agents and political activists. As the mission and goals of the community psychology grew, community psychologists formed the 27th Division of the APA. Today, Division 27 is the Society for Community Research and Action: Division of Community Psychology. Division 27 launched its journal, the *American Journal of Community Psychology*, in 1973. In the same year, the *Journal of Community Psychology* was first published, reflecting the rapid growth of the new specialty within just a few years.

Community psychologists and others interested in prevention were instrumental in founding the annual Conference on Primary Prevention of Psychopathology at the University of Vermont. Under the leadership of George Albee, Justin Joffee, and Marc Kessler, the first conference was held in 1975, with Emory Cowen as keynote speaker. A review of the major themes of the conference over the years shows them to be reflective of some of the major issues facing the United States, as well as issues in psychology and other mental health professions. This is not surprising given the social activism promoted by conference organizers. Examples of conference themes include developing competence in children, political action and social change, and prevention of AIDS. An outgrowth of the Vermont Conference was the *Journal of Primary Prevention*, which published its inaugural issue in 1980 under the editorship of Tom Gullotta, who remained as editor for the next 20 years.

Counseling and Prevention

Other mental health professions, in addition to psychology, have played important roles in the history and development of prevention. Some, such as social work, arose from a strong social justice and social advocacy foundation. Others, such as counseling and college student development, originated in the early 20th century vocational guidance movement and have long been identified with human development and prevention perspectives. The American

Counseling Association (ACA; formerly the American Personnel and Guidance Association) enjoys a rich history of prevention and also traces its roots to the vocational guidance movement. Over the years, ACA members have shared many professional interests and activities with members of APA's Division 17, the Society of Counseling Psychology (Heppner, Casas, Carter, & Stone, 2000).

In the 1970s, a renewed conceptualization of counseling specifically included prevention as an important component of services (Morrill & Hurst, 1971; Morrill, Oetting, & Hurst, 1974). In this model, prevention services are offered both directly (e.g., direct contact with clientele) and indirectly (e.g., information dissemination). College and university counselors and student affairs personnel provided such diverse prevention services as problem-solving skills (Heppner, Neal, & Larson, 1984), alcohol education (Conyne, 1984), and stress management (Romano, 1984). A professional division within ACA, the American School Counseling Association (ASCA), promoted prevention through school-based services and professional frameworks for the practice of school counseling (ASCA, 2003; Baker & Gerler, 2004).

Social Work and Prevention

The history of prevention in mental health, social activism, and advocacy would not be complete without a discussion of the early beginnings of social work, a profession founded on serving the poor and disenfranchised members of society. Social work as a profession traces its history to 1898, when the first social work courses were offered at Columbia University in New York City. However, as with other human services professions, the origins of social work services predate formal training programs. The profession of social work was strongly influenced by two major social movements to serve the poor and disenfranchised during the late 19th and early 20th century: the Settlement Movement and the Charity Organization Societies (Gitterman & Germain, 2008). Although the movements had somewhat different methods and philosophies, they both were instrumental in addressing social injustices in the United States, a country that was rapidly becoming industrialized with a large influx of immigrants settling in urban areas.

The Settlement Movement, originating in London, was supported by affluent members of the community and provided shelter, food, education, and other services to the poor. In addition to serving individuals in need, the Settlement Movement was strongly dedicated to social activism, social reform, and political change to bring about better living conditions for the poor (Gitterman & Germain, 2008). Jane Addams, a social and peace activist, cofounded the first U.S. settlement house in 1889 in Chicago. The Settlement House Movement promoted a democratic philosophy in which workers lived in close proximity with those they served to demonstrate equality between the server and the served. Addams was the corecipient of the Nobel Peace Prize in 1931 for her work as a social reformer and peace activist. During the height of the Settlement Movement, settlement houses were popular in many parts of the United States. The settlement house concept has continued in different forms to this day, as exemplified by comprehensive community centers and neighborhood shelters that provide a range of prevention and intervention services for those in need. The Settlement Movement also spurred the development of radical social work, which focuses on the causes of social injustices and discrimination across society and attempts to correct them (Reisch & Andrews, 2002).

Also at the start of the 20th century, another social work pioneer, social reformer, and advocate for children and families, Mary Richmond, was instrumental in the formation of the Charity Organization Societies. The Societies emphasized the importance of personal empowerment to break the cycle of poverty and to reduce the dependency on charitable donations of those receiving them. The goals of the Charity Organization Societies emphasized a scientific basis for reducing and eliminating poverty by assisting individuals through efficient and careful distribution of resources (Gitterman & Germain, 2008). The Societies used case work methods to give information and make referrals to needed services. Modern descendants of the Charity Organization Societies are community agencies that provide a range of services that can be accessed by those in need of them.

Society for Prevention Research

A milestone in the field of prevention occurred in Pittsburgh during the spring of 1991 at a meeting of prevention researchers. The meeting was sponsored by the National Institute of Drug Abuse, and it marked the beginning of the Society for Prevention Research (SPR). Several years later, the journal *Prevention Science* was born as the official journal of the Society (Botvin, 2000). The organization is dedicated to advancing research on the etiology and prevention of social, health, and academic problems, and translating research to promote health and well-being (www.preventionresearch.org). An interdisciplinary organization that attracts scholars, practitioners, and policymakers, SPR hosts an annual convention that has grown from 25 attendees in 1991 to more than 800 in 2012, demonstrating the rapid growth of prevention as a specialty.

THEORETICAL MODELS THAT ADVANCE PREVENTION

Detailed descriptions of prevention theories are presented in Chapter 3. However, mention of them here is important because they are integrally connected to the history of prevention. Psychological theories and perspectives with strong prevention components were advanced in the second half of the 20th century, including a developmental model (Ivey, Ivey, & Zalaquett, 2009), a multicultural framework (Sue, Arredondo, & McDavis, 1992), and a social justice orientation (Albee, 1986). These models address practice, research, and training issues across the helping professions and highlight the importance of contextual, environmental, and political factors in facilitating the health and well-being of individuals, groups, and society. The advancements in theory have helped to mobilize the psychology and counseling professions from giving almost exclusive attention to traditional theories of psychotherapy (e.g., psychodynamic, behavioral, person centered) to broader conceptualizations of human development, human behavior, and change processes that recognize the importance of demographic variables such as ethnicity, culture, gender, and social and economic status in the pursuit of well-being.

Other theoretical models with strong implications for prevention research and practice were advanced in the late 20th century (Schinke, 1994). The more popular theories included the transtheoretical model of change (Prochaska, DiClemente, & Norcross, 1992), the theory of planned behavior (Ajzen, 1991), the theory of reasoned action (TRA; Fishbein & Ajzen, 1975), social learning theory (Bandura, 1986), and the health belief model (Janz, Champion, & Strecher, 2002). Other more recent conceptualizations relevant to prevention that have informed practice and research include positive psychology and positive human functioning (Lopez et al., 2006; Seligman & Csikszentmihalyi, 2000), strength-based counseling (Smith, 2006), and motivational interviewing (W. R. Miller & Rollnick, 2002). Many of these theories and perspectives are referred to and discussed in the chapters that follow.

The advances in psychological theory gave increased attention to the importance of prevention and spurred additional models of change that incorporated prevention (Hage, Barnett, & Schwartz, 2008). It is unfortunate, however, that several of these newer models and theories are not taught with regularity in many applied counseling and psychology training programs (Conyne, Newmeyer, Kenny, Romano, & Matthews, 2008); therefore, graduate students and new professionals may not be familiar with them. The lack of exposure to prevention theory, application, and research serves to increase the influence of traditional models that emphasize remediation (Snyder & Elliott, 2005). The omission of prevention as an important component of the training of psychologists and counselors historically has created the situation in which the professions' words about prevention have been much more abundant than their actions to move it to the center of their work (Holden & Black, 1999; Kleist & White, 1997; O'Byrne, Brammer, Davidson, & Poston, 2002). However, given the recent prevention initiatives identified above, and throughout this book, this state of affairs may be changing.

SUMMARY

As detailed in this historical review, different professions within the human services field have responded to major social conditions that influenced the health and well-being of the U.S. population. At the beginning of the 20th century, the United States experienced social upheaval that gave rise to finding ways to address the physical and emotional needs of its citizens. Throughout the 20th century, major historical events helped to advance interest and actions related to prevention, including the economic depression years of the 1930s, the needs of soldiers returning from World War II and those of their families, and the rapid social changes of the 1960s and 1970s. Some of the social disruptions of the last half of the 20th century added to the burdens and reduced the influence of societal institutions that have traditionally served as protectors for individuals and groups at risk for problems, such as families, schools, and religious and spiritual centers.

The latter years of the 20th century saw a renewed focus on youth, schools, and communities, to combat a number of child and adolescent problems that spread rapidly across the United States and affected children at increasingly younger ages. These problems include use of illegal substances (e.g., tobacco, alcohol, drugs), increased sexual activity leading to sexually transmitted diseases and pregnancy, incidents of violence in and outside of school from bullying to murder, and increased emotional and behavioral disturbances (McWhirter, McWhirter, McWhirter, & McWhirter, 2007). These problems have persisted into the 21st century, but advances in prevention research and practice, as discussed in the following chapters, have helped to reduce some of them.

3

PREVENTION THEORIES FOR BEHAVIOR CHANGE

The cause of prevention has been strengthened to some extent by theoretical frameworks that support prevention interventions. However, theoretical models as frameworks for prevention research are often lacking. For example, Painter, Borba, Hynes, Mays, and Glanz (2008) studied the use of theory in health behavior research from 2000 to 2005 and found that the use of theory in empirical research had not changed significantly since the mid-1990s. Only about one third of the 193 studies they reviewed used a theoretical framework, most often the transtheoretical model of change (TTM), social cognitive theory (SCT), or the health belief model (HBM). For prevention research to move forward, prevention interventions must be grounded in theoretical frameworks to examine their efficacy and to improve their application across population groups and problem areas. The implementation of prevention requires that people and institutions change to bring about enhanced protections and/or reduced risks to health and psychological well-being. Theories

DOI: 10.1037/14442-003
Prevention Psychology: Enhancing Personal and Social Well-Being, by J. L. Romano
Copyright © 2015 by the American Psychological Association. All rights reserved.

that focus on how people and institutions change are extremely important in explaining processes that bring about such change.

The theories that I summarize in this chapter are TTM; the theory of reasoned action and planned behavior; HBM; and motivational interviewing (MI), an approach that is based on person-centered theory. Although other theories could also be included in this chapter, the four that are reviewed support the underlying assumptions and principles of prevention interventions, and they are often not given much attention in the training of applied psychologists and counselors. The presentation of each theory will follow a similar structure: background and major theoretical concepts, empirical research of the theory used in prevention interventions, and strengths and limitations of the theory. The summary also provides resources that prevention specialists can access if they deem the theoretical framework relevant to their work.

TRANSTHEORETICAL MODEL OF BEHAVIOR CHANGE

Prevention interventions help people make changes that will enhance their personal well-being and prevent the development of problems. Prochaska, DiClemente, and Norcross (1992) described a stage theory of change that they called the transtheoretical model of behavior change (TTM). TTM, according to Prochaska, Johnson, and Lee (2009), is an integrative theory that incorporates several leading theories of psychotherapy and behavior change. Since the early 1980s, investigators have been studying and refining TTM to identify variables that bring about change. TTM purports to answer the following questions: How do people make behavioral changes, and why are some people more successful than others in making behavioral changes with or without professional assistance? TTM is arguably the most dominant theory of health behavior change in psychology, and it has been used as a theoretical framework to bring about change in diverse problem areas (Armitage, 2009; Weinstein, Rothman, & Sutton, 1998).

According to TTM, people eventually engage in change as they move through different stages in the change process. TTM was initially developed to explain the process of change related to cigarette smoking cessation. However, use of the theory rapidly expanded to explain and bring about positive change in the reduction of other addictive behaviors (e.g., alcohol use), and it has been applied to still other problem areas and diverse populations (Prochaska, Evers, Prochaska, Van Marter, & Johnson, 2007). A sample of these areas and groups includes physical activity among African American college women (Juniper, Oman, Hamm, & Kerby, 2004), college student alcohol abuse (Oswalt, Shutt, English, & Little, 2007), condom use and other contraceptive methods (Galavotti et al., 1995), stress management and depression (Evers et al., 2006), and prevention of bullying in schools (Prochaska et al., 2007).

TTM is based on a set of foundational assumptions: that behavioral change is a process that occurs in stages; that the stages are both stable and open to change; that planned behavioral interventions are necessary to assist individuals in moving from an early stage to later stages of action and maintenance; and that without assistance and guidance, people will remain at the early stages of change (Prochaska, Johnson, Lee, et al., 2009). In addition, TTM assumes that most individuals at risk for a problem are not immediately ready to engage in action-oriented prevention interventions and that intervention programs should be matched to the person's or group's stage of change. Further, although behavioral change may involve a combination of biological, social, and self-control processes, stage-matched interventions are most often designed to effect self-control processes (Prochaska et al., 2009). However, biological and social contexts should also be considered when designing prevention interventions, for example, attending to physical cravings in nicotine addiction and alcohol availability at social gatherings. In these cases, a nicotine patch may be used in smoking cessation interventions to reduce physical cravings, and beverages other than alcohol are available at social gatherings.

The five core concepts of TTM that emanate from these assumptions are (a) stages of change, (b) processes of change, (c) pros and cons of changing behavior (decisional balance), (d) self-efficacy, and (e) temptation. These core concepts are discussed next.

Stages of Change

Prochaska et al. (1992) identified five stages of change. During the earlier years of their research, the authors suggested a five-stage model, but when these stages were not supported by research, they defined a four-stage model. However, after further review of their research methods, they settled on six stages (Prochaska et al., 2009). Although the researchers initially believed that people progressed through the stages in a linear progression, further examination showed that individuals most often cycled in and out of the stages during their change process (Prochaska et al., 1992). This nonlinear process is common in behavioral change, as people make progress then revert to prior behaviors, make progress again, and revert, until the new behavior is maintained. The six TTM stages are described below.

Precontemplation

In this stage, there is no intention to make any changes in the near future, and a person may not even be aware that any changes are necessary. For example, a person may not be aware that a problem exists and therefore sees no need to make changes. At times a person may express a desire to change, but only because of pressure from others, as when someone agrees to participate in an intervention or suffer the consequences (e.g., the choice between losing one's driver's license or participating in a DWI intervention).

Contemplation

In this second stage, a person is planning to make a change within the next 6 months (Prochaska et al., 2009). He or she may recognize that a problem exists and that something needs to be done but has not taken any action to bring about change. For example, people in this stage may believe that they must lose weight, exercise more, or stop smoking to improve their health, but they have not acted on their belief. One could say that New Year's resolutions that never get acted on are made by people in the contemplation stage. Some people may remain in this stage for months or even years before taking action (DiClemente & Prochaska, 1985). People in this stage typically engage in a decision-making process, weighing the pros and cons of engaging in behavior to bring about change.

Preparation

Individuals in this stage have engaged in a decision process and are preparing to take major action in the near future, usually measured as within a month (Prochaska et al., 2009). They may also have developed a plan for change and begun to make small changes in behavior, such as parking farther away from their office to increase physical exercise, reducing the number of cigarettes smoked per day, or searching for a physical fitness center to join. Originally, Prochaska, DiClemente, and Norcross (1992) called this stage *decision-making*.

Action

In this stage, individuals make major changes in their behavior. Their commitment and motivation to make change are considerable, as are the time and energy needed to do so. Their actions are often the most visible, for example, stopping smoking, beginning a regular exercise routine, or not using alcohol. The goal of the action stage is to make changes that are acceptable to promote better health and well-being. For example, reducing cigarette smoking from 20 to 10 cigarettes per day would not be considered an acceptable goal in the action stage (because of nicotine addiction), but engaging in moderate to vigorous exercise three times per week would be an acceptable goal.

Maintenance

Prochaska et al. (1992) viewed the maintenance stage as a continuation of the action stage and not a discrete stage. The main goal of the maintenance stage is to sustain the gains made in the action stage and avoid relapse to previous dysfunctional or addictive behaviors. Individuals will continue to engage in healthy behaviors that support the changes that were made. Some of the new behaviors may last a lifetime, such as refraining from cigarette smoking or using drugs. Others may be modified as a person's life changes, such as changing diet and exercise activities as the person grows older. Prochaska et al. (2009) estimated that the maintenance stage can last from 6 months to 5 years.

Termination

In this stage, persons are confident that they will not revert to the problem behavior. However, Prochaska et al. (2009) found that this may be an unrealistic goal for most people; a more realistic goal is lifetime maintenance of the new behavior. For example, people may need to continue to monitor new habits of diet and exercise years after initial changes were made, or they may still crave tobacco after quitting the habit. The termination stage has been given much less attention in the literature than the other stages, and it was not even identified as one of the stages in earlier descriptions of TTM (Prochaska et al., 1992). Researching this stage is also problematic because people receiving a TTM-based intervention would need to be followed years after the intervention.

Processes of Change

Processes of change are activities that people use as they move through the stages of change. The processes of change are important, as they provide guidance for the application of the theory to behavioral change. Prochaska et al. (2009) identified 10 processes of change that have received the most empirical support: (a) consciousness raising, which increases awareness about the problem, such as through media messages; (b) dramatic relief, which moves people emotionally, such as personal testimonials; (c) self-reevaluation or self-assessment related to the behavior, such as improved self-image as a result of weight loss; (d) environmental reevaluation, assessment of the effect of the behavior on others, for example, secondhand smoke; (e) self-liberation, commitment to change and to act on the commitment; (f) social liberation, social opportunities or alternatives to support the desired change, such as school-sponsored all-night high school graduation parties to keep kids safe; (g) counter-conditioning, learning healthy behaviors to replace unhealthy ones, such as relaxation training to combat anxiety; (h) stimulus control, environmental reminders to support healthy behaviors or discourage unhealthy ones, such as "notes to self" to discourage snacking; (i) contingency management, using consequences to reward new behavior or punish old behavior; and (j) helping relationships, social networks, and caring relationships to support desired behavior change, such as might be developed with professional counseling or peers.

Prochaska et al. (1992) reported that their research on smoking cessation and dietary behavior changes showed that the stages of change and processes of change interact. The processes of consciousness raising, dramatic relief, and environmental reevaluation were the ones most emphasized at the contemplation stage, although environmental reevaluation helped to move individuals from contemplation to preparation. Counterconditioning, stimulus control, contingency management, and helping relationships were emphasized at the action stage. The processes of change continue to support behavior changes made during the maintenance stage.

Pros and Cons of Changing (Decisional Balance)

This construct refers to the individual's positive and negative reasons for making a change. Although studies have attempted to verify eight categories (four each) of pros and cons for making the behavioral change, Prochaska et al. (2009) settled on a decisional balance of simply pros and cons for making a change. Theoretically, the more positively a person evaluates the importance of making a change, the more likely it is that she or he will engage in trying to change the behavior.

Self-Efficacy

Adopted from Bandura (1986), the construct of *self-efficacy* refers to the individual's confidence that he or she can make a needed change and/or maintain the new behavior, especially in situations where there is a high risk of reverting to old behavior. For example, a college student who has recently decided to refrain from using alcohol decides not to join a group of friends to celebrate a 21st birthday, knowing that alcohol will be available and its use encouraged during the evening. Because of low self-efficacy related to alcohol use, the student decides not to risk recent changes related to alcohol use and thus decides not to attend the celebration. As a person gains confidence in maintaining a behavior change, even in situations or events that pose risks for reverting to old behavior, she or he is more likely to participate in those situations, as her or his self-efficacy related to the new behavior has strengthened.

Temptation

This construct refers to strong urges that tempt someone to engage in unhealthy behaviors. Prochaska et al. (2009) found that the most common temptations were emotional distress, social situations that the person values, and cravings.

Strengths and Limitations

TTM is widely used as a theoretical framework for prevention interventions, especially with interventions designed to change health-related behaviors (Armitage, 2009). However, TTM is not without its detractors (Bridle et al., 2005; Herzog, 2008; Van Sluijs, Van Poppel, & Van Mechelen, 2004). For example, Bridle et al. (2005) reviewed 37 randomized-trial TTM studies across seven target behaviors, with 25 of the 37 studies focused on smoking cessation, physical exercise, and diet. They found limited evidence in support of TTM, and they questioned the methodological quality of the studies that they reviewed. Similarly, Van Sluijs et al. (2004) reviewed 29 studies that used TTM to bring about behavioral changes in physical activity, diet, and smoking. They also found limited support for the model, and they raised questions about its internal validity and the uneven attention to methodological issues in the studies reviewed. Herzog's (2008) review of TTM studies of only smoking cessation concluded that TTM does not meet necessary criteria for a stage model of change. Specifically, Herzog faulted TTM because the stages of change are not qualitatively distinct categories, specificity of moving from one stage to another is lacking, and the research and intervention studies of the model are inadequate.

Despite these critiques, Armitage (2009) emphasized that criticism of TTM focuses almost exclusively on the one core concept of stages of change while neglecting the other four components of the model. Armitage specifically identified the processes of change component of TTM as meriting more research and study, as including this component in interventions has been shown to yield positive results in a few studies on behavior change. Researchers have emphasized that motivation and intention to change merit further study within TTM and may increase the effectiveness of behavioral change interventions (Arden & Armitage, 2008; Armitage & Arden, 2008)

Although the stage design of TTM is intuitively attractive and has enjoyed widespread use, additional research, with stronger methodologies, is needed to more fully support the viability of the theory. However, as foundational to prevention interventions, TTM merits continued use, with perhaps greater attention given to all of its components. Prevention interventions that are tailored to the readiness for change of an individual or group have the potential to be most efficacious, as a one-size-fits-all intervention may not be the most effective or economical. For example, universal prevention interventions, where problem awareness is important, focusing an intervention on the early stages of change activities, may be most important. However, in selective and indicated prevention interventions, when symptoms of problem behaviors have occurred, interventions appropriate for the preparation and action stages may be most effective. Finally, by attending to other components of TTM (i.e., the change process, pros and cons of changing behavior, self-efficacy, and temptation), prevention specialists are likely to strengthen the interventions they use, while empirical studies of these components will lead to an increased understanding of TTM as a framework to guide prevention interventions.

THEORY OF REASONED ACTION AND PLANNED BEHAVIOR

TRA was first proposed by Fishbein (1967) to better understand the relationships between personal beliefs, attitudes, and behaviors (Montaño & Kasprzyk, 2002). TRA is based on the assumptions that humans are rational and can use information to make reasonable decisions (Aronson, Wilson, & Akert, 2003). The theory has received considerable attention in the social psychology literature (Ajzen & Fishbein, 1980; Fishbein & Ajzen, 1975). In the development of TRA, Fishbein differentiated between an attitude toward an object and an attitude toward a behavior related to that object (Montaño & Kasprzyk, 2002). For example, in terms of a prevention intervention, an attitude toward an object would be lung cancer, and an attitude toward a behavior is to stop smoking. Fishbein and Ajzen (1975; as cited by Montaño & Kasprzyk, 2002) demonstrated that a person's attitude about a behavior (e.g., stop smoking) is a much better predictor of behavior change than one's attitude toward the object that the behavior is designed to prevent (e.g., lung cancer). In another example from a prevention perspective, TRA suggests that an adolescent's attitude toward condom use is a much better predictor of actually using condoms than is his attitude about fathering a child. An adolescent boy may not wish to father a child but may also have an unfavorable attitude toward using condoms. In this scenario, the latter would predict, according to TRA, that he would not use condoms. TRA is based on the assumption that humans are rational and can use information to make reasonable decisions (Aronson, Wilson, and Akert, 2003).

Attitudes and Subjective Norms

As originally conceptualized, TRA proposed that behavior is a function of an individual's willingness to carry out a behavioral intention. However, the intention to carry out a behavior is a function of a person's attitudes and subjective norms about the behavior (Romano & Netland, 2008).

Attitudes refer to a person's beliefs about the behavior, beliefs about the relationship between the behavior and the outcome, and the value associated with the outcome. For example, in terms of smoking prevention programs for school-age youth, programs that emphasize the health consequences of cigarette smokers 20 years into the future will not be convincing in light of the immediate needs and desires of adolescents. However, programs that show how smoking leads to poor hygiene, such as stained teeth, bad breath, and the smell of tobacco in hair and clothing, may be a more convincing means to change adolescent attitudes about smoking (Lantz et al., 2000). Smoking attitudes of adolescents may also be impacted by showing how tobacco use can negatively affect athletic skills and by the cost of cigarettes (i.e., money that would be spent on cigarettes can be used for other valued purchases, e.g., clothing, concerts).

Subjective norms or *social norms* refer to an individual's beliefs about what others think about a behavior and the importance of others' approval or disapproval of that behavior. In the smoking example, social norms may be important to measure. For example, strong social deterrents to an adolescent's cigarette smoking may be disapproval from parents, a coach or other valued adult role-model, or most powerfully, an adolescent's peer group. It is illegal for youth under 18 years old to purchase cigarettes, which can be another deterrent related to broader social norms. The social norms for adults are different in many instances. For example, the prohibition against smoking inside buildings, and in some communities, in outdoor public spaces, can motivate adults to stop smoking, as these policies show public disapproval of smokers. In addition, adults may become more conscious of the health consequences of smoking and of others' attitudes toward a person who ignores such health risks.

Attitudes and subjective norms are created through a process of evaluating one's beliefs related to a particular behavior. Therefore, beliefs emanate from personal attitudes and social norms, which in turn support behavioral intentions to carry out a desired behavior. Fishbein (1967) made clear distinctions among beliefs, attitudes, intentions, and behaviors in terms of definitions and measurement (Montaño & Kasprzyk, 2002).

Theory of Planned Behavior

Ajzen (1991) proposed the theory of planned behavior (TPB) as an extension of TRA to account for behaviors that are not completely under an individual's control. Ajzen added the component of perceived behavioral control (PBC), based on a person's belief (control beliefs) about his or her ability to carry out a particular behavior. A person who has strong beliefs that she or he can complete a behavior will have high PBC, which strengthens behavioral intentions and engagement in the behavior; the reverse is true for a person who has negative beliefs about completing the behavior. The beliefs can be internal or external to the person. Examples of internal beliefs may be a person's estimate of his or her ability to carry out a behavior, and external control beliefs could be perceived lack of money to carry out a behavior. The combination of TRA and TPB (TRA/PB) suggests that the more favorable the attitudes, subjective norms, and perceived control, the stronger will be the intention to perform a behavior targeted for change, and hence the more likely that the targeted behavior will be performed. Symbolically, the relationships among these variables can be expressed as

$$Behavior \approx Intentions \approx (Attitudes + Norms + Control).$$

In some situations, a person may be motivated to perform a behavior, but environmental or contextual factors may reduce his or her perceived control. For example, religious or cultural beliefs may reduce a person's perceived control, such as beliefs that prohibit members of a religious organization from undergoing a medical procedure or using birth control. Adolescents may refrain from using condoms because of strong social sanctions against sexual intercourse, thus risking pregnancy and sexually transmitted infections. Therefore, people may believe that they do not have control over changing a behavior because of pressure they receive to maintain the status quo from peers, family, or community members. For example, resistance to change may occur among adolescent peers at school or among adult coworkers on the job. The pressures of adolescent peers to engage in unhealthy behaviors can be intense, and adults also may lose perceived control over behavioral changes they wish to make— for instance, one spouse purchases high-calorie foods while the other spouse is attempting to lose weight.

Ajzen (1991) and Albarracín, Fishbein, Johnson, and Muellerleile (2001) found that PBC directly affects behavioral intentions, as well as the targeted behavior itself, especially when PBC is accurate and volitional control is low. In their meta-analysis of 185 studies, Armitage and Connor (2001) found support for the construct of PBC. They concluded that TPB was more effective with TRA than TRA alone in predicting intentions and behavior when there is low volitional control. When there is complete volitional control, PBC does not have an effect on behavioral intention. However, the effect of PBC on behavior is problematic when the estimation of behavioral control is incorrect or inaccurate (Armitage & Connor, 2001). For example, a man may believe that he has more control about a behavior than he actually does, such as being able to stop using alcohol whenever he wishes. In their 2002 article, Montaño and Kasprzyk cited a variety of studies that have applied TPB to various health behaviors, including health screenings, prevention of sexually transmitted diseases, and exercise behavior. The studies have generally supported PBC as a predictor of intention to perform a given behavior as well as actually performing the behavior itself.

Elicitation Research

TRA/PB offers a research procedure that is extremely useful and important in prevention work. The procedure is called *elicitation research*, which measures and detects specific within-group variables that are important to TRA/PB variables. Through elicitation research, belief variables (i.e., behavioral beliefs, social norm beliefs, and control beliefs) about the targeted behavior are assessed before the development of a prevention intervention so as to better understand the attitudes and beliefs, social norms, PBC, and behavioral intentions of the population for whom the prevention intervention is being considered. Prevention specialists and researchers can use elicitation research to obtain information about the most salient influences that can facilitate or hinder behavioral change before they finalize an intervention (Romano & Netland, 2008). Elicitation research is unique to TRA/PB and is an especially important procedure for prevention interventions delivered to minority group members and/or low-incidence behaviors (Montaño & Kasprzyk, 2002). It elicits an understanding of variables important to the group that will receive the prevention intervention. For example, before developing an eating disorders prevention program for middle-school girls, it is important to gather information about the girls' beliefs about food and nutrition. However, gathering this information from a subgroup of middle school girls who, for instance, are new immigrants to the United States may be especially important because their attitudes, beliefs, and norms about food and self-perception may be different from those of U.S.-born students. Elicitation research provides information that enables the intervention developed to respond to the eating beliefs of all girls. Romano and Netland (2008) provided an explicit example of elicitation research and its application within a TRA/PB framework.

Strengths and Limitations

TRA/PB is particularly adaptable to prevention interventions with multicultural and multinational populations, as its elicitation research component provides knowledge of cultural beliefs about the targeted behavior. For example, Ramirez, Bravo, and Katsikas (2005) found that perceived social support was an important factor in Colombian women's decisions to breastfeed their children, compared with mothers in the United States. In another example, TRA/PB formed the basis of an HIV prevention program for low-income Latina adolescents (Koniak-Griffin et al., 2003). The prevention program, called Project CHARM, emphasized maternal protectiveness and the devastating effects of HIV/AIDS on communities. Among the findings of a 6-month follow-up were that the Latina girls showed increased intention to use condoms and had fewer sex partners. Further, Montaño and Kasprzyk (2002) conducted a study to identify the best predictors of behavioral intentions to use condoms among a sample of Black, Hispanic, and White women. The researchers used elicitation research of the TRA/TPB variables with the three ethnic groups. Although they found differences among the three groups of women, they reported that the model "led to very accurate prediction of condom use intentions" (p. 88). Montaño and Kasprzyk provided intervention examples that may be salient for each group of women in their study. For example, they suggested that one of the interventions for Black women would be to increase their normative belief that their partners should use condoms; for Hispanic women, an intervention may increase their behavioral belief that using condoms will increase their relaxation during sex; and for White women, an intervention may increase their behavioral control by focusing on the belief that they have control over condom use during sex. These examples demonstrate the importance of conducting elicitation research before finalizing a prevention intervention.

Romano and Netland (2008) summarized the conceptual and research limitations of TRA/PB. According to these authors, one conceptual limitation is the assumption that behavior is solely influenced by intentions. In fact, past behavior may be the best predictor of future behavior (Sutton, McVey, & Glarz, 1999). This may occur because environmental stimuli or cues that supported old behaviors have not changed, making it difficult to act in new ways that are not supported by the environment. However, careful attention to the social norms surrounding a behavior targeted for change may help to reduce or alleviate this limitation. Abraham and Sheeran (2003) noted that because TRA/PB focuses on a single behavior, other less desirable behaviors may be attractive and compete with the desired behavior targeted for change.

One of the limitations of TRA/PB empirical research is that many of the research studies use cross-sectional, rather than longitudinal, designs. Thus, studies may accurately assess behavioral intentions but not behavioral change (Romano & Netland, 2008). Poorly designed or nonexistent elicitation research can reduce awareness and understanding of participant beliefs about the behavior targeted for change, thus compromising the prevention intervention. Although Ajzen and Fishbein (2004) and O'Connor and Armitage (2003) argued that behavioral intentions can substitute for actual behaviors when direct measures of behavioral change cannot be collected, a major goal of prevention interventions is to change actual behaviors. Although well-designed longitudinal studies may be costly and difficult to maintain, it is important to strive for an understanding of the most salient TRA/PB variables and their relationships to actual behavior change when designing and implementing prevention interventions.

HEALTH BELIEF MODEL

HBM was developed during the 1950s by social psychologists at the U.S. Public Health Service (Hochbaum, 1958; Rosenstock, 1974). Observing the low turnouts for tuberculosis screenings, researchers sought to understand why people will or will not participate in illness prevention procedures that promote early disease detection. They found that beliefs about the illness and about screening procedures helped to differentiate those who participated from those who did not.

Health Beliefs

HBM is a cognitive model that views early prevention, screening, and illness as functions of four subjective and personal beliefs about one's health: (a) perceived susceptibility, (b) perceived severity, (c) perceived benefits, and (d) perceived barriers (Janz et al., 2002).

- *Perceived susceptibility* is the extent to which an individual believes he or she is at risk of contracting a disease (or having a relapse) or engaging in behavior that leads to a problem.
- *Perceived severity* refers to beliefs about the severity of the consequences of contracting an illness (or leaving it untreated) or developing a problem.
- *Perceived benefits* are beliefs about whether a preventive behavior will reduce the risk of developing a disease or problem, as well as its severity; they are also beliefs about benefits unrelated to health.
- *Perceived barriers* represent the disadvantages of or obstacles to taking a preventive action. The barriers may include time, cost, inconvenience, pain, and emotional upset.

Together, perceived susceptibility and perceived severity constitute *perceived threat*, which provides motivation to act, although the course of action depends on perceived benefits and barriers (Rosenstock, 1974). Demographic, psychological, and cultural variables may affect health-related behaviors indirectly by influencing health beliefs. Educational level, for example, has been of interest to HBM researchers as a variable that might influence health behaviors by helping to shape health beliefs (Janz et al., 2002). HBM suggests that people will carry out a behavior to prevent, detect, or manage a condition if they believe that (a) they are susceptible to the condition, (b) the condition has serious consequences, (c) the preventive behavior is effective in reducing risk or consequences of the condition, and (d) benefits of performing the behavior outweigh costs.

Cues to Action

In addition to the four belief constructs, HBM also considers *cues to action*: any events, internal or external, that trigger an individual to act on his or her health beliefs. Examples include a reminder from friends not to drink and drive, a media story about an alcohol-related car accident, or encouragement to increase physical activity after a physical exam.

HBM and Social Cognitive Theory

Rosenstock, Strecher, and Becker (1988) examined similarities between HBM and SCT (Bandura, 1986) and proposed an expanded HBM that incorporates the SCT concept of self-efficacy. SCT and HBM are cognitive psychology theories, as they hypothesize that acting on a behavior depends on the value that an individual places on an outcome of the behavior, on that individual's assessment of his or her ability to perform the behavior, and on whether the behavior will lead to a desired outcome. Janz and Becker (1984) suggested that self-efficacy could be considered a barrier if a person lacks confidence in being able to perform a preventive behavior or, alternatively, a benefit if a person has confidence in being able to perform the behavior.

Rosenstock et al. (1988) proposed that the inclusion of self-efficacy in HBM might extend the model's application from short-term, one-time health preventive behaviors, such as participating in a health screening, to longer and more complex behavioral goals, such as engaging in regular physical exercise or changing eating habits, which often require greater self-efficacy to achieve. Rosenstock et al. suggested that self-efficacy be incorporated as a distinct variable along with the four health beliefs and cues to action variables in HBM preventive interventions. Studies that have examined HBM with the addition of self-efficacy have reported that greater self-efficacy for performing a preventive behavior is associated with an increased likelihood of performing or intending to perform the behavior, suggesting that the inclusion of self-efficacy can enhance the model (e.g., de Paoli, Manongi, & Klepp, 2004; Kloeblen, 1999; Zak-Place & Stern, 2004). Zak-Place and Stern (2004) found self-efficacy to be the strongest and most consistent predictor of preventive behavior among HBM variables.

Although HBM has been extensively researched, much of the literature focuses on behaviors that are directly related to physical health preventive outcomes, for example, cancer screening behaviors (Champion, Ray, Heilman, & Springston, 2000; Janz, Wren, Schottenfeld, & Guire, 2003). Harrison, Mullen, and Green (1992) conducted a meta-analysis of HBM research published between 1966 and 1987, on adult preventive behaviors. Using 16 studies that met inclusion criteria, Harrison et al. concluded that the HBM constructs show significant associations in the expected directions with preventive health behaviors. However, the relationships tended to be weak, with any given health belief accounting for a relatively small amount of variance in preventive health behaviors. There has been limited research about the role of cues to action in predicting preventive behavior, perhaps because cues to action are often fleeting and difficult to identify and measure (Janz et al., 2002). Janz and Becker (1984) reviewed the HBM literature and concluded that perceived barriers were the strongest predictors of the likelihood of engaging in health preventive behaviors, whereas perceived severity was the weakest. Demographic, psychological, and cultural variables also affect health beliefs, and thus health and health-related behaviors.

Although much of the early HBM research focused on physical health behaviors, more recent studies have addressed preventive behaviors that are more directly relevant in counseling and psychology. These include studies to prevent or detect HIV and other sexually transmitted infections (de Paoli et al., 2004; Maguen, Armistead, & Kalichman, 2000; Thato, Charron-Prochownik, Dorn, Albrecht, & Stone, 2003) and studies that examine dietary behaviors (Kloeblen, 1999) and physical activity (Juniper et al., 2004), teen pregnancy prevention (Out & Lafreniere, 2001), behaviors to prevent violent victimization (Hammig & Moranetz, 2000), health beliefs about exposure to secondhand cigarette smoke among adolescents (Li et al., 2003), and health beliefs in predicting medication adherence among people with mental disorders (Adams & Scott, 2000).

In one unique study, Spoth and Redman (1995) used HBM as a framework to examine the relationship between health beliefs and parents' intentions to participate in parent skills training. The study also assessed whether contextual factors, such as income, number of children, and degree of child problem behaviors, influenced health beliefs and behavioral intentions. Study participants included 1,129 parents of fifth graders attending school in the rural Midwest. The parents completed a telephone interview survey regarding relevant health beliefs, provided contextual information, and conveyed intentions to enroll in a parenting skills program. Health beliefs were measured with separate scales: (a) Perceived Susceptibility, in which parents were asked to rate the probability that their child would exhibit each of eight problem behaviors as a teenager, such as alcohol use, poor school grades, and risky sexual behavior; (b) Perceived Severity, which was based on how concerned the parents would be if, as a teenager, their child were to experience any of the same eight problems; (c) Perceived Benefits, in which parents were asked how helpful they would find information on each of the parenting program topics (e.g., family communication, effective discipline, child peer pressures); and (d) Perceived Barriers, in which parents rated obstacles that might prevent them from enrolling in the parenting program, such as lack of child care, travel to meetings, and costs. The researchers found that parents who perceived greater benefits of parenting skills training and fewer barriers to participation showed a stronger intention to participate in the program. Moreover, parents who perceived potential teen behavior problems as more severe tended to attribute greater benefits to such a program. Thus, perceived severity had an indirect influence on behavioral intention through its effects on perceived benefits. Perceived susceptibility of their child to develop future adolescent behavior problems, however, was not related to perceived benefits. Contextual factors, such as lower household income and number of children, were associated with higher perceived barriers to participation.

The Spoth and Redmond (1995) study carries the limitations of being cross-sectional and assessing behavioral intentions rather than actual behavior change, that is, enrolling in the parenting program. However, the results show that health beliefs about the severity of teen problems and the benefits of and barriers to participating in a parenting program influenced parents' intention to enroll in the program. The results also show that contextual variables are important influences on health beliefs. The results are largely consistent with HBM.

Juniper et al. (2004) investigated the relationship between HBM and the TTM stages of change. In this cross-sectional study of 233 African American college women, Juniper et al. analyzed whether relevant health beliefs differed among individuals at different stages of change related to physical activity. The authors found that compared with women at earlier stages of change, those at later stages of change reported greater perceived severity associated with the consequences of not being physically active, more cues to action, higher levels of self-efficacy for physical activity, and fewer barriers to physical activity. These findings are consistent with the combined predictions of HBM and TTM and suggest an interesting link between the two models. Other researchers have designed interventions based on HBM and TTM to increase mammography screening by tailoring intervention messages to health beliefs and stage of change (Champion et al., 2000).

Strengths and Limitations

HBM research has investigated the model within a multicultural context by examining cultural similarities and differences of health beliefs and their underlying assumptions in different cultures (Champion et al., 2000; de Paoli et al., 2004; A. S. James, Campbell, & Hudson, 2002; Juniper et al., 2004; Thato et al., 2003). The research suggests that HBM is a useful framework in a multicultural context but that the salience of beliefs is important to assess, as in elicitation research, with appropriate measures (Champion &

Scott, 1997; Dignan et al., 1994; Janz et al., 2002; A. M. Miller & Champion, 1997). The variation of relevant health beliefs across cultures encourages pilot research to identify salient health beliefs about the behaviors targeted for change in a prevention intervention.

Some conceptual limitations of HBM have been noted. For example, HBM, unlike TRA/PB, does not directly incorporate social influences on behavior (Weinstein, 1993). However, Janz and Becker (1984) suggested that the TRA construct of social norms is a refinement of the HBM constructs of perceived benefits and barriers, as social approval may be a perceived benefit of behavior change, whereas social disapproval is a perceived barrier. In addition, Weinstein (1993) noted that because HBM is not a stage theory, it may oversimplify the behavioral change process. It is likely that different factors and influences are important when making a decision to change a behavior, compared with actually performing and maintaining a new behavior. Thus, combining HBM with other models, such as TTM and TRA/PB, may offer more comprehensive prevention interventions (Champion et al., 2000; Juniper et al., 2004).

There have also been problems with the methodology of HBM research. For example, Harrison et al. (1992) identified only 16 studies out of 147 that met all of their criteria for inclusion in their HBM meta-analysis. Many studies were eliminated because they did not assess all of the HBM variables or because they did not report measurement reliability. Other limitations arise frequently in HBM research.

- Much of the research is cross-sectional. However, because HBM aims to predict changes in behavior, cross-sectional studies provide a less rigorous test of the model than do longitudinal studies that can measure behavioral change (Janz et al., 2002; Weinstein, 1993).
- Measurement of HBM variables varies widely across studies, creating inconsistencies in the literature and leading to the use of measures with uncertain reliability and validity (Janz et al., 2002; Poss, 2001; Weinstein, 1993).
- Studies do not treat HBM as an integrated model. For example, perceived threat (combination of perceived susceptibility and severity) may not directly influence behavior, whereas perceived benefits and barriers may have direct influence on preventive behaviors. Thus, researchers have encouraged the examination of direct and indirect influences on HBM variables (Janz et al., 2002; Poss, 2001; Weinstein, 1993).
- Few studies have used pilot research to identify relevant health beliefs to emphasize in prevention interventions. Similar to

elicitation research, pilot research is important because salient beliefs vary by population and targeted preventive behavioral change (Dignan et al., 1994; Janz et al., 2002). For example, Miller and Champion (1997) assessed health beliefs related to breast cancer and mammography in a sample of 1,083 women. They reported that African American women were more likely than Caucasian women to report fear of radiation as a barrier to mammography, and women with low incomes were more likely than women with higher incomes to view cost as a barrier to screenings. Failure to identify salient health beliefs in the population could lead researchers and practitioners to focus on beliefs that are not relevant to the participants and ignore those that are.

- A number of studies have assessed the relationship between HBM variables and behavioral intention, rather than actual behavior change. Because intention does not necessarily translate into action, findings from these studies may or may not extend to actual behavioral changes. Relatedly, studies may examine the impact of an intervention on either behavior (Champion et al., 2000) or health beliefs (Out & Lafreniere, 2001), rather than measuring both health beliefs and behavior change to assess whether the prevention intervention changed health beliefs and also changed behavior.

MOTIVATIONAL INTERVIEWING

MI is a personal change strategy that was developed with people desiring to make changes in their addictive behaviors. MI was introduced by Miller and colleagues (W. R. Miller & Rollnick, 2002; W. R. Miller & Rose, 2009) more than 30 years ago as a result of surprising findings that therapist interpersonal style had a strong influence on client outcomes in addiction counseling. W. R. Miller and Rollnick (2002) defined MI as "a client-centered, directive method for enhancing intrinsic motivation to change by exploring and resolving ambivalence" (p. 25). Although C. R. Rogers's (1951) person-centered theory and counseling are foundational to MI, MI differs from Rogerian nondirective theory and counseling in that it is specifically directive. In MI, the counselor directs the conversation toward reducing the client's ambivalence about making changes to reduce problematic behavior. For example, the counselor may attempt to help a client focus on resistance to changing abusive alcohol use, while encouraging the client to increase motivation to refrain from abusing alcohol.

MI is an interpersonal intervention, based on person-centered theory, that emphasizes collaboration between client and counselor. It attempts to elicit from clients intrinsic motivations for change, and the MI model holds that clients have the capability and freedom to make informed choices (W. R. Miller & Rollnick, 2002). As such, W. R. Miller and Rollnick (2002) discussed four general principles that guide MI: (a) express empathy, (b) develop discrepancy, (c) roll with resistance, and (d) support self-efficacy.

- *Express empathy* is similar to the Rogerian concept of communicating empathy with a client, such as developing an understanding of the client's perspective and not imposing the counselor's will.
- *Develop discrepancy* is a departure from traditional person-centered, nondirective counseling, as the phrase refers to directive discussion with clients about their motivations to continue problem behaviors. In this principle, the counselor discusses the client's ambivalence about replacing problem behaviors with health-enhancing ones. Although MI is more directive than nondirective therapeutic approaches, it does not impose counselor values and desires on clients but, rather, helps clients explore internal motivations to either maintain current problem behavior or make positive changes.
- *Roll with resistance* is related to developing discrepancy. However, resistance is accepted by the counselor, and the counselor attempts to understand the client's resistance to change. MI encourages the client to discuss resistance to change, and the counselor is accepting of that perspective while also helping the client consider how the resistance may relate to his or her broader life goals and personal values.
- *Support self-efficacy*, a concept from Bandura's (1986) SCT, refers to a client's beliefs about his or her abilities and competencies to perform new behaviors. MI theory understands that clients must have expectations that they have the necessary skills and competencies to engage in new behaviors that are being promoted. The MI counselor helps clients gain an appreciation of the skills they possess to make change, perhaps through a discussion of changes they made previously that required similar skills or by sharing information about how others have made similar changes.

MI Research

MI was initially developed through clinical trials to stop addictive behaviors. However, MI has since been applied across a broad spectrum of problem behaviors, including eating disorders (Price-Evans & Treasure, 2011), gambling

(Carlbring, Jonsson, Josephson, & Forsberg, 2010), and low academic achievement (Strait et al., 2012). As a framework for prevention interventions, MI has been most used with selective and indicated interventions. MI has been used as an intervention at different life stages, for example, with adolescents who abuse drugs (Jensen et al., 2011), with young adults and college students (Ceperich & Ingersoll, 2011; LaBrie, Pedersen, Lamb, & Quinlan, 2007; Naar-King & Suarez, 2010), and with older adults (Campbell et al., 2009).

Several excellent literature reviews of MI have been published, and they often focus on specific population groups. For example, D. R. Thompson et al. (2011) surveyed the MI literature from 1999 to 2009 pertaining to cardiovascular health. They concluded that MI is a stronger intervention for behavior change than is traditional advice and that MI is especially effective in eliciting intrinsic motivation to change. However, they also noted that MI research is often compromised by methodological problems such as small sample sizes, uneven application of MI, and weak attention to the fidelity of treatment applications. D. R. Thompson et al. also reviewed summaries of several other MI treatment applications and concluded that meta-analyses across different problem areas, for example, smoking, drug, and diet and exercise, were generally positive in support of MI. However, results of primary studies using MI with specific problem areas have been mixed.

Barnett, Sussman, Smith, Rohrbach, and Spruijt-Metz (2012) reviewed 39 studies that used MI with adolescents with substance abuse problems. Two thirds showed significant reduction of adolescent substance abuse, and no differences were found between studies that used MI alone or in combination with other interventions. In their review of nine studies that used MI as an intervention with men at risk for HIV, Berg, Ross, and Tikkanen (2011) found no difference between the MI and the control conditions. However, in a review of overweight and obese patients, MI promoted weight loss and body mass reduction in this population (Armstrong et al., 2011). Yet, of the 101 potential studies, only 12 met inclusion criteria for the review, suggesting weaknesses in research methods in this body of MI research.

Lundahl and Burke (2009) examined four meta-analyses of MI across a range of clinical areas, including illegal substance and tobacco use, risk behaviors, and client engagement in therapy. The researchers concluded that MI is more effective than no treatment and is equally effective with other treatments. They also found that group MI interventions were less effective than individual therapy and that client variables, such as age and severity of problem, were not related to MI outcomes. In some cases, MI was enhanced when used in combination with other therapeutic interventions.

In a clinical trial of a study comparing MI with brief advice to stop adolescents from smoking cigarettes, Colby et al. (2012) found that MI reduced student smoking, compared with brief advice, but neither treatment led to smoking cessation. In this well-controlled study, 162 adolescents, ages 14 to 18, received one in-person treatment session and telephone follow-up sessions at 1, 3, and 6 months. The MI group showed significant decreases in smoking from baseline to 1-month follow-up, and adolescent and adult smoking norms were perceived more accurately after the MI intervention. However, Colby et al. concluded that the study yielded only modest support for MI.

MI has been used in school settings to improve academic achievement. Strait et al. (2012) used one MI session with 50 middle school students and compared their academic performance with a wait-list control group ($n = 53$). In comparison with the control group, students who received MI showed significant improvements in class participation, positive academic behaviors, and higher math grades.

Other applications of MI include brief interventions delivered to college students with problem drinking incidents (Borsari & Carey, 2000; LaBrie, Lamb, Pederson, & Quinlan, 2006). J. G. Murphy et al. (2012) conducted a randomized controlled study with 82 college freshmen in which brief MI was combined with either one substance-free activity session (SFAS) or relaxation training. The SFAS included discussion of career and academic goals, and gave students encouragement to participate in alcohol-free activities (e.g., exercise, creative arts). MI combined with SFAS showed significant reductions of alcohol problems at 1- and 6-month follow-ups, compared with MI with relaxation training.

A web-based application of a wellness and alcohol risk reduction program (MyStudentBody.com) offers online motivational feedback and wellness education for subscribers. The program has been implemented by more than 195 colleges in the United States and abroad for high-risk alcohol users. In a study of persistently heavy college student drinkers, Chiauzzi, Green, Lord, Thum, and Goldstein (2005) reported a decrease in heavy drinking by participants, compared with students who received an attention control condition.

Seal et al. (2012) applied MI to Iraq and Afghanistan war veterans who were positively screened with a telephone-administered assessment for mental health problems. Over a 3-year period, 73 veterans who had at least one mental health problem and who were not receiving treatment were assessed. The veterans were randomly assigned to either a four-telephone-session MI intervention to encourage referral for mental health services or four neutral telephone check-in sessions (control). The MI intervention and control sessions occurred four times over an 8-week period. Veterans receiving the MI intervention were more than twice as likely as control group members to express intent to seek treatment. They also had higher retention rates once in treatment than did controls. The authors concluded that telephone-administered MI treatment enhances veterans' willingness to engage in mental health services, compared with a more standard telephone-administered referral.

Dray and Wade (2012) reviewed studies that combined TTM with MI as treatment for eating disorders. They concluded that, overall, MI added little to the treatment efficacy for eating disorders when used in combination with TTM. However, MI was found to increase motivation for change in studies with binge eating disorder and bulimia nervosa. Generally, however, the research reviewed found inconsistency in procedures and methods, outcome measures, and research design. Thus, reliable conclusions about the efficacy of TTM with MI in the treatment of eating disorders could not be reached, and the authors asserted that more rigorous research is needed here.

C. Murphy, Linehan, Reyner, Musser, and Taft (2012) applied a two-session MI intervention with cognitive behavioral therapy (CBT) with partner-violent men. MI was compared with a standard intake session. With men who were initially reluctant to change, MI produced more willingness to change; for those who claimed to have solved their problem were more likely to comply with CBT homework assignments. In addition, MI contributed to a stronger working alliance for men who were high in the contemplation stage of change, and better attendance at group sessions by those with high trait anger. The researchers found modest support for the benefits of MI with CBT among men who were initially reluctant to change.

Martins and McNeil (2009) reviewed the literature on MI used to influence health promotion behaviors. Specifically, they reviewed a total of 37 studies, of which 24 focused on diet and exercise; nine, on diabetes; and four, on oral health. Generally, they found that MI was shown to be effective in promoting behavior change across the areas of focus reviewed. Although more study is needed, the review also found that when followed over a period of 1 to 2 years, the behavior changes were maintained. Martins and McNeil addressed several methodological issues that need attention before fully sanctioning the effectiveness of MI, including training for those delivering MI and reporting treatment assessments, treatment content, and treatment dose. Also, some studies lacked a control group, and MI was combined with other treatments, thus limiting conclusions based on the effectiveness of MI as a single treatment. These limitations were also revealed in previous reviews of MI as reported by Martins and McNeil. Despite these limitations, the authors concluded that MI shows promise as a viable treatment for behavior change in medical and dental settings.

Strengths and Limitations

MI has received much attention as a theoretical framework for prevention work, especially with selective and indicated prevention interventions. Since it was initially developed, applications of MI have expanded tremendously into many different areas across population groups. The number of literature reviews and meta-analyses of MI is impressive and shows the breadth of MI application, especially for a theoretical model that is fairly new. Health care professionals can be successfully trained in MI (Barwick, Bennett, & Johnson, 2012), and paraprofessionals have been trained in MI to promote peer support for patients with cancer (Allicock et al., 2012). Thus, MI can be taught to professionals who practice outside of the mental health fields, as well as to nonprofessionals to improve health outcomes.

As previously noted, MI has received much less interest as a framework for universal prevention interventions, and there is much less use of MI with elementary school children. MI appears to be most applicable with people who are already experiencing risk behaviors and with people who are comfortable with a less directive and more action-oriented intervention. Young children may respond better to more active and directive interventions.

MI seems to have even greater potential in prevention when used in combination with other theoretical models and constructs, such as self-efficacy, TTM, and CBT. However, much more research is needed to evaluate the extent to which MI is more effective in combination with other interventions. Research is also needed to fully evaluate MI's contribution to behavior change. Although MI has been used with different population groups and problem areas, there is no clear consensus about the contributions of parts of the theory to behavior change. However, because interest in MI is very strong, improved research methods and applications of MI, either by itself or in combination with other models, are likely to lead to a greater understanding of MI in behavior change.

SUMMARY

It is important to articulate a theoretical framework during the design and implementation of prevention interventions. This chapter has presented four models and theoretical perspectives that have received considerable attention in the literature but are not often discussed in training programs for applied psychologists, counselors, and other mental health professionals. Therefore, the chapter provided prevention specialists with several theories that may be applicable to their activities. Prevention specialists may investigate other theories to guide their interventions, and they are encouraged to do so. The theories and models summarized in this chapter can be used alone or in combination with other theoretical perspectives to advance the science of prevention.

It is unfortunate that prevention interventions are often developed and implemented without one or more theoretical frameworks to guide them. Without a theoretical base, it is more difficult to assess which of an intervention's components are most efficacious with a given behavior and/or population group.

4

PROTECTIVE FACTORS: PROMOTING STRENGTHS AND BUILDING POSITIVE BEHAVIORS

An integral component of a prevention framework is the promotion of personal strengths and positive characteristics and behaviors that serve as buffers or protectors against the development of problem behaviors at the individual and systemic levels. Thus, a prevention framework includes not only working to prevent problem behaviors but also actively working to increase behaviors and strengthen characteristics that are protections against potential problems. Thus, one can think of protective factors as helping to inoculate individuals and larger systems against the development of risk behaviors that can lead to problems. Examples of prevention interventions that promote protections include strengthening interpersonal skills, teaching safe-sex practices, developing healthy leisure activities, improving decision making, supporting families, improving access to health care, and reducing neighborhood crime.

In this chapter, I identify risk and protective factors at individual and systemic levels for various behavior problems and population groups. I also

DOI: 10.1037/14442-004
Prevention Psychology: Enhancing Personal and Social Well-Being, by J. L. Romano
Copyright © 2015 by the American Psychological Association. All rights reserved.

summarize research and activities that target such factors to reduce risks and prevent problem behaviors.

BACKGROUND

The importance of giving increased attention to protective factors in prevention was recognized in the National Research Council and Institute of Medicine's (2009) *Preventing Mental, Emotional, and Behavioral Disorders Among Young People: Progress and Possibilities*. In this 2009 volume, the Committee on the Prevention of Mental Disorders and Substance Abuse Among Children, Youth, and Young Adults added mental health promotion as necessary for healthy development in the prevention of behavioral and mental disorders. In distinguishing between prevention and health promotion, the Committee wrote

> Prevention emphasizes the avoidance of risk factors; promotion strives to promote supportive family, school, and community environments and to identify and imbue in young people protective factors, which are traits that enhance well-being and provide the tools to avoid adverse emotions and behaviors. (p. xv)

More specifically, the Committee defined a *protective factor* as "a characteristic at the biological, psychological, family, or community (including peers and culture) level that is associated with a lower likelihood of problem outcomes or that reduces the negative impact of a risk factor on problem outcomes" (p. xxvii). Protective factors are important to highlight because their promotion has historically been given less attention in prevention work than preventing problem behaviors.

PROTECTIVE AND RISK FACTORS

A discussion of protective factors in prevention must be considered in relation to risk factors. The National Research Council and Institute of Medicine's (2009) Committee on the Prevention of Mental Disorders and Substance Abuse Among Children, Youth, and Young Adults defined a *risk factor* as "a characteristic at the biological, psychological, family, or community or cultural level that precedes and is associated with a higher likelihood of problem outcomes" (p. xxviii). This definition, similar to the definition of protective factors, includes individual and systemic risks. The definitions of risk and protective factors may be considered as opposite poles of specific variables, such that the absence of a protective variable can be considered as contributing to the risk of a problem, and the presence of such a variable is considered protection. For example, positive and healthy family dynamics and strong parenting skills are considered protective in reducing problems of youth, whereas their opposites are considered to be risk factors (Flores, Cicchetti, & Rogosch, 2005; Spoth, Kavanagh, & Dishion, 2002).

The relationship between risk and protective variables in the development of problem behaviors was refined by Lösel and Farrington (2012). Although Lösel and Farrington focused on youth violence, their conceptualization of risk and protective factors can apply to other problem behaviors and conditions. In their review, they differentiated between direct protective factors and buffering protective factors against violence. *Buffering protective factors* produce lower probability of youth engaging in violence despite risk factors being present, whereas *direct protective factors* result in a lower probability of problem behavior without considering the presence of risk factors. In their review of more than 100 studies of violence and aggression, Lösel and Farrington identified six categories of personal and environmental characteristics that protect youth against violence if they are present in a health-enhancing context. However, if they are not present or exist in an unhealthy way, they can contribute to risks of violent and aggressive behaviors. The six categories are (a) biological, (b) personality, (c) family, (d) school, (e) peers, and (f) community.

- *Biological* factors may be genetic, prenatal, and perinatal influences on the child.
- *Personality* characteristics include temperament, risk taking, and impulsivity.
- *Family* considerations include quality of family relationships, especially parental relationships, family support, and parental supervision.
- Characteristics of the *school* environment can also be considered as both risk and protection variables. These characteristics include school achievement, student's connectedness to school, motivation to achieve, and teacher support and supervision.
- *Peer* relationships may create protections or risks, depending on whether peers are supportive (protection) of nondeviate behaviors, which would be protective peer relationships, or if peers engage in deviate behaviors, they would constitute peer relationships that add to risk. Also, peers who affiliate with groups and activities that enhance health and well-being, such as religious groups and school organizations, are protective, whereas affiliation with peers who have very little involvement with health-enhancing activities may constitute a risk.

School-based activities may include participation in athletics, in peer governance and student clubs, and in service learning opportunities.

- *Community* protective factors include broader environmental social contexts that are nonviolent, demonstrate cohesiveness through healthy neighborhood gatherings, and promote personal safety, and community space that demonstrates an appreciation for maintaining the pleasing appearance of physical space.

As exemplified by Lösel and Farrington's (2012) review, risk and protective variables as predictive of problem behaviors are not necessarily mutually exclusive. In the majority of situations, especially when dealing with multiple factors and layers of context, from the individual to the family to the larger community, risk and protective factors related to problem behaviors exist. Risk and protective factors tend to overlap across different types of problem areas, whether at the personal, institutional, or larger environmental levels. Both types of factors exist at multiple levels and in different contextual environments, such as in families, schools, workplaces, and communities across national and international contexts (Viner et al., 2012). The goal of prevention, therefore, is to strengthen protections while alleviating risks.

Coie et al. (1993), reporting from a panel of a 1991 National Prevention Conference sponsored by the National Institute of Mental Health, identified protective factors as mitigating against risk factors through direct or indirect means. Direct influences of protections include characteristics or behaviors that prevent the problem directly, and indirect influences buffer the risks associated with a problem. An example of the former may include structured alcohol prevention programs that develop decision-making skills and assertive behaviors. An example of the latter would be community-level protections that rigorously enforce legal age to purchase and consume alcohol. Coie et al. identified two major types of protective factors that may limit problems in childhood: (a) *individual* characteristics, such as cognitive skills and temperament, as well as genetic and biological characteristics; and (b) *environmental* factors that may include positive family characteristics, such as support and resources of parents and caregivers.

Coie et al. (1993) identified protective and risk factors as critically important to prevention science. As protective factors, they specifically identified psychological resilience, skills, strengths, and environmental advantages. They further emphasized the importance of giving attention to protective and risk factors that are common to multiple disorders and of addressing protective factors with adult populations, especially with universal prevention interventions recommended to all people in the population (e.g., seat belt use).

Protective and Risk Factors in Adolescent Problem Behaviors

Jessor, Van Den Bos, Vanderryn, Costa, and Turbin (1995) studied protective factors in adolescent problem behaviors, such as alcohol and drug use, delinquent behaviors, and early sexual activity. They conceptualized protective factors as those that decrease the likelihood of engaging in problem behaviors, such as through personal and social controls (e.g., parental and religious sanctions), activities that are incompatible with problem behaviors (e.g., family or religious activities), and positive involvement with societal institutions (e.g., schools, families). Contrasting protective factors with risk factors, Jessor et al. conceptualized risk factors as increasing the likelihood of engaging in problem behaviors. Examples of risk factors include direct encouragement from peers to engage in problem behaviors; personal vulnerability, such as low self-esteem; and opportunities to engage in problem behaviors, such as availability of alcohol and lack of adult supervision. The researchers studied the moderating effect of protective and risk factors on problem behaviors of students in Grades 7 through 9. Their analysis included White, Hispanic, and Black students (representing 94% of the sample), who completed measures of risk and protection factors over the 4-year period of the study ($N = 1,486$). Four problem behaviors were investigated: alcohol use, delinquent-type behavior, marijuana use, and sexual intercourse. Six measures of risk were obtained, and seven measures of protection. The seven protective factors measured three related to the personality system (i.e., positive orientation to school, positive orientation toward health, and intolerance for deviance), three represented the perceived environment system (i.e., positive adult relationships, regulatory controls [e.g., curfews, dating], friends who engage conventional behaviors [e.g., religious activities, school clubs, academics]), and one represented the involvement and time in prosocial activities (e.g., sports, social service involvements). A total of six risk factors were represented by three of the personality system (i.e., low expectations for success, low self-esteem, and high hopelessness), two of the perceived environment system (i.e., friends who model problem behaviors and high influence of friends compared with parents), and one risk factor of the behavior system (i.e., low grade point average [GPA]). Their results showed that psychosocial protective factors are important in moderating adolescent problem behaviors. Specifically, protections mitigate problem behaviors and moderate the impact of risk factors. This study was an early comprehensive study of protective factors with adolescents during a period when most of the research attention on adolescent problems focused on risk factors.

A particularly interesting national study on risk and protective factors predictive of substance use and misuse was conducted with youth involved with the child welfare system (Traube, James, Zhang, & Landsverk, 2012).

A large national U.S. study was conducted with a sample of youth ages 11 to 14, using the social development model (Catalano, Kosterman, Hawkins, Newcomb, & Abbott, 1996) as its theoretical foundation. The researchers undertook the study at least partially because of the paucity of research on risk and protective factors in this vulnerable population. However, the study did not shed much new light on risk and protective factors for substance use and abuse with this population, as the findings on the roles of demographic and psychosocial risk and protective factors were not conclusive. Only a limited role was found for protective factors for substance use, as caregiver connectedness impacted use, and no protective factors affected the major substance use in the future. The sparse findings of this study on risk and protections were somewhat similar to those of an earlier study of similar youth that assessed risk and protective variables predictive of sexual risk behaviors (S. James, Montgomery, Leslie, & Zhang, 2009). In that study, the researchers found that protective factors of caregiver monitoring and caregiver connectedness had a limited role in moderating sexual intercourse and using contraception during intercourse.

Protective and Risk Factors for Youth Violence

A series of papers published in the *American Journal of Preventive Medicine* examined protective factors in the prevention of youth violence across four large-scale U.S. research programs (Hall et al., 2012). An expert panel of the Centers for Disease Control and Prevention summarized the studies and considered the important protections that directly influence youth violence, as well as those that serve as buffering protections (Hall et al., 2012). The panel also noted that much research has been conducted on risk factors for youth violence but that more research on protective factors is needed. They also emphasized that risk and protective factors are not simply opposites but distinct variables that may predict youth violence.

In a study of risk and protective factors for youth violence using data from the National Longitudinal Study of Adolescent Health, Bernat, Oakes, Pettingell, and Resnick (2012) identified several characteristics that serve as protections for 14-year-olds becoming involved with violent behaviors. Protections for violent behaviors—defined as one act of using a weapon or serious fighting on three or more occasions—included low levels of attention-deficit/hyperactivity disorder (ADHD) symptoms, low emotional distress, high educational aspirations, and high GPA. Risk factors for violent behaviors at the same age included early ADHD symptoms, weak connections to school, high levels of delinquency in peers, and low GPA. However, for older youth, ages 18 to 20, the only direct protective effect for violent behaviors was low peer delinquency. No other risk and protective factors studied were present, demonstrating difficulties with predicting youth involvement with violence and the need to search for additional risk and protective variables of youth involvement in violent behaviors (Bernat et al., 2012).

In another study of youth violence prevention, Henry, Tolan, Gorman-Smith, and Schoeny (2012) studied more than 4,000 middle school youth across multiple school sites, measuring a variety of factors, including depression, delinquency, involvement with alcohol and drugs, school attitudes and school achievement, and involvement with family activities. The researchers found that only higher study skills were associated with lower involvement with violence across all ethnic groups and genders. They concluded that it is important to consider ethnicity in identifying protective and risk factors for violent behaviors, as their study found that affiliation with peer delinquents was a risk factor for students identified as White and Other, but this risk factor was only marginally associated with violent behaviors of African American students and was not related to violent behaviors of Latino youth.

Promoting Protective Factors in Schools

Prevention programs in schools that are long term, comprehensive, and coordinated across a school or system have yielded positive results (Espelage & Poteat, 2012; Greenberg et al., 2003; Nation et al., 2003). Promoting protective factors in school-based youth prevention programs has been highlighted by Romano (1996, 1997). Evaluating the efficacy of school personnel training designed to strengthen student protections against drug and alcohol use, Romano (1997) defined the concept of *student well-being* (SWB) as "the development of knowledge, attitudes, skills, and behaviors that maximize student's functioning (i.e., academic, inter- and intrapersonal, and physical and emotional health) in environments where they live and work (i.e., school, home, and community)" (p. 246). SWB is a holistic conceptual framework that facilitates the promotion of student protective factors at the individual and environmental levels, as implemented by school-based educators, who are closely connected to the students. Therefore, in this educator training model of drug and alcohol prevention, the emphasis is on helping educators develop protections for the student and the larger environment, rather than focusing only on the prevention of risks associated with the problem behaviors. The SWB training model has been shown to increase educators' self-efficacy in promoting SWB immediately after the training and at follow-up (Romano, 1996).

Romano's (1997) model supports the necessity to consider actual and potential protections of individuals and larger contexts to mitigate the impact of risk factors that may exist at the individual, systems, and environmental levels. An emphasis on risk factors to the neglect of protective factors can create an unbalanced situation in which those at risk may be victimized and incur blame for their problems. Also, some students might be considered at risk because of environmental or biological factors beyond the control of the individual. If students are considered at risk for school failure because of the socio-economic conditions in which they find themselves, there is little they can do to improve their situation. Therefore, rather than only focusing on risk conditions, it is important to address potential protections that can be strengthened in the adolescent and/or in his or her environment. For example, educators and parents can assist the student to focus on his or her interpersonal skills that may help him or her develop positive relational influences with adults and peers. Similarly, by educators and parents assessing the student's nonacademic skills, such as those, for example, that are important in theater production, music, or athletics, the student will be encouraged to engage in school-based activities that give meaning to school beyond academics while also strengthening positive intrapersonal characteristics, developing healthy relationships, and promoting skill development.

Protective and Risk Factors for Substance Use in Adolescence and Young Adulthood

Much of the research on risk and protective factors in prevention has been conducted with children and adolescents. However, A. L. Stone, Becker, Huber, and Catalano (2012) examined risk protective factors for substance use in young adults ages 18 to 26. The results of their literature review were similar to results on risk and protective factors with younger ages. However, age-related life events, such as marriage, legally obtaining alcohol, and postsecondary education, influenced risk and protections for this age group. A. L. Stone et al. used a similar framework to investigate risk and protective factors as presented 20 years earlier by Hawkins, Catalano, and Miller (1992) and required that at least two longitudinal studies demonstrate an association with a prediction of risk or protection of a variable. Interestingly, the two reviews of protective factors and risks associated with substance use and abuse problems were similar despite being conducted 20 years apart. In the A. L. Stone et al. study, the risk and protective factors that had an impact included those that were fixed (e.g., sex and race/ethnicity), contextual (e.g., social norms, laws, taxation of substances), or individual and interpersonal (e.g., family relations, peer relationships, marriage or cohabitation). Longitudinal studies are needed to more fully evaluate the impact of military service, college attendance, parental attitudes, and social engagement and volunteerism. Young adults experience unique risks, such as increased independence from parents and living outside of the parental home, but they also have increased protections, such as being married or cohabitating and graduating from college. The two studies, two decades apart, show the range and number of risk and protective factors that are associated with predicting adolescent and young adult use and misuse of substances such as drugs, alcohol, and tobacco. Developmental periods of youth and young adults must be considered when identifying risk and protections as predictors of problem behaviors. A similar conclusion was reached from a large-scale study of adolescents and young adults, 11 to 24 years old, across 30 Tennessee counties (Harris Abadi, Shamblen, Thompson, Collins, & Johnson, 2011).

When considering predictors for problem behaviors, one must also consider in addition to age the environmental context, especially as individuals gain increased autonomy and independence from caregivers and legal sanctions. For example, alcohol use is legal at 21 years of age, as is marijuana use in some U.S. jurisdictions.

Protective Factors for Depression in Older Adulthood

Beyond considering the emerging adulthood years, researchers are giving increased attention to protections and risks in predicting mental health problems in later life. For example, C. F. Reynolds et al.'s (2012) review of studies found success for selective and indicated prevention interventions for older adults at risk for depression. In high-income countries, psychoeducational and psychological interventions reduced the rate of depression from 20% to 25%. In addition, psychological and psychopharmaceutical interventions reduced the recurrence of major depression. In middle- and low-income countries, lay health counselors offer promise in delivering psychoeducational prevention interventions in collaboration with health care professionals. Prevention interventions for older adults designed to reduce risks and strengthen protections include social support groups, life reviews and remembrances, cognitive behavioral interventions, and medications. Prevention with older populations, specifically the prevention of depression, is critically important given the aging populations throughout the world and the high incidence of depression, which can lead to other health complications (C. F. Reynolds, 2009). Although demonstration trials of prevention interventions have yielded positive results in higher income countries, there is less evidence of their success when adopted for similar prevention interventions but with limited funding, especially in middle and lower income countries.

Older adults without symptoms or disease are also encouraged and provided with opportunities to develop protective behaviors that can help to inoculate them against physical and mental health problems. The protective behaviors can be implemented by health care personnel at personal and environmental levels. At a personal level, older adults can receive periodic messages and support to exercise, to eat healthfully, and to manage stress, to name only a few. At environmental levels, protections can be implemented and supported through indoor and outdoor cigarette-free environments, healthy food choice options in places where seniors gather, and community programs and activities that support wellness and address the needs of the older population.

Resilience

Resilience is one protective factor that has received considerable attention in the literature since it was first introduced by Werner, Bierman, and French (1971). Werner et al. studied Hawaiian youth who were raised in very difficult situations but who managed to succeed despite overwhelming odds against them. In their critical analysis of resilience research, Luthar, Cicchetti, and Becker (2000) defined *resilience* as "a dynamic process encompassing positive adaptation within the context of significant adversity" (p. 543). Although resilience as a psychological construct has been studied extensively, the construct is not without difficulties, as shown by Luthar et al. These authors addressed several problem areas, including inconsistencies in theoretical frameworks, definitions, and terminology, and research methods. However, despite these challenges, Luthar et al. showed the need to continue to clarify and address problematic issues related to the construct of resiliency and to not abandon the construct, recognizing its importance within a prevention framework and especially as a protective factor in reducing risks for problem behaviors.

Resilience and Ethnic Minority Youth and Young Adults

A 2008 American Psychological Association (APA) report on resilience and strengths in Black youth emphasized strengths and protective factors of this demographic. This is an important emphasis because the majority of research conducted with Black youth, as with other minority groups, focuses on reducing risk factors. As the report makes clear, it is important to acknowledge protections that this population group possesses and to further develop these protections in youth (APA Task Force on Resilience and Strength in Black Children and Adolescents, 2008). In the report, the authors identified how factors that are traditionally thought of as risk factors for this group can be considered as adaptive and protective.

In the APA Task Force on Resilience and Strength in Black Children and Adolescents (2008) report, studies of African American youth ages 5 to 21 across all socioeconomic groups and regions of the United States were reviewed to examine how factors such as racial identity, racial socialization, emotional regulation and expression, religiosity, and school and family support can prepare African American youth to thrive despite societal challenges. The report describes characteristics of optimal functioning for African American youth that include the themes of active engagement, flexibility, communalism, and critical-mindedness, and shows how these themes cut across the following five developmental domains.

1. *Identity development.* Positive racial identity is essential to the well-being of African American youth and they must be encouraged to develop a positive sense of self in a society that often devalues them through negative stereotypes.
2. *Emotional development.* Coping with emotions effectively is directly related to self-esteem and better mental health. African American youth need to be made aware of how their emotional expressions resonate across all situations and circumstances.
3. *Social development.* Family and community interaction is crucial to these young people's social development, as is having access to high-quality child care, after-school programs, and religious institutions.
4. *Cognitive development.* African American youth must believe in their abilities in the classroom. Parents should avoid harsh parenting styles, and schools should continue to look at ways to infuse culturally relevant themes into the classroom as a way to improve academic performance.
5. *Physical health and development.* A wide range of health conditions disproportionately affect African American youth, including obesity, poor oral health, asthma, violent injury, sickle cell anemia, diabetes, and HIV/AIDS. Research has proven that improved physical health is more likely to lead to improved mental health as well (American Psychological Association, 2008).

Others have also focused on resilience on ethnic minority youth. Flores et al. (2005) studied predictors of resilience in maltreated and non-maltreated Latino youth to gain a greater understanding of how resilience may be promoted in this demographic. It is not surprising that maltreated Latino youth experienced more difficulties and lower levels of resilience compared with a matched group of Latino children who were not maltreated. On interpersonal variables, maltreated youth experienced more difficulties in interpersonal functioning, especially with developing a strong relationship with an adult, a characteristic that is associated with the development of resiliency in youth. This study was important because it is one of the few studies that addressed the protective factor of resilience in Latino children, a growing population in the United States.

In a study of protective factors against the effects of discrimination among Korean American college students, R. M. Lee (2005) found partial support for ethnic identity as a moderating influence on the negative effects of discrimination on depression and social connectedness. In this study, Korean Americans who experienced high ethnic pride in the face of discrimination had fewer depressive symptoms and higher social connectedness. However, when higher levels of discrimination were present, ethnic pride did not moderate depression and social connectedness. However, in Korean Americans, higher levels of depression and lower social connectedness were associated with high and low levels of discrimination, regardless of their levels of ethnic pride. Therefore, the development of ethnic pride in this population group may not be protective in the face of higher levels of discrimination against the group. Given the relatively small sample size ($N = 84$) of Korean American college students in the study, R. M. Lee acknowledged that the variables studied may not yield similar results with other ethnic groups or even with other groups of Korean Americans with different demographics. However, this research supports the need for additional study of protective factors for different population demographic groups.

ENHANCING SYSTEMIC PROTECTIVE FACTORS

Supporting and facilitating protective factors beyond the individual level into systemic levels, Vera and Shin (2006) discussed the importance of addressing socially toxic environments in which people live. Citing work from Garbarino and colleagues (Garbarino, 1995; Garbarino & Bedard, 2001), Vera and Shin noted that social toxins such as poverty, racism, lack of adult supervision, isolation from community, and violence impede the development of strengths and protective factors in youth. However, psychologists' and other mental health professionals' shift to a preventive focus will require a movement away from traditional, crisis-oriented counseling and psychotherapy to a greater emphasis on using professional knowledge and talents to positively impact larger social systems, such as families, schools, and neighborhoods. This will require that mental health and human development professionals receive training on influencing public policies to reduce or eliminate social toxins in society and to develop policies that enhance personal and institutional protections, such as reducing crime, improving health care, and providing increased access to educational opportunities. This type of advocacy is aligned with the social justice perspective of prevention discussed in Chapter 5.

POSITIVE PSYCHOLOGY

Positive psychology as a specialty area of psychological research and practice has received considerable attention in the social sciences since the 1990s, although topics under the umbrella of positive psychology (e.g., creativity, happiness, hope, wisdom) have been explored throughout history in many disciplines, including philosophy, religion, literature, and the social sciences (Peterson, Park, & Seligman, 2005). Nevertheless, during the past 20 years, scholars have brought renewed attention and excitement to what is often referred to as *positive psychology* (Clifton & Nelson, 1992; Lopez & Snyder, 2009; Peterson & Seligman, 2004; Seligman & Csikszentmihalyi, 2000; Snyder & Lopez, 2007).

Positive psychology refers to the study of the positive characteristics of people and the study of positive human functioning. The focus on the positive is contrasted with psychology's historical emphasis on negative aspects of human functioning (e.g., depression, anxiety, abuse, addiction). The domain of positive psychology studies questions such as how people achieve positive states of being, for example, happiness, hope, resiliency, creativity, and emotional well-being. Snyder and Lopez (2007) defined positive psychology as the "scientific and applied approach to uncovering people's strengths and promoting their positive functioning" (p. 3). Seligman, Steen, Park, and Peterson (2005) offered a broader definition of positive psychology as "an umbrella term for the study of positive emotions, positive character traits, and enabling institutions" (p. 410). Scholars also emphasize that positive psychology is not intended to replace psychology's historical emphasize on deficits, weaknesses, and problems but is instead intended to balance the study of human emotions and experiences to include positive aspects of human functioning (A. H. S. Harris, Thoresen, & Lopez, 2007).

Positive psychology as a conceptual framework for prevention is quite appropriate (Seligman & Csikszentmihalyi, 2000). The definition of prevention used in this book includes the promotion of individual, group, and institutional strengths and assets, and the promotion of factors that serve as protections from human difficulties and suffering. Protective factors are important components of a comprehensive framework for prevention because they serve to shield individuals and institutions against the effects of personal risk characteristics (e.g., temperament, skill deficiency) and exposure to unhealthy environments (e.g., poverty, family instability, crime) (Coie et al., 1993). Therefore, positive psychology can inform prevention interventions that promote positive aspects of individuals, groups, and communities in order to strengthen their ability to resist problem behaviors through protective factors. Seligman and Csikszentmihalyi (2000) echoed Albee's (1983) contention that neither the disease model of care in psychology and the health sciences nor the emphasis on personal deficits has served to further the prevention of psychological disorders and human distress. The enhanced study of personal and institutional strengths and positive characteristics gives the helping professions a viable avenue through which to develop preventive interventions to reduce psychological dysfunction and human suffering.

During the first decade of the 21st century, the study of positive psychology has yielded numerous journal articles, journal special issues, books, websites, conferences, and college courses devoted to the topic (e.g., *Journal of Positive Psychology, Journal of Happiness Studies, Handbook of Positive Psychology* [Lopez & Snyder, 2009]). Seligman and Csikszentmihalyi (2000) edited one of the first special journal issues on positive human functioning to reach a broad readership of psychologists. Articles in this special issue of *American Psychologist* included those by Buss (2000) and Myers (2000) on happiness, subjective well-being by Diener (2000), and Simonton (2000) on creativity; more recently, special issues of *The Counseling Psychologist* on optimal human functioning (Lopez et al., 2006) and strength-based counseling (Smith, 2006) investigated both theoretical and applied aspects of positive psychology as it applies to areas as diverse as vocational psychology (Robitschek & Woodson, 2006) and multiculturalism (Constantine & Sue, 2006). A special issue of the *Journal of Social and Clinical Psychology* addressed sources of human strengths and their relationship to variables of positive human functioning, such as wisdom, forgiveness, and hope (McCullough & Snyder, 2000). Positive psychology has excited the profession, as evidenced by its popularity and scholarly works. Positive psychology can be used as a framework to better understand the human experience and to aid in the prevention of psychological disorders and the enhancement of emotional well-being (Seligman et al., 2005).

A major contribution to the application of positive psychology was made by Peterson and Seligman (2004), who developed a classification scheme for positive human characteristics or strengths that they hoped would rival the *Diagnostic and Statistical Manual of Mental Disorders* (e.g., American Psychiatric Association, 2000) classification for emotional disturbance. Peterson and Seligman called their classification system Character Strengths and Virtues (CSV). More recently, Peterson and Park (2009) referred to the CSV classification as the Virtues in Action (VIA) classification, consisting of 24 strengths of character organized within six core virtues. According to Peterson and Park, VIA describes "a vocabulary for psychologically informed discourse on the qualities of a person worthy of moral praise" (p. 26). The VIA's six core virtues and character strengths associated with each value (in parentheses) are (a) wisdom and knowledge (creativity, curiosity, open mindedness, love of learning, perspective), (b) courage (authenticity, bravery, perseverance, zest), (c) humanity (kindness, love, social intelligence), (d) justice (fairness, leadership, teamwork), (e) temperance (forgiveness, modesty, prudence, self-regulation), and (f) transcendence (appreciation of beauty and excellence, gratitude, hope, humor, religiousness). Measures to assess VIA character strengths have been developed and refined over several years of empirical study, with data collected in multiple ways, including Internet surveys (Peterson & Park, 2009). The measure is called the Values in Action Survey of Character (or VIA Inventory of Strengths; Snyder & Lopez, 2007) and is available online (see http://www.viacharacter.org). The adult version of the VIA Inventory of Strengths consists of 240 questions, 10 questions for each strength; a shorter adolescent version is also available (Park & Peterson, 2005; Snyder & Lopez, 2007). Seligman et al. (2005) cited endorsements and empirical evidence for the six virtues and 24 character strengths in various countries and cultures.

In addition to the VIA classification, Snyder and Lopez (2007) summarized two other widely used classifications and measures of human strengths: Gallup's Clifton StrengthsFinder and the Search Institute's 40 Developmental Assets.

Clifton StrengthsFinder

The StrengthsFinder classification was developed by Donald Clifton at the University of Nebraska and the Gallup Organization. Clifton began his investigations on career success and what is "right" with people in the 1950s, years before the current wave of enthusiasm for positive psychology (Snyder & Lopez, 2007). Clifton's small organizational consulting firm eventually acquired the Gallup Organization in 1988, and he remained as its board chair until 1999. His significant contributions to human strengths were recognized by APA in 2002 through an APA Presidential Commendation that honored Donald Clifton as the "father of strength-based psychology."

Conceptually, Clifton aligned success with a person's talents, strengths, and intelligence, and after a few iterations, his StrengthsFinder classification was finalized, and currently includes 34 themes, with 180 paired items. The StrengthsFinder is a web-based assessment that informs several best-selling books (see http://www.strengths.gallup.com). Examples of the StrengthsFinder 34 themes and brief definitions (in parentheses) as reported by Snyder and Lopez (2007) are (a) achiever (much stamina, work hard, and productive), (b) belief (strong core values that define their life's purpose), (c) focus (follow through and stay on track), (d) harmony (seek consensus), (e) positivity (enthusiastic about their activities which rubs off on others), (f) responsibility (take ownership and possess values of honesty and loyalty, (g) significance (independent and want to be recognized by others).

StrengthsFinder has been translated into several languages, and the Clifton Youth StrengthsExplorer is available for children and adolescents from 10 to 14 years old. The youth version is also web-based and includes resources for parents and educators.

Much psychometric research has been conducted with the Strengths-Finder, and it has been found to have strong psychometric properties (Lopez, Hodges, & Harter, 2005). Limitations of the StrengthsFinder are that only an individual's top five themes (top three for youth) are ranked, and it is not sensitive to pre–post change and should not be used as a measure in this way (Snyder & Lopez, 2007).

Search Institute Developmental Assets

The Search Institute, a Minneapolis-based organization founded in 1958, partners with community institutions and organizations to promote healthy children and adolescents by focusing on community and youth assets through programs of education, training, research, and leadership (Search Institute, n.d.). In 1990, the Search Institute conducted a national survey (Profiles of Student Life: Attitudes and Behaviors) of adolescents in Grades 6 through 12 across 111 communities in the United States. The results of the survey were reported in a landmark publication, *Troubled Journey: A Portrait of 6th–12th Grade Youth*, which identified 30 assets of healthy youth development (Benson, 1993). The assets are presented as building blocks that can help to prevent youth participation in risk behaviors and promote success in school and other aspects of life. On the basis of subsequent survey research, the original set of developmental assets was expanded from 30 to 40 assets, with 20 assets identified as internal and 20 as external. *Internal assets* are personal characteristics and behaviors such as achievement motivation, caring, and self-esteem. *External assets* include support and caring environments in which adolescents live, creative use of time and leisure, and community resources and services (Snyder & Lopez, 2007). The Search Institute continues to conduct research on adolescents, and its work has expanded to include developmental assets of younger children. The Search Institute's framework of developmental assets has been applied to entire communities to strengthen community involvement in the promotion of youth asset development. One such project, Children First, was initiated in 1993 in St. Louis Park, Minnesota, and remains active in the city. Characteristics of Children First are that it (a) is referred to as a philosophy and not a program; (b) focuses on the positive attributes of youth and not on negative, risk behaviors; (c) targets all youth from birth to 18 years; (d) supports active community-wide partnerships with business, city, education, health, and faith communities; and (e) calls on all community members to support youth (www.children-first.org). This type of collaborative community initiative exemplifies the often quoted phrase "It takes a village to raise a child," recognizing the importance of a community working together to promote youth development and reduce problem behaviors. Children First is a good example of a systemic community program to promote protective factors among youth.

Conceptually, positive psychology and the promotion of optimal human functioning have proven to be exceptionally fertile topics for scholarly inquiry and applications with children, youth, and adults in diverse settings (Lopez & Snyder, 2009). The ideas surrounding investigations of positive traits in people and institutions hold much merit and attraction for professional communities and the lay public. Positive psychology offers a model that can serve as a foundation for strength-based preventive interventions with children, youth, and adults (Galassi & Akos, 2007; Lopez & Snyder, 2009; Smith, 2006).

SUMMARY

Protective factors in mitigating risks for problem behaviors are important in prevention. Although scholarship on protective factors has been increasing, historically, much more attention has been given to risk factors. There is much more research conducted on both risks to, and protection of, children and adolescents compared with other age groups. However, risk and protection research with later adolescents and early adulthood is a growing area. Beyond early adulthood, research on risk and protective factors during the middle and later years of life is scarce. Protective and risk factor research with older adults is needed and important, given the aging population in the United States and across the globe.

As reviewed in this chapter, protective factors for problem behaviors are not necessarily the positive side of risk factors in all situations. In some contexts, they may offer very different perspectives on reducing problem behaviors. In other words, reducing risks does not necessarily enhance protections; similarly, strengthening protections does not necessarily reduce risks. Therefore, prevention researchers and practitioners need to consider both risk and protection variables in prevention research and applications.

The perspective of the specialty area of positive psychology offers a useful theoretical foundation in the consideration of protective factors. Researchers and prevention specialists can use concepts from positive psychology to anchor interventions that promote protections against particular problems. For example, at the individual level, personal strengths may be enhanced if they are shown to be protective against particular problems. Similarly, institutional and environmental strengths can be promoted as a means to reduce problem behaviors. The use of positive psychology as foundation in the prevention of problems is at a very early stage, but this strengths-based orientation offers much promise in prevention research and applications.

5

SOCIAL JUSTICE AND PUBLIC POLICY ADVOCACY

During the 20th century, the development of prevention in the mental health professions has been fueled by strong social justice and advocacy orientations. Social justice, prevention, and advocacy of public policies that enrich lives are related. As summarized in Chapter 2, early 20th century social reformers from the fields of mental health, social work, and vocational guidance articulated their principles, ideals, and activities from social justice and social advocacy perspectives.

Social justice as a foundation for prevention gained increased attention in psychology during the 1960s and 1970s (Fondacaro & Weinberg, 2002). This period in U.S. history was marked by much social upheaval and social justice advocacy for less empowered members of society. One of the outcomes of the social movements was a new psychological specialty, community psychology. Community Psychology, the 27th Division

DOI: 10.1037/14442-005
Prevention Psychology: Enhancing Personal and Social Well-Being, by J. L. Romano

of the American Psychological Association (APA), was formed in 1965. The division, currently named the Society for Community Research and Action (SCRA)—Community Psychology, continues to promote a vision of social justice and prevention goals. The division promotes "a strong, global impact on enhancing well-being and promoting social justice for all people by fostering collaboration where there is division and empowerment where there is oppression," and one of its goals is "to promote the use of social and behavioral science to enhance the well-being of people and their communities and to prevent harmful outcomes" (SCRA, n.d.).

In the 21st century, there has been continued emphasis on and interest in the relationship between social justice and prevention in psychology and human development (Goodman et al., 2004; Kenny & Hage, 2009; Kenny, Horne, Orpinas, & Reese, 2009a; Pieterse, Hanus, & Gale, 2013; Reese & Vera, 2007; Vera & Kenny, 2013). The relationship between prevention and social justice is complex. Kenny and Hage (2009) described prevention as "an instrument of social justice" (p. 1). However, it can also be argued that social justice and advocacy enhance a prevention perspective and influence actions across many domains of society. Nevertheless, there is a very strong interrelationship between social justice, public policy advocacy, and prevention, as I delineate in this chapter. Social justice and its promotion through public policy advocacy advance a preventive perspective, and the goals of prevention are embedded in the promotion and support of practices and policies that empower people and reduce oppression.

A history of social justice and prevention clearly shows the interplay between the two, starting with early 20th social reform movements to improve the lives of less empowered members of U.S. society. However, relationships between social justice, public policy advocacy, and prevention are complex, in that people have different values and beliefs associated with how best to prevent problems (e.g., health care and gun control debates in the United States). Nevertheless, it is important to recognize and understand the promotion of social justice through prevention and vice versa within a broader conceptualization of prevention.

This chapter begins with John Rawls's (1971) theory of a just society, which provides a framework for the integration of prevention and social justice. This integration is then highlighted in the work of two psychologists, George Albee and Isaac Prilleltensky. As a follow-up to the perspectives offered by these scholars, I discuss the role of psychologists and other mental health professionals in public policy advocacy to support prevention initiatives that promote individual and institutional well-being.

JOHN RAWLS: DISTRIBUTIVE JUSTICE AND THE PROMOTION OF A JUST SOCIETY

Distributive justice as a concept in scholarly discourse has a long history, dating back to antiquity (Englard, 2009; Frohlich, 2007). Distributive justice is concerned with the fair and equitable distribution of goods, services, and resources to promote a just society. A theoretical foundation that articulates the relationship between distributive justice and a just society was proposed by Rawls (1971).

John Rawls, an American moral and political philosopher, wrote the classic treatise *A Theory of Justice* (1971), in which he described a theoretical foundation for a just society. According to Rawls, social justice is anchored in two basic principles. The first principle states that members of society should have equal rights and liberties to participate fully in the structures and institutions of society, for example, political and legal structures. The second principle has two parts. One part states that all members of society have equal opportunities to obtain positions of power and authority in society. The second part of Rawls's second principle is referred to as the *difference principle* and states that social and economic inequalities in society should be arranged so that they provide the greatest benefit to the least advantaged members of society. The difference principle endorses the idea that the least advantaged members of society benefit from the successes of the more advantaged members of society. Therefore, Rawls's principles for a just society endorse equal rights and freedoms for all, provide equal opportunities for all members of society, and arrange inequalities in social and economic resources to maximize benefits to the least advantaged members of society.

GEORGE ALBEE: SOCIAL JUSTICE AND PREVENTION

A major leader in the promotion of prevention in psychology during the last half of the 20th century was George Albee, who served as APA president in 1969. In 1959, Albee published his first book, *Mental Health Manpower Trends*, which argued for prevention as the only viable way to reduce the incidence of mental disorders. His passionate calls for changes in the social order through social justice initiatives to reduce the incidence of emotional distress continued throughout his life in many publications, arguing for a revolution in psychology and psychiatry to reduce the incidence of mental illness (Albee, 2005). Albee made a considerable impact on prevention, and he received several awards for his contributions. He served on the President's Commission on Mental Health during the Dwight Eisenhower and Jimmy Carter administrations, and he received the APA Distinguished Professional Contribution Award and the Lifetime Achievement Award in Applied Preventive Psychology. In addition, in 2008, Albee was posthumously recognized by the Prevention Section of APA's Society of Counseling Psychology for his enormous contributions to psychology, prevention, and social justice.

Albee advocated that psychology address social injustices and attend to the needs of disenfranchised members of society through proactive and social actions. At times, he was one of only a few who took this position. His work was a major force in the development of the specialty of community psychology, and he was one of the cofounders of the Vermont Conference on Primary Prevention. Albee's (1970) APA Presidential Address questioned the future of clinical psychology if the profession continued to ascribe to the medical model of care, which emphasizes diagnosis and treatment to the neglect of prevention in the practice of psychology.

In promoting a prevention perspective as opposed to a crisis intervention model, Albee (2000) stated on more than one occasion that no disease or psychological problem was ever eliminated by treating only one afflicted person at a time. He strongly believed that it is necessary to attend to social conditions that foster mental illness if there is any hope of eliminating the tragedy of mental illness and psychological dysfunction. Despite Albee's passionate pleas to the profession to give greater voice to prevention and social justice, toward the end of his career, he lamented that individual treatment and a remedial model of care continued to be the model of choice in the training and practice of applied psychologists (Albee, 2000). Throughout his distinguished career, Albee argued for an end to racism, sexism, poverty, and other social conditions that create psychological problems for individuals and contribute to the disintegration of communities. During his lifetime, Albee was the most influential voice for a theoretical perspective that informs a social justice prevention framework within psychology and other mental health professions. His legacy remains, carried forward by others within and outside of psychology.

Albee (2009) maintained that much of what is called *psychopathology* is rooted in highly toxic social conditions, such as poverty, discrimination, and powerlessness, that create environments that lead to dysfunctional and abnormal behaviors of individuals (Albee, 1983, 1986). Although Albee acknowledged that some mental illness is organic and genetic in nature, he maintained that the majority of mental health problems are associated with negative social conditions that can be reduced, if not eliminated. He further argued that biological explanations for mental illness among psychiatrists and other mental health professionals are overemphasized, and he suggested that the social and financial benefits reaped from practicing within a medical model benefit the most powerful in society. To support his arguments, Albee cited numerous examples and studies demonstrating that the most vulnerable members of society are those most afflicted with mental health problems, emotional disturbances, and dysfunctional behaviors. Therefore, he argued for a primary prevention agenda that emphasizes a just society where all members have equal rights and equal access to financial gain and power. Thus, the major goal of primary prevention, according to Albee, is to address the underlying social conditions that contribute to psychological distress and human dysfunction. These underlying conditions include poverty, discrimination, and the disenfranchisement of large segments of the population within the United States and across the globe.

In support of Albee's (e.g., 1983, 1986) contentions, educational and health disparities between the majority Caucasian population and ethnic minority groups in the United States exist. For example, the U.S. Department of Education, National Center for Education Statistics (2012), reported that Caucasian students are more than twice as likely to complete high school as Black, Hispanic, and Native American students. U.S. ethnic minority populations and people from lower socioeconomic levels also endure poorer health care and poorer health outcomes, compared with White and higher socioeconomic populations, as reported by an agency of the U.S. Department of Health and Human Services (Agency for Healthcare Research and Quality, 2004). Education and health disparities have a profound impact on the population groups who are negatively affected. For example, lack of a high school diploma limits access to further education, job opportunities, and future income. Without adequate health care insurance, preventive health care and treatments become much less accessible, affecting quality of life and life expectancies. One major example is the absence of prenatal care, which can lead to infant mortality, low birth weight, and birth complications that can negatively impact a child for many years (Hack et al., 2002; Rickards, Kelly, Doyle, & Callanan, 2001). The U.S. Patient Protection and Affordable Health Care Act (2010) provides for improved health insurance for lower socioeconomic groups in society, and the law also provides funding for preventive services across the life span, from prenatal care to preventive services for older adults. However, passage of a national health care law in the United States took many years, and the value and merits of the current law continue to be fiercely debated. Although the U.S. Affordable Health Care Act was initially passed into law in 2010, various parts of the legislation are being phased into law until it becomes fully implemented.

Albee (1983) and Albee and Canetto (1996) argued that prevention must reduce the incidence of mental health disorders; to do so, Albee and colleagues proposed the formula below, showing relationships among the primary variables associated with mental disorders. The incidence of mental health disturbances is reduced as numerator variables are reduced and denominator variables increase.

$$\text{Incidence of Mental Disorders} = \frac{\text{Organic Factors} + \text{Stress} + \text{Exploitation}}{\text{Competence} + \text{Self-Esteem} + \text{Support Networks}}$$

In the formula, *Organic Factors* refer to physiological events that may be prevented, such as brain damage caused by lead poisoning, occupational environmental hazards that may lead to disability, and the prevention of strokes through public health education campaigns. *Stress* is captured in different ways (e.g., personal stress, environmental stress) and is also managed differently. For example, personal stress may be reduced by teaching stress management skills and by providing education about the relationship between managing stress and improving lifestyle behaviors (e.g., regular exercise, getting sufficient sleep). Techniques from cognitive behavioral theory are also helpful in managing stress, and they can be taught in prevention interventions. Environmental stress may require changes to institutions and systems where people live and work. For example, stress may be reduced by limiting noise volume in the workplace, providing training to improve communication among coworkers, and offering financial incentives to motivate employees to participate in health enhancement activities (e.g., gym membership). Environmental stress can also be reduced through the promotion of safe neighborhoods and crime prevention activities and by providing opportunities for leisure and recreational activities for all members of the community. *Exploitation* within a smaller or larger unit of society, such as a neighborhood or a country, can be reduced through laws that protect children and through legislation and enforcement of laws that give all members of society equal rights (principles espoused by Rawls, 1971). Equally important is the elimination of behavior or inaction that exploits members of the community, such as activities that sexually exploit girls and women, inattention toward and neglect of older adults, and weak enforcement of laws pertaining to the purchase of alcohol by minors.

By increasing the variables in the denominator of the formula, the incidences of mental illness will decrease, according to Albee and colleagues (Albee, 1983; Albee & Canetto, 1996). In the formula above, *Competence* refers to the development of skills that assist people in navigating the world in which they live. Academic, interpersonal, and career-oriented competencies can be developed in any number of ways, but the development of such competencies is best begun during early life. Development of competencies across the school-age years can lead to improved academic achievement and other outcomes (Durlak, Weissberg, Dymnicki, Taylor, & Schellinger, 2011). Strengthening competencies provides greater access to postsecondary education, employment, and financial gain. *Self-Esteem* (see the formula above) can be enhanced through skill development and participation in activities and organizations that promote personal development. For youth, activities may include participation in leisure and recreational activities, such as scouting, athletics, dance, and theatre, and membership in youth and religious organizations though which youth develop new skills, receive adult mentoring, and may become involved in social justice and social advocacy activities. *Support Networks* (see the formula above) are important at all ages, and they can serve as protections against emotional distress and mental health problems throughout life (Konnert, Gatz, & Hertzsprung Meyen, 1999).

Albee (1983) acknowledged that one shortcoming of the model as represented by the formula is the lack of specific attention to improvements and changes within institutions and systems to prevent psychological problems. However, systemic changes—such as legislation to reduce childhood exposure to lead paint, health and wellness programs offered to employees by employers and insurance providers, and school-based programs to help children develop friendships and social supports—are implicit in the model (Albee & Canetto, 1996).

To reduce discrimination and to empower less powerful members of society, Albee's social justice as prevention perspective supports universal health care and legalization of gay marriage. A just society would also include government support to sufficiently fund schools and communities and to provide for older adults and less powerful members of society, to name just a few of the issues that are currently being debated in the United States. These issues of social justice, among others, have the potential to reduce emotional distress and improve mental health outcomes. They offer tremendous potential to enhance the lives of people who are negatively affected by the effects of discrimination, poverty and low income, insufficient opportunities for advancement, and personal exploitation.

The innovative philosophy of Albee's positions on prevention and social justice is summarized below. The ideas were published more than 30 years ago, when such ideas were much less popular than they are today:

1. God is not male. And any religion that attributes superiority to one sex over the other is a psychological pollutant that causes endless pain and suffering, and emotional distress.
2. Any economic institution that profits from the exploitation of workers who are underpaid, that exposes workers to dangerous and life-shortening conditions, that can move factories to areas of cheap labor with no consideration for the human devastation left behind—in short, corporation without conscience—is psychologically devastating and must be changed.

3. Widespread "cultural patterns" that result in the mutilation of the bodies and spirits of women and children must be identified as psychologically devastating and must be changed. (Albee, 1983, p. 38)

Albee continued to write and share his passion for primary prevention after his retirement as a university professor in 1991. He died in 2006 at the age of 84. Shortly after his death, the *Journal of Primary Prevention*, which he was instrumental in founding, devoted several articles to the impact of his passing. One paper, written by Trickett (2007), summed up Albee's contributions particularly well, commenting on Albee's "unbending focus on social disenfranchisement and poverty as root causes of human misery" (p. 62).

Historically, Albee has been the most visible voice articulating social justice as prevention for more than 50 years; however, others have expanded upon his early work as well as early work by his contemporaries (e.g., Hage & Kenny, 2009; Kenny, Horne, Orpinas, & Reese, 2009b; Kenny & Medvide, 2013; Nelson & Prilleltensky, 2005; Pieterse et al., 2013; Prilleltensky, 2001; Prilleltensky & Nelson, 2013; Reese & Vera, 2007; Vera & Kenny, 2013; Vera & Speight, 2003).

ISAAC PRILLELTENSKY: COLLECTIVE WELLNESS

Prilleltensky (2001) has articulated a "value-based praxis" (p. 747), which promotes the value of social justice and argues for values within psychology and human development that promote collective wellness, such as social justice, rather than the more commonly ascribed value of individual or personal wellness (Prilleltensky & Nelson, 2013). Prilleltensky referred to praxis as the unity of theory and action and built a framework designed to unite values, research, and social action. Too often, he argued, psychologists work in isolation, are not explicit about their values, and emphasize research, all to the detriment of social action and a social justice agenda. The explicit discussion of values is important because social justice requires adjustments to the prevailing social order (a perspective that would be shared by Rawls, 1971), which in turn are difficult to change due to powerful forces in society that benefit from the status quo. Numerous examples in U.S. history, such as laws to promote racial and gender equality, to reduce exposure to tobacco products, and to reform health care, required several years or decades of debate before legislation was enacted. It is unfortunate that differences in values that support different positions during these debates are not often discussed openly and respectfully.

Values, according to Prilleltensky (2001), should meet four criteria: (a) guide processes and mechanisms that lead to an ideal outcome; (b) avoid dogmatism and relativism; (c) be complementary and not contradictory; and (d) promote personal, collective, and relational wellness. He identified seven values that meet the criterion for the promotion of personal, collective, and relational wellness: (a) self-determination, (b) health, (c) personal growth, (d) social justice, (e) support of community structures, (f) respect for diversity, and (g) collaboration and democratic participation. Prilleltensky acknowledged that people hold different values on specific issues (e.g., bans on cigarette smoking in public places), the importance of self-determination, and the need for public health promotion campaigns. However, the underlying premise of collective wellness supports the principle of the common good, similar to Rawls's (1971) difference principle. Thus, a healthy community benefits everyone in the community, although the reverse is also true: Unhealthy community environments negatively impact everyone in the community. Prilleltensky understood that the importance placed on a specific value or several values within a particular environment may differ with respect to a given community and context. Therefore, engaging in meaningful conversation about relevant values, especially when discussing concepts of social justice, is particularly important to undertake with those affected by proposed changes.

The concept of praxis (i.e., unity of theory and action) is designed to complement the role of values in Prilleltensky's (2001) framework. Therefore, Prilleltensky proposed four criteria for praxis: (a) balance the philosophical and grounded reality, (b) balance understanding and actions, (c) balance processes and outcomes, and (d) balance voices of the powerful with those less powerful. Based on these criteria, the praxis framework consists of four considerations: philosophical, contextual, needs, and pragmatic. To complete the cycle of theory to action, the cycle begins with philosophical reflections on values, followed by research on context and needs, and the process ends with practical considerations for actions. Prilleltensky described each of these, complete with examples, in some detail. For example, balancing the philosophical with grounded reality requires actions that reflect the realities of the situation or people involved. Balancing understanding with actions means that the impacts of actions, both positive and negative, are addressed as much as possible before taking action. Attending to process and outcomes is important to understand the impact of actions on the people involved. And, all voices, the empowered and the less powerful, are listened to and considered in prevention interventions. Prilleltensky believed that his complementary frameworks of values and praxis would advance social action and a prevention social justice agenda, especially in the development of social policies that benefit the common good.

MULTICULTURALISM, SOCIAL JUSTICE, AND PREVENTION

In the 21st century, scholars have advanced the integration of prevention and social justice with a focus on multiculturalism (e.g., Goodman et al., 2004; Reese & Vera, 2007; Vera & Speight, 2003). Scholars have emphasized health and education disparities between the dominant and minority cultures and the importance of delivering culturally competent prevention interventions to communities of color (Shin & Kendall, 2013; Tucker et al., 2007). Reese and Vera (2007) emphasized that prevention researchers and practitioners (a) possess knowledge of the community within which they are working so as to develop positive working relationships with community members; (b) develop and implement prevention programs that the community values; and (c) engage members of the community in the different phases of a prevention intervention: beginning, end, and follow-up.

Shin and Kendall (2013) recommended that school dropout prevention programs intervene at multiple levels to correct social injustices, such as poverty and oppression, that may reduce students' motivation to graduate from high school. They encouraged psychologists and other mental health professionals to develop collaborative partnerships with school personnel and community members in developing effective school dropout prevention interventions. The prevention interventions are especially important in urban schools. Given the previous discussion on values by Prilleltensky (2001), understanding values and goals is critically important when prevention specialists are outsiders and not familiar with a community. The importance of the issue is magnified in communities where the majority of the population is of a different ethnic group than the prevention specialists. Culturally sensitive prevention programs are exemplified in recent prevention literature, such as interventions to strengthen personal and academic effectiveness with multiethnic urban youth (Rivera-Mosquera, Phillips, Castelino, Martin, & Dobran, 2007; Vera et al., 2007) and parenting skills for African American caregivers (Coard, Foy-Watson, Zimmer, & Wallace, 2007).

A special millennium issue of the *Journal of Primary Prevention* highlighted three themes that were addressed in the articles of the special issue on multiculturalism (McIntosh, Jason, Robinson, & Brzezinski, 2004). The themes were (a) culturally affirmative conceptualizations of prevention; (b) selecting ecologically valid variables important to the target population; and (c) personal and contextual influences, including those of the researcher. The special issue articles included HIV prevention in Thailand and health promotion in New Zealand, as well as prevention with immigrant populations in the United States. Therefore, the theme of cultural affirmations of prevention was considered in contexts outside of the United States, as well as within ethnic minority populations in the United States. The concept of prevention and the interventions used will vary in different cultures, whether in the United States or elsewhere. Examples currently being widely and passionately debated in the United States are the most effective ways to prevent gun violence and how best to reform U.S. immigration policy. Divergent views are held across the United States, with differences between geographical areas, rural and urban areas, and among people from different population demographics.

McIntosh et al. (2004) summarized prevention interventions that attend to cultural differences, and they emphasized that the theories used and the variables studied be understood by the group receiving the intervention. One way to help ensure the cultural appropriateness of an intervention is through the creation of a group of major stakeholders who are attentive to the cultural attitudes and beliefs of the population, especially when the leaders of the prevention intervention are from outside the community. In addition, culturally appropriate research methodology and measurements are needed to adequately study the processes, outcomes, and impact of prevention interventions.

Vera and Kenny (2013) provided frameworks for and outstanding examples of applying social justice and cultural relevancy to prevention. In their volume, they summarized relationships among the perspectives of social justice, culture, and prevention, noting that all of these concepts are relatively new in the field of psychology and that attention to them has been inconsistent during their brief history of use. They also addressed the scarcity of empirical studies that fully integrate these three perspectives. Vera and Kenny noted the tensions and challenges that prevention researchers may face by attempting to be scientifically rigorous and culturally relevant at the same time. However, they emphasized that "being culturally responsive and scientifically rigorous are not necessarily incompatible goals" (p. 16) and that prevention researchers and practitioners must be attentive to both rigor and relevancy. Vera and Kenny proposed prevention program evaluation models that are less structured and more inclusive of evaluation methods and the type of data collected. They also stressed the importance of collecting information from all parties who have a stake in the prevention intervention, such as is used in participatory evaluation methods that collect information from multiple sources (Upshur & Barreto-Cortez, 1995). It is also important to carefully assess research goals and objectives of prevention interventions and to attend to research methodologies that holistically study the social justice and cultural relevancy of the intervention.

Vera and Kenny (2013) summarized two school-based case studies from their own experience that show the strengths and limitations associated with prevention activities in inner-city schools. The first case study gathered information from students and teachers in an effort to better understand the low retention rate of Mexican American high school students. The project yielded important information that the school and district can use in the development of prevention activities to strengthen school completion rates. The project also provided opportunities for members of the project team to engage with stakeholders outside of the school in attempts to influence school and government policies (e.g., Development, Relief, and Education for Alien Minors [DREAM] Act of 2011) that have a strong potential to support Latino students graduating from high school with motivations for postsecondary education.

The second case study reported by Vera and Kenny (2013) is described as a universal school-based prevention program to promote an understanding of the relationship between school success and career aspirations. This intervention study delivered a psychoeducational curriculum to all ninth-grade students. The curriculum is designed to prevent school dropout and to enhance student school engagement (Kenny, Sparks, & Jackson, 2007). The prevention program was implemented through a strong partnership between university faculty and graduate students, school-based personnel, and recent graduates of the schools involved. Efforts were also made to collaborate with parents of the students, but these efforts met with less success. Several different evaluation strategies, qualitative and quantitative methods with participants and stakeholders, were used to assess program processes, outcomes, and impact. Evaluation of the project revealed realities and challenges associated with collecting data from the school-based and community initiative. However, the project evaluation collected process data that proved helpful in making program modifications and also in assessing participant awareness and attitudes. It is surprising that outcome data to assess school dropouts were difficult to access, as it was unclear whether students left school completely or transferred to another school. The project also had some limited impact on stakeholders' participation in promoting broader systemic changes that impact the educational process. Vera and Kenny commented on the difficulties in making sustained and meaningful change across multiple contextual levels (e.g., individual, school, community).

There has been increased attention to the integration of prevention, cultural relevancy, and social justice in recent years. However, the relationships between these concepts and perspectives are complex and not easily discerned. Even in countries with a fairly homogeneous ethnic and religious population (e.g., Thailand), there may be cultural and socioeconomic differences across geographic regions. Such differences are amplified tremendously in a country as large and diverse as the United States. However, despite challenges, developing scientifically sound and meaningful prevention interventions across diverse populations remains a major goal of prevention research and practice.

PREVENTION AND PUBLIC POLICY ADVOCACY

Prevention and advocacy for public policies that advance the health and well-being of the citizenry are clearly linked (Coates & Szekeres, 2004; Jason, 2012; Kiselica, 2004; Levant, Tolan, & Dodgen, 2002). Public policies designed to improve health and well-being are inherently preventive, and they strengthen communities, states, and nations. However, they are not without controversy, as exemplified by discussions surrounding cigarette smoking bans, gun control legislation, immigration reforms, and national health care policy, to name a few of the policy debates ongoing in the United States and other countries. The debates are usually contentious, and they often focus on issues related to individual responsibility, or state control versus central government mandates. The conversations also address issues related to perspectives of a common good within a community or other entity, and financial implications of implementing a public policy.

Embedded in the economic issues is the extent that prevention policy will save money in the long run compared with initial expenditures to implement a policy. Such issues are debated in arguments to promote and fund more extensive early childhood education programs (A. J. Reynolds, Rolnick, Englund, & Temple, 2010). The debates are also intertwined with the personal values and beliefs of the people who would be affected either directly or indirectly by a policy. The controversies about major policy changes often continue for several years until there is sufficient political strength on one side or another to either pass or reject legislation or institutional policy. Final decisions to adopt a proposal are usually approved after amendments and compromises have been made to the original policy proposal.

One prominent example of public policy that has dominated political discourse on large and small scales for decades in the United States is the use of tobacco in buildings and public spaces. Despite more than a half century of research showing associations between cigarette smoking and exposure to secondary smoke with the onset of many illnesses and health problems, controversies about cigarette smoking continue across communities and states in the United States (U.S. Department of Health and Human Services, 2014). Although indoor smoking bans have become commonplace across the United States, some communities, work settings, and educational institutions are advocating for outdoor smoking bans to further reduce exposure to second-hand smoke and environmental litter. Some outdoor smoking bans have been successful, others have not, but the debate continues.

The controversies surrounding tobacco use continue despite research showing that a country without cigarette smoking would greatly improve the health of the nation, resulting in improved health outcomes for the population. For decades, U.S. surgeon generals have identified tobacco use as the leading preventable cause of premature death in the United States, and tobacco use contributes enormously to economic and social burdens of illness and premature death (U.S. Department of Health and Human Services, 2010c, 2012). Some states have attempted to regulate and reduce the use of tobacco products by strict age enforcement of tobacco purchases, where and how tobacco can be advertised, and by increasing sales taxes on tobacco products. The U.S. government has attempted to strengthen warning labels on cigarette packages, but with limited success compared with other countries (e.g., Canada). Some communities restrict tobacco use in public buildings, such as athletic stadiums, and also in outdoor parks and recreational areas. Some colleges and universities ban cigarette smoking anywhere on campus, inside and outside of buildings. Recently, electronic cigarettes (e-cigarettes) have appeared on the scene as an alternative to traditional cigarettes. E-cigarettes are designed to simulate traditional cigarettes with fewer health risks and as aids to stop using tobacco. However, according to the World Health Organization (WHO; 2013), the health risks of e-cigarettes are not known, and their value in smoking cessation has not been determined. WHO strongly advises against the use of e-cigarettes.

The tobacco wars are only one example of the major public health issues that have been debated and that impact the health and well-being of the nation. Much progress has been made since the 1964 U.S. Surgeon General Report (U.S. Public Health Service, 1964) that documented the relationship between smoking and health, but more can and should be done to curtail the use of cigarettes and exposure to their by-products in support of health promotion and disease prevention. Psychologists and other health professionals have contributed much to these debates, including informing policymakers about research on the addictive nature of tobacco, evaluations of smoking cessation interventions, and the impact on youth of cigarette marketing strategies that target youth.

During the past 50 years, legislation and policy regulations, in addition to those regarding tobacco, have been debated with much intensity in various public forums; some have met with legislative success and others have not. Counted among the successes are the 1964 civil rights legislation and federal programs developed as part of President Johnson's War on Poverty in the 1960s. One example is the federally funded Head Start program, which provides funding for preschool education to improve school readiness for children from lower socioeconomic communities (Ripple & Zigler, 2003; Styfco & Zigler, 2003). As an example of the intense debates that revolve around these types of publicly funded programs, Head Start continues to be evaluated nearly 50 years after its inception. The Head Start controversy focuses on its effectiveness in preparing children for long-term success in school. For example, one recent government-sponsored evaluation found that Head Start had a positive impact on children's cognitive development at preschool and through kindergarten, but the gains were largely dissipated by the end of the first grade (U.S. Department of Health and Human Services, 2010a). As controversy continues about Head Start's cost-effectiveness, public commentators have called for its elimination (Klein, 2011).

The issues surrounding Head Start may be similar to those of other prevention programs that attempt to change behaviors and improve outcomes. There must be thorough and sophisticated discussions and research about whether a program is effective. For example, with children who completed preschool Head Start programs, the gains made before the start of school will be difficult to maintain without continued educational support and enrichments, and consideration of the impact of environmental contexts in which education occurs (V. E. Lee & Loeb, 1995). Similar to other prevention efforts in schools (e.g., drug prevention programs), school-based prevention interventions are best implemented as early as appropriate and administered throughout the years of schooling. The impact of a one-time-only preventive intervention will not be sustained over time, as was demonstrated with the popular school-based Drug Abuse Resistance Education (D.A.R.E.) alcohol and drug prevention program (Vincus, Ringwalt, Harris, & Shamblen, 2010).

In addition to their review of Head Start, Ripple and Zigler (2003) reviewed four other federal policy initiatives important to the promotion of health and well-being of children and families, including the 1965 Medicare and Medicaid program (LBJ Presidential Library, 2012), the Lead Contamination Control Act of 1988, and the Earned Income tax credit (initially enacted in 1975 and expanded in subsequent years as an antipoverty measure; Hotz & Scholz, 2001). According to Ripple and Zigler, the programs reviewed have been successful in health promotion and prevention, but they also are limited because they often implemented in fragmented components to limited segments of the population. They also lack comprehensive evaluations. Ripple and Zigler suggested that stronger efforts be made in communicating evaluations and research of the programs to policymakers. Psychology and other disciplines have much to offer in the design and methods of program evaluations, and in communicating results of the evaluations to policymakers. It is important that advocacy positions supported by psychological research be concise and delineated in nontechnical language for use by decision makers (Coates & Szekeres, 2004).

U.S. policies that relate directly to prevention have been approved in several areas, including the Mental Health Parity and Addiction Equity Act of 2008, the Individuals with Disabilities Act (2004), the U.S. Patient Protection and Affordable Health Care Act (2010), and the Garrett Lee Smith Memorial Act (2004) for suicide prevention and mental health promotion. Gun control is another topic fiercely debated in the United States, and several laws have been either introduced or passed in the U.S. Congress and in state legislatures to prevent gun violence. Among the issues debated in legislative bodies are laws that propose improved enforcement of access to and availability of guns by expanding background checks on people purchasing guns, banning the sale of high-powered weapons and ammunition, and improving access to mental health services for those identified as risks for committing violent acts. Thus, these public policy debates and actions are designed as preventive measures to reduce gun violence.

The U.S. Patient Protection and Affordable Health Care Act of 2010 authorizes benefits for many preventive services within physical and mental health domains, including areas such as depression screening, tobacco screening and smoking cessation interventions, domestic and interpersonal violence screening and counseling, and well-woman visits (see http://www. HealthCare.gov/prevention). Collectively, the Act provides for 16 preventive service benefits for adults, 22 for women, and 27 for children and adolescents. Among the benefits for children and adolescents are assessments for drug use and depression, obesity counseling, and sexually transmitted disease screening and counseling. In addition, senior preventive benefits, through Medicare coverage, include depression screening and mental health services. The range of benefits outlined in the Act attests to the importance of prevention in promoting health and reducing illness and disability in the United States. The law supports the overall National Prevention Strategy (National Prevention Council, 2011).

As the examples demonstrate, a comprehensive prevention framework must include public policies that advocate for prevention services, benefits, and behaviors that support the common good. Psychologists and other mental health professionals can play a major role in advocating for such policies. APA's Public Interest Directorate applies psychology to the fundamental problems of human welfare and social justice, and supports the equitable and fair treatment of all members of society through education, training, and public policy (see http://www.apa.org/pi). The Directorate has been a strong voice advocating for the passage of public policies that address the common good, such as the Patient Protection and Affordable Health Care Act (2010), the Violence Against Women Reauthorization Act (2013), and legislation to promote mental health services in schools. Other mental health organizations, such as the American Counseling Association, the National Association of Social Workers, and the American Psychiatric Association, have similar offices within their organizational structures that advocate for public policies and legislation that promote health and well-being and the prevention of problems across the population.

As the number of examples summarized above demonstrate, there are many public policy issues that merit advocacy to enrich the lives of individuals and promote healthy societal institutions. However, one must also recognize that examples such as those above will generate much discussion, and at times heated disagreements, among the general population, as well as among psychologists and other mental health providers. Disagreements often arise because of differing values related to how a particular problem may be prevented. The teaching of sex education in schools is one example, including how best to prevent teen pregnancy and sexually transmitted infections. Some argue for an abstinence-only approach to teaching sex education, whereas others may view abstinence as unrealistic and recommend a comprehensive approach that includes providing teens with information about birth control methods. In this example, all parties desire to prevent pregnancy and sexually transmitted infections, but discussions are framed by values and spiritual beliefs associated with the best ways to prevent precocious sexual behaviors. In addition, some may believe that sex education does not belong in the school curriculum, arguing that it is best taught at home.

Intense policy debates may also occur about less emotionally charged issues, such as school cafeteria food options and school vending machine choices. Some will recommend more healthy food choices. Similar discussions may occur in workplace cafeterias. Discussions about these issues often emphasize individual freedom, responsibility, and choice, versus decisions based on a collectivist orientation of the common good. Financial consequences of policy change also often enter into these debates.

Obviously, all mental health providers do not hold similar values and opinions about the impact of policy decisions on health promotion and prevention. However, as much as possible, it is important for prevention specialists to become informed about the issues and to use their expertise to contribute to the policy discussions. Contributions can be made at local levels when policies are discussed and at larger community and national levels through advocacy statements and communications to policy and decision makers.

SUMMARY

Social justice and public policy advocacy as prevention have emerged as philosophical and action-oriented approaches to prevention. At a basic level, a social justice framework in support of prevention requires societal changes to realize more equal distributions of power and resources among the population to bring about reductions in health, education, and economic disparities. Further, public policies that reduce risks to members of society and enhance well-being are intricately linked to both social justice and prevention. Such policies have the promise of being the strongest prevention interventions because they affect large numbers of people across demographics and geographical regions and institutions. Three contemporary examples, and there are many more, about which intense public policy discussions are occurring are (a) how to reduce gun violence in the United States, (b) how to prevent bullying behaviors in schools, and (c) how to reduce poverty and protect the most vulnerable members of society. The ultimate goal of these discussions is a society whose members enjoy enhanced physical and emotional health as a result of reducing risks and promoting health.

People differ about the best ways to reach these ultimate goals. Differences are often rooted in strong values and religious beliefs, and are not easily amenable to change. In addition, information and research evaluative data may be contradictory and not persuasive. Psychologists and other mental health professionals can adopt more focused social justice and public advocacy prevention positions in their employment settings and professional activities. However, they can also actively participate in discussions about social change proposals debated in legislatures and in other policymaking groups. Prevention specialists who ascribe to a social justice and public advocacy perspective work at micro- and macrolevels of society and institutions to enhance the lives of people and communities.

6

PREVENTION APPLICATIONS IN EDUCATIONAL SETTINGS

Prevention applications in educational settings have a long history. In this chapter, I briefly summarize this history and focus on recent and exemplary prevention interventions in prekindergarten through college (preK–16) educational settings. Most of the applications selected articulate a theoretical framework and are evidenced based. I summarize each prevention intervention, including (a) target population and information about what is being prevented and/or promoted, (b) goals and objectives of the application, (c) theoretical concepts or framework to support the intervention, (d) details about intervention components, (e) evaluation and outcome data, and (f) newer supplements to the intervention design, as appropriate.

DOI: 10.1037/14442-006
Prevention Psychology: Enhancing Personal and Social Well-Being, by J. L. Romano

PREVENTION IN PREK–16 SCHOOLS: BRIEF HISTORY

Educational settings are logical places to develop and implement prevention interventions. Historically, prevention interventions have focused on some of the most severe and complex problem behaviors that affect youth, including alcohol and drug use, early sexual activity, cigarette smoking, school bullying, and poor academic achievement (Nation et al., 2003). Among other school-based prevention initiatives are those that focus on promoting positive youth development behaviors and positive school climates (Bosworth, Orpinas, & Hein, 2009; Espelage & Poteat, 2012).

Durlak (1995) emphasized the growth of published outcome studies on school-based prevention activities, showing dramatic increases from 1960 to the mid-1990s. Although the growth is impressive, Durlak also noted that schools have been delivering health education preventive programs for much longer, and his data do not include a large number of prevention programs that either have not been evaluated or published. Therefore, prevention activities in the schools have existed for a long time but not in their current form. For example, Baker and Shaw (1987) traced the history of primary prevention in the schools from the early 1940s and highlighted school-based prevention in subsequent decades, especially noting the work of Mosher and Sprinthall (1970), which emphasized developmental education to promote student development.

In their meta-analysis of primary prevention programs with children and adolescents, Durlak and Wells (1997) stated that numerous reports of prevention activities and studies appeared in school counseling journals. This is not surprising, because the U.S. school counseling professional association (i.e., American School Counseling Association [ASCA]) has encouraged school counselors to engage in prevention, and the ASCA National Model for school counseling programs recommends that preventive and developmental services be major components of school counseling services (ASCA, 2003; Dahir, 2008). Similarly, school psychologists are increasingly emphasizing prevention as an important focus of their work in schools (Sheridan & D'Amato, 2004).

Although school-based prevention programs and activities have been offered for many years, too many are developed and delivered without strong theoretical foundations, with little evaluation, and in fragmented components (Greenberg et al., 2003). The evolution of school-based alcohol and drug prevention programs included early programs that emphasized scare tactics, followed by programs that featured people in recovery, and more recent peer-based programs often delivered by older, trained student peers. However, because many school prevention programs have been atheoretical, fragmented, and conducted with little evaluation, it is difficult to measure their outcomes and impact. Historically, prevention programs have focused on a particular problem for several years, then more often than not, because of a national crisis, another problem targeted for prevention is addressed. Prevention topics are often given impetus because of federal and state grants that support prevention of a problem behavior, such as early alcohol and drug prevention programs and more recent school bullying prevention initiatives.

Students are at risk for various problems as they navigate their childhood and adolescent years, and problems are often interrelated. Therefore, comprehensive prevention programs are needed across the years of schooling. Although a comprehensive review of all topics that have been addressed through prevention and health promotion programs in schools is beyond the scope of this chapter, exemplary prevention and health promotion programs that address major problems for children and adolescents are highlighted.

Colleges and universities have developed and implemented prevention interventions to address a range of student problems for many years. Over 40 years ago, Morrill, Oetting, and Hurst (1974) articulated a model for campus student development service delivery that included prevention to strengthen the campus ecology. Prevention initiatives have been developed by different units and professionals on campuses, including counseling center professionals, student affairs personnel, and residence life staff. Colleges and universities offer prevention interventions to impact the behavior of students who are at risk for problems (i.e., selective and indicated prevention), as well as programs for the general campus population (i.e., universal prevention) designed to influence attitudes and change behaviors.

The need to continue to develop and implement prevention interventions on college campuses has been demonstrated by surveys showing college students to be at risk for a number of problems related to their health and well-being. In one survey conducted by the University of Minnesota (2007), college and university students from across the state of Minnesota were surveyed about their health and personal habits. A total of 24,000 students were invited to participate in the survey, and 10,000 students completed and returned the survey. The institutions represented included all campuses of the University of Minnesota; several Minnesota state colleges and universities, including 2-year colleges; and one private college. Survey results revealed that 27.1% of the students had been diagnosed with a mental illness during their lifetime, and 15.7% had been diagnosed during the past 12 months. Depression and anxiety were the most common diagnoses reported. In addition, the results showed that 37.1% of students had engaged in high-risk drinking behavior during the past 2 weeks; 25% used tobacco during the past month; and 6.8% reported illicit drug use. In addition, 22.4% of women reported experiencing at least one sexual assault during their lifetime, and 6.8% of female students had experienced a sexual assault during the past 12 months. Sexual assaults experienced by men were lower, at 5% during their lifetime and 1.9% in the past 12 months. Nearly 40% of the students reported being overweight or obese. Students used various forms of technology to such an extent that the excessive use affected their academic work. The study authors reported that the survey results were similar to survey trends of college student behaviors in other parts of the United States. These survey data provide documentation that supports the need for prevention interventions in different areas of student life on college campuses.

Therefore, it is not surprising that prevention interventions have addressed different student problems, and interventions have also been designed to promote behaviors that encourage health and wellness behaviors and academic success. Prevention interventions that have been offered, and sometimes required, for college students include those to prevent use and abuse of alcohol and drugs (Baer, Kivlahan, Blum, McKnight, & Marlatt, 2001; LaBrie, Lamb, Pederson, & Quinlan, 2006; Oswalt, Shutt, English, & Little, 2007; West & Graham, 2005), to prevent sexual harassment and assaults (Foubert, 2000; Foubert, Tatum, & Godin, 2010; Lonsway, 1996; Rothman & Silverman, 2007), to prevent eating disorders (Stice, Rohde, Shaw, & Marti, 2013; Stice, Shaw, & Marti, 2007), to increase suicide awareness and prevent suicide (Haas et al., 2008), and to reduce depression (e.g., Seligman, Schulman, & Tryon, 2007). Although some programs are designed as selective and indicated prevention programs, others are offered for the entire campus community. For example, a campus may set aside time during the academic year to highlight a topic and provide information and workshops about the topic to increase awareness. The campus may also offer screenings and suggest referrals to students who are at risk for the problem. National screening and awareness days are popular on college campuses, such as those that address depression, alcohol abuse, and sexual assault.

In addition to programs that prevent student problems, colleges and universities also offer programs, activities, and courses that teach skills and behaviors that serve as protections against developing psychosocial problems. Examples of these types of interventions include career development courses to assist students in selecting a college major and career path (P. Johnson, Nichols, Buboltz, & Riedesel, 2002), programs to educate students about sexual health (Kanekar & Sharma, 2010), activities and policies that promote responsible use of alcohol and safety on campus and in the larger community adjacent to campus (Glider, Midyett, Mills-Novoa, Johannessen, & Collins, 2001; Saltz, 2011), interventions to enhance academic success (Cerezo & McWhirter, 2012; Morrow & Ackermann, 2012; M. N. Thompson & Phillips, 2013), interventions to promote student engagement (Hausmann, Schofield, & Woods, 2007), campus programs that promote health and wellness (Donovan et al., 2012; Haines et al., 2007; Werch et al., 2008), and campus consultation teams organized to respond to threatening campus situations (Stark, 2013). These types of prevention programs are often available to the entire campus or to a subgroup of students. Programs to strengthen student protective factors against developing problem behaviors increase awareness and knowledge about the topic, influence student attitudes about the topic, strengthen personal skills important to the topic, and promote behaviors that enhance student health and well-being.

The Substance Abuse and Mental Health Services Administration (SAMHSA) National Registry of Evidence Based Programs and Practices (NREPP) is a clearinghouse (see http://www.nrepp.samhsa.gov) of prevention programs that provides detailed descriptions of prevention programs. The NREPP clearinghouse is the primary resource used to identify exemplary prevention school-based programs in this chapter.

EXEMPLARY PROGRAMS FOR CHILDREN, ADOLESCENTS, AND COLLEGE STUDENTS

Preschool

School-based prevention interventions for preschool children are reported less often compared with school-based prevention programs with older students (Humphries & Keenan, 2006). This is surprising, given the importance of learning prosocial behaviors and preventing emotional and educational difficulties during the preschool years. Much attention is given during early childhood to preventing health and physical problems (e.g., infant vaccination programs), and these measures have improved the health of children. However, programs that promote the emotional, educational, and social development of all preschool children are also important, and they must be given priority and funded appropriately.

Humphries and Keenan (2006) conducted a review of preschool-based prevention programs for children ages 3 to 5 years. Only programs that appeared in the literature from 1986 to 2006 and that were empirically evaluated were included in their review. Humphries and Keenan identified six programs that met their criteria of being theory based, developmentally appropriate, and culturally sensitive and included both behavior promotion and symptom reduction components. The six programs that Humphries and Keenan reviewed were Incredible Years: Parent and Teacher Training Program (Webster-Stratton, Reid, & Hammond, 2001), Social–Emotional Intervention for At-Risk 4-Year-Olds (Denham & Burton, 1996), Peaceful Kids Early Childhood Social–Emotional Learning (Sandy & Boardman, 2000), Resilient Children Making Healthy Choices (Dubas, Lynch, Galano, Geller, & Hunt, 1998), The High/Scope Preschool Curriculum (hereinafter

"HighScope"; Schweinhart, & Weikart, 1997), and Chicago Child–Parent Center & Expansion Program (A. J. Reynolds, 1994). These programs target disruptive behavior, social and emotional competence, and educational instruction. It is unclear from the Humphries and Keenan review whether these were the only programs that met their criteria for inclusion or whether they were a sample of programs that they choose to highlight.

Humphries and Keenan (2006) cautioned that the preschool programs they reviewed were based on Eurocentric and middle-class theories of development, and the programs were primarily implemented with ethnic minority children and children from low-income families. The researchers concluded that more research must be conducted so that there is a more balanced alignment between the theoretical models on which the prevention programs are based and the demographic characteristics of children who receive them.

NREPP lists 17 school-based preschool programs (as of April 2013), and two of the programs were also reviewed by Humphries and Keenan (2006): Incredible Years and HighScope. Both programs have been in existence for many years and have been empirically supported through numerous research studies. HighScope is summarized to represent an evidence-based prevention program for children 3 to 5 years old, and Incredible Years is reviewed under elementary-school-based programs. HighScope also offers specific curricula for infants (0–3 years) and elementary school students.

HighScope

HighScope (see http://www.highscope.org) was developed in the 1960s by Dr. David Weikart and his colleagues, and the program was more formally established in 1970 in Ypsilanti, Michigan. The program has been implemented in schools and preschools across the United States and abroad (Peyton, 2004). The program is based on Piaget and Dewey principles that emphasize children as active participants in their learning, rather than passive recipients of knowledge dispensed by another (Dewey, 1938; Piaget & Inhelder, 1969). HighScope includes components of child-initiated and experiential learning, the development of strong relationships with adult caregivers, and the development of children's social and emotional competencies (Humphries & Keenan, 2006). The program is delivered through small- and large-group activities for children and outreach activities to parents and caregivers (Schweinhart & Weikart, 1999). Schweinhart and Weikart (1999) reported on longitudinal studies of children who participated in HighScope, compared with children who received traditional teacher-directed or child-centered programs. The follow-up studies found that, as young adults, HighScope participants showed more prosocial behaviors than did children who had participated in alternative preschool programs.

Elementary School

Compared with preschool prevention programs, there are many more prevention programs developed for elementary and middle school students. NREPP identifies 80 prevention programs (as of April 2013) that are school based for children ages 6 to 12 years, ages that span elementary through middle school settings. Most of the programs in the SAMHSA registry are multifaceted and universal and selective prevention interventions. As might be expected from prevention programs at this educational level, the emphases are on building social and emotional competencies and preventing risk behaviors, such as tobacco, alcohol, and other drug use; bullying and aggressive behaviors; and conduct problems. The programs in this group usually include classroom components delivered by the classroom teacher or educational specialist, activities with parents, and activities to connect the children to the community. Therefore, the programs connect schools, families, and communities to strengthen protections for youth and prevent at-risk behaviors. One of the NREPP programs, Incredible Years, that is elementary-school-based is summarized next to highlight some of the unique features of prevention programs with this age group.

Incredible Years

This multifaceted program has components for parents and teachers, and social skills training for children who are at risk for conduct problems (Reid, Webster-Stratton, & Hammond, 2007; Webster-Stratton & Reid, 2003; Webster-Stratton et al., 2001). The program has demonstrated improved parental skills and decreased problem behavior in children (Reid, Webster-Stratton, & Baydar, 2004). The program is driven by developmental theory, emphasizing children's social and emotional learning that serve as protective behaviors to reduce conduct problems. The goals are to promote emotional and social competence among children and prevent, reduce, or treat emotional and behavioral problems in children. The child curriculum, aided by puppets, teaches a variety of skills, such as communication skills, problem-solving strategies, and appropriate classroom behavior. Teacher training components include classroom management skills, promoting children's social skills, and effective communication with parents and peers. Parent training includes encouraging parental school involvement and skills to promote prosocial and academic success of their children. A recent follow-up study of children who received the Incredible Years program as young children (3–8 years) found that adolescents (8–12 years after receiving the program) were well adjusted and their risk behaviors were within normal limits (Webster-Stratton, Rinaldi, & Reid, 2011). Although the study did not use a comparison control group, which is a limitation of many follow-up studies like this one, the study showed evidence that the Incredible Years program is beneficial to children as they progress through childhood, especially with children who demonstrated conduct problems early in life.

To make the Incredible Years more accessible to families of young children, Taylor et al. (2008) developed a technology-enhanced parent training version of the program. Recruiting families of 4-year-olds from Head Start programs in rural and urban Oregon, the researchers used 178 families who met the eligibility criteria, which included the home having a telephone contact, members of the family being English speaking, and children scoring in the top third of all children screened on the Oppositional Defiant Scale of the Child and Adolescent Disruptive Behavior Inventory (Burns, Taylor, & Rusby, 2001). Eighty-eight families were randomized into a control group, and 90 families received the intervention. The technology-enhanced version of the Incredible Years program offered a hybrid model, in which parents could watch training modules on their computer (either loaded on a disc or streaming on the Internet), along with participating through online message groups with other parents enrolled in the program. In addition, each family was assigned a coach who attempted to visit the family five times during the program's implementation. The coach was a trained professional who helped parents set goals for their participation in the program, role-played with parents the skills demonstrated in the training modules, discussed strategies to implement the skills, and served as a resource to answer questions.

Taylor et al. (2008) analyzed data only from the second cohort ($n = 45$ families), as much data were missing from the first cohort ($n = 45$ families). From the second cohort, results showed that families in the intervention group made major progress toward their goals. Thirty families reported achieving at least one goal at 100%, and 30 families reported making 50% progress on all goals. Seventeen families reported achieving all of their self-selected goals during the program. In addition, 76% felt confident in their ability to manage their children's disruptive behaviors, although 80% said they felt confident in their ability to handle future behavior problems of their children. Parents were satisfied with the program, as 87% were very satisfied and 93% would recommend the program to a friend. The results of this web-based study demonstrated that electronic interventions can be useful in parental skills training. However, as the authors pointed out, the results of the data collected do not demonstrate program efficacy, as the data were subjective self-reports of parental strategies and skills and satisfaction with the program, rather than objective measures of changes in children's problem behaviors and direct observation of parental behaviors. Further, although the study initially enrolled 90 families, data were analyzed with only 45 families. Despite these limitations, which likely can be corrected in future evaluations of the program, this technology-enhanced

Incredible Years program shows promise as an innovative prevention program with potential to reach more parents who are not available for out-of-home prevention interventions.

Early Risers

The Early Risers program was developed to reduce aggressive behaviors in children by targeting those who were identified as high risk in kindergarten. The program is based on a "developmental–ecological perspective" framework to reduce risks and promote protections to prevent childhood antisocial behavior (August, Realmuto, Winters, & Hektner, 2001, p. 142). The developmental–ecological framework addresses disruptive behaviors of children and intervenes within communities in which children live (e.g., family, school) to reduce these behaviors. A major goal of the program is to help children return to more normal developmental behaviors and move away from aggressive behaviors and conduct problems through participation in school, community, and family programs that emphasize skills and competencies designed to reduce risks and strengthen protections. Therefore, Early Risers components target academic competence, behavioral self-regulation, social competence, and parental investments in their children through participation in school and community enrichment programs (August, Realmuto, Hektner, & Bloomquist, 2001).

Kindergarten children who were identified as high risk for behavioral problems were recruited from 20 schools in two different communities to participate in a study on child development. The schools were randomized to intervention and control conditions. All children in the intervention schools participated in core programming that included classroom interventions comprising a life skills curriculum, individualized academic and social skills training, parenting skills training, and family activities to strengthen parent–child relationships. A select number of students were selected to attend a summer camp focusing on building academic and social skills. These children subsequently served as peer mentors during the school year. In addition, supplemental individualized programs were offered to children at higher risk to meet their additional needs and those of their families (August, Realmuto, Winters, & Hektner, 2001).

Results from this study found that after 2 years, the children receiving the intervention significantly improved in reading and math achievement and classroom concentration compared with children in the control group. However, the main outcome variable of behavior self-regulation (as measured by parent and teacher rating scales) did not yield significant differences between children in the intervention group and those in the control group (August, Realmuto, Hektner, & Bloomquist, 2001). Six-year outcomes on oppositional defiant disorder (ODD) and conduct disorder (CD) diagnoses of the children in the study revealed that children in the control group were more likely to receive these diagnoses than intervention children, but the results were not statistically significant. However, significant differences were found in the amount of ODD or CD symptoms displayed, with intervention children less likely to engage in these behaviors (Bernat, August, Hektner, & Bloomquist, 2007). In addition, using mediation analysis, researchers found that social skills and effective discipline served as mediators in reducing ODD symptoms in sixth graders who had participated for 5 years of the program (Bernat et al., 2012).

In a follow-up study of the institutional (nonprofit community agency) sustainability of the Early Risers program, the results showed less effectiveness than those at the early stage effectiveness trial of the program (August, Bloomquist, Lee, Realmuto, & Hektner, 2006). Despite training, technical support, and oversight by program developers, program effectiveness was much less evident. Compared with the earlier trial, attendance rates were lower for program participants, and only one positive outcome was found, that is, program children had improved teacher-rated problem behaviors, compared with the control group children. No differences were found on other variables, such as academic achievement and social adjustment. The authors discussed the potential reasons for the lack of program sustainability, such as agency staff turnover, reduced funding, and poor community and school collaboration. This study demonstrates the importance of developing and maintaining prevention program strategies, including funding streams, to sustain programs after the initial trial periods end.

Middle School

Many programs identified through NREPP address the later childhood and early adolescent years. More than 80 school-based programs, for children ages 13 to 17, are listed on the NREPP site (as of April 2013). One exemplary program, Project Northland, designed for later childhood and early adolescents is summarized.

Project Northland

This multiyear, school-based, communitywide, and multicomponent program is designed to prevent alcohol use in the middle and junior high school years (i.e., Grades 6–8). The program offers multilevel components that require school and community participation. Project Northland components, as described below, incorporate principles from child and adolescent development, experiential and active learning, and positive community engagement. The program has been in existence since the early 1990s, with a history of empirical research supporting the intervention (Komro et al., 2001, 2004; C. L. Perry et al., 1996). The program was offered in school districts across northern Minnesota, initially to a cohort of children in the sixth grade ($n = 2,351$); and it was later extended to children through the eighth grade. The program has also been adapted for urban youth (Komro et al., 2004). Program components include grade-appropriate classroom curricula to teach students alcohol resistance skills and to develop peer leadership skills, and to provide parent education. Project Northland also includes reinforcing the importance of adhering to laws against alcohol sales to minors and supporting community ordinances to reduce youth access to alcohol. The program initiated a gold card program in which students receive discounts from community merchants if they made alcohol-free pledges (C. L. Perry et al., 1996).

Students in the intervention and the control school districts completed researcher-generated questionnaires at baseline and at the end of each school year. The questionnaires asked about alcohol, tobacco, and other drug use; psychosocial factors (e.g., peer influence, self-efficacy, parental communication); and participation in Project Northland activities. Results of the 3-year intervention showed that students who participated in Project Northland reported significantly less likelihood of alcohol use, compared with those in the control condition. Intervention students who had not used alcohol at baseline were significantly less likely to use alcohol, compared with the control group (C. L. Perry et al., 1996). Students who participated in the intervention were also significantly more likely to resist alcohol at a party. Overall, Project Northland was most successful with students who had not begun using alcohol before the start of the program; children who had already started using alcohol at baseline were less likely to benefit from the program.

Although research data have shown positive results of Project Northland, they are based on self-report measures. However, C. L. Perry et al. (1996) contended that self-report measures are reliable, and they cited an earlier study that showed less likelihood of intervention students underreporting information compared with students in a control condition (Komro, Kelder, Perry, & Klepp, 1993). Project Northland has been shown to delay middle school students' alcohol use, and a high school curriculum has been developed.

Life Skills Training

Life Skills Training (LST; see http://www.lifeskillstraining.com) is a short-term, evidence-based universal prevention program that has been shown to reduce use of alcohol, tobacco, and other drugs (Botvin, Baker, Dunesbury, Botvin, & Diaz, 1995; Griffin, Botvin, Nichols, & Doyle, 2003; Zollinger et al., 2003). Similar to other prevention programs described in this chapter, LST uses a skill-based, participatory, active learning curriculum to educate students about substance use and abuse. More than 30 evaluation studies have been conducted on the program, and LST has been implemented with age-specific curricula with elementary through high school students. Several organizations, including the U.S. Department of Education and the Center for Substance Abuse and Prevention, have recognized LST as an exemplary program.

Botvin et al. (1995) studied the effectiveness of LST with a large sample of predominantly White 7th-grade students. The students were initially given the 15 LST lesson curriculum delivered by regular classroom teachers. Booster sessions were given in Grades 8 (10 lessons) and 9 (five lessons). The lessons, using cognitive behavior theory, included topics such as building self-esteem, managing anxiety, assertiveness training, communication skills training, and developing healthy interpersonal relationships. The lessons also included specific skills to resist social and peer influences to use drugs. Sixty percent of the original seventh-grade participants were reassessed in the 12th grade on measures of cigarette smoking and alcohol and marijuana use. Results showed a significant reduction in drug and polydrug use in the intervention groups compared with control groups (defined as "treatment as usual") at follow-up. Limitations of the study are the predominately White, middle-class population studied and that 40% of the original sample were not assessed at follow-up. Perhaps the students most at risk for substance use and abuse are also most at risk for irregular school attendance. Strengths of the study include the use of booster lessons in Grades 8 and 9, regular classroom teachers trained to implement the program, and regular monitoring to assess program fidelity during implementation.

LST has been implemented with middle school youth to prevent drug use and aggressive behaviors that often co-occur (Botvin, Griffin, & Nichols, 2006). In this application, the program included information about anger management and taught conflict resolution skills. Students who received the 3-month LST curriculum reported reduced aggressive behaviors in the past year, compared with control students who completed the standard health education curriculum. Similar to earlier LST studies, outcome measures were based on student self-reports. LST has also been conducted internationally in Spain (Fraguela, Martin, & Trinanes, 2003) and in combination with the Strengthening Families Program (Spoth, Randall, Trudeau, Shin, & Redmond, 2008). The results of these controlled follow-up studies showed reduced illegal substance use for the treatment groups; however, in the Fraguela et al. (2003) study, the positive effects decreased over time.

LST is well researched and has received endorsements by professional organizations and government agencies. Although LST has shown positive results through longitudinal research studies (Griffin, Botvin, & Nichols, 2006), many studies use self-reports as outcome measures. Outcome measures of program participant behaviors, as reported by others (e.g., teachers, parents, friends, law enforcement) would add substantially to the body of knowledge about LST reported to date.

High School

Many of the NREPP programs listed for younger students have also been adopted for high-school-age youth. High school prevention programs tend to emphasize the prevention of alcohol and drug use. Two of the NREPP programs summarized next were selected because they target suicide prevention, one with a general population of students and the other with Native American youth. In addition, a steroid use prevention program for male athletes is also summarized. Suicide and steroid use are topics that are given less attention in high schools, compared with more general programs that target alcohol and drug prevention.

Coping and Support Training, and Care, Assess, Respond, Empower

Coping and Support Training (CAST) and Care, Assess, Respond, Empower (CARE) are companion selective and indicated suicide prevention programs. E. A. Thompson, Moody, and Eggert (1994) initially created the programs on the basis of research that showed that brief interventions were as effective as longer interventions in reducing suicide risk and in strengthening student levels of self-control (Eggert, Thompson, Herting, & Nicholas, 1995). E. A. Thompson and Eggert (1999) reported that students at risk for suicide were also at risk for dropping out of school. Therefore, studies have also implemented the programs with students at risk for dropping out of high school (Randell, Eggert, & Pike, 2001).

CAST uses a small-group counseling format for students at risk for suicide behavior. The small-group intervention delivered by trained group counselors offers guidance, support, and skill training using positive group influences to support behavior change. CAST goals are to improve mood, reduce alcohol and drug use, and improve school performance through twelve 55-minute small-group sessions that focus on topics such as setting goals, decision making, academic performance, anger management, and relapse prevention.

CARE is a 4-hour counseling program, consisting of 2 hours of assessment and 2 hours of counseling. CARE is conducted by mental health professionals for students at risk for suicide behavior (www.reconnectingyouth.com). The programs have been recognized for excellence by several organizations, and they are listed on the Suicide Prevention Resource Center Best Practices Registry (see http://www.sprc.org/pbr).

To assess the effectiveness of CAST and CARE, E. A. Thompson, Eggert, Randell, and Pike (2001) selected 460 students at risk for suicide from a pool of potential high school dropouts from across seven high schools. The students were randomly assigned to one of three conditions: (a) CARE, a brief 4-hour intervention to assess for suicide and a brief therapeutic intervention to inform about student resources and support networks in school and at home; (b) CARE program followed by the CAST program of twelve 1-hour group sessions of skills training; and (c) Usual Care, one brief 15- to 30-minute assessment interview and intervention with school personnel and parents. Students completed The High School Questionnaire: A Profile of Experiences (HSQ; Eggert, Herting, & Thompson, 1995) at baseline, 4 weeks after the Usual Care and CARE interventions were completed, again weeks later to coincide with the completion of the CAST program, and finally at 9-month follow-up from baseline measures. HSQ, which has been used for many years in several studies, assessed for suicide risk behaviors; the related risk factors of hopelessness, depression, anxiety, and anger; and protective factors, including a sense of personal control, problem-solving ability, and family support.

Results showed that students participating in all three conditions demonstrated reductions in suicidal risk behaviors, which included reports of suicidal ideation, threats, and attempts, during the study. Students in all conditions also showed significant reductions in drug involvement, particularly in hard drug use, and reductions in depressive symptoms. Students participating in the CARE and CARE + CAST differed significantly from those in Usual Care with significantly lower levels of depression, and these students also maintained decreases in suicidal ideation, depression, and hopelessness across time. The results of the study showed that a limited intervention (Usual Care) led to decreases in suicide risk behaviors, but the experimental CARE and CAST programs were more effective in reducing depression and suicidal ideation over time.

To further the development of a theoretical model of suicide prevention of youth, E. A. Thompson, Mazza, Herting, Randell, and Eggert (2005) examined the mediating roles of depression, anxiety, and hopelessness on suicidal behavior among 1,287 potential high school dropouts. Hopelessness had direct effects on suicide behavior for boys and girls, whereas depression had a direct effect on boys, but not girls. For both genders, anxiety was related to depression and hopelessness, and drug use was directly and indirectly related to suicide behavior. The lack of family support also played a role in suicide behavior, with indirect influences on anxiety. This study is important for future suicide prevention program development, and the results suggest that different variables may need to be incorporated into high school suicide prevention programs according to the gender of participants.

The Zuni Life Skills Development

The Zuni Life Skills Development (ZLSD) curriculum is a unique suicide prevention intervention designed around the cultural mores and ideology of the Zuni Pueblo living in New Mexico (LaFromboise & Howard-Pitney, 1995). The ZLSD curriculum intervention uses culturally specific activities and education to support and build personal, social, and educational skills that serve as protections against suicide for this population. This type of culture-specific program is important, given the high suicide rates among American Indian adolescents and young adults (Centers for Disease Control and Prevention [CDC], 2012). ZLSD is listed on the NREPP as a universal prevention program.

The ZLSD curriculum consists of classes that meet three times each week for 30 weeks during the school year. The curriculum focuses on seven areas: building self-esteem, increasing problem-solving abilities, identifying emotions and stress, recognizing and eliminating self-destructive behavior, receiving suicide information, suicide intervention training, and setting personal and community goals (LaFromboise, 2006; LaFromboise & Howard-Pitney, 1995; LaFromboise, Medoff, Lee, & Harris, 2007).

LaFromboise and Howard-Pitney (1995) implemented and evaluated the ZLSD curriculum in a tribal high school with 69 freshman and junior students participating in the ZLSD curriculum, which was supplemental to the language arts curriculum. Fifty-nine students participated in a control condition, and they received the regular language arts curriculum. Students in both conditions completed pre- and posttest questionnaires designed to assess suicide probability, hopelessness, depression, and self-efficacy in a number of areas, including suicide prevention skills, problem solving, anger management, and stress management. Thirty-one students from the intervention and 31 students from the control group were randomly selected to participate in a behavioral intervention after the curriculum was completed. Two independent judges watched videotaped segments of students role-playing scenarios with a suicidal confederate and rated their performance. Students also rated their peers on suicide intervention skills and problem solving abilities.

Because of attrition and differences between the intervention and control groups, investigators matched students into 31 pairs based on hopelessness and suicidal probability. Results showed that students in the intervention group reported significantly less feelings of hopelessness after the intervention. The researchers also reported that the intervention group was less suicidal but results were not significant. However, students in the intervention group demonstrated more suicide prevention skills. The researchers also reported a higher level of problem-solving abilities in intervention students, although this did not reach significance. There were no significant differences between groups on peer ratings.

The results of the study showed some indication of the effectiveness of the ZLSD curriculum. Even though the study had some methodological limitations based on small sample size and lack of randomization, the measures used were reliable and validated.

The results suggest that the ZLSD curriculum may reduce hopelessness in American Indian high school students and increase suicide prevention skills. However, further research with more rigorous methodology is required to substantiate the effectiveness of the curriculum. Beyond the outcome results, the researchers learned a great deal about using an intervention program in a culturally specific context. They described the difficulties that they encountered, including developing partnerships with community leaders, gaining trust within the community, and learning to work in a culturally competent and professional manner to maximize the impact of the program (LaFromboise & Lewis, 2008).

Adolescents Training and Learning to Avoid Steroids

The Adolescents Training and Learning to Avoid Steroids (ATLAS) program was designed to deter high school athletes from using steroids or other substances to enhance their athletic skills (Goldberg et al., 2000). This education-based program provides information and skills training to give athletes necessary tools to resist using steroids and other substances. ATLAS is based on social learning theory (Bandura, 1986), with a sports team (e.g., football team) as the social unit. ATLAS includes a classroom curriculum of mostly small-group discussions of alternatives to anabolic steroid (AS) and alcohol and other drug (AOD) use, and consequences of using those substances, and it used role-plays to practice drug refusal skills. In addition, students received weight-room skill training sessions, which outlined proper nutrition and strength training techniques. Students also received sports nutrition guides and weight-training materials. Peer educators, coaches, and strength trainers delivered and facilitated the intervention.

In a randomized trial, 31 high schools in the Pacific Northwest were pair matched and randomized to the ATLAS experimental ($n = 15$ schools) and control ($n = 16$ schools) groups during three football seasons (1994–1996). All students participating in football programs during the 3 years were recruited to participate, and 1,145 male students received the ATLAS program. The control students ($n = 1,371$) received only pamphlets on adverse effects of steroid use and proper sports nutrition. All three cohorts (i.e., 1994–1996) of ATLAS and control group students completed self-report questionnaires before and after the football season. The first and second cohorts (1995–1996) also completed 1-year follow up questionnaires. These self-report measures asked about attitudes and behaviors related to AS and AOD. Students completed the questionnaires anonymously.

Results of the ATLAS intervention showed that students who participated in ATLAS reported significantly less likelihood of intending to use and actual use of AS compared with participants in the control group. At 1-year follow up, intention to use remained significantly lower for students who had received the ATLAS program. Use of other substances, including alcohol and marijuana, was reduced at 1-year follow-up for students in the ATLAS group, although it was not significantly lower at the end of the season. Students in the ATLAS group reported better nutrition and increased self-efficacy with strength training, when compared with control students at the end of the season and at 1-year follow up. Students receiving ATLAS also reported reduced incidences of drinking and driving at 1-year follow up, compared with participants in the control group.

In a later study of ATLAS, Fritz et al. (2005) found consistent Baseline × Treatment interactions for knowledge of the effects of steroid use and intention to use steroids by athletes who participated in the program. These results suggest that ATLAS is beneficial for athletes at greater risk for steroid use, especially if they have less knowledge about steroids and higher intentions to use steroids compared with other athletes.

ATLAS is a unique prevention intervention for high school athletes, and the program has shown effectiveness in reducing AS and other drug use. It addresses an important topic relevant to high school athletes, and the prevention of steroid use merits increased attention by educators and others, such as coaches and trainers, who work with adolescent athletes. The ATLAS program includes classroom and experiential learning components to increase knowledge about steroids and other drugs, while educating about nutrition and strength training.

Postsecondary School

Although colleges and universities have been developing and implementing prevention programs and interventions for many years, only approximately 20 prevention interventions designed for young adults and college students have been reviewed and recommended for dissemination by NREPP (as of April 2013), and some are extensions of interventions originally developed for younger students One reason for the relatively few programs listed by NREPP may be that campus prevention programs developed because of a need to prevent an escalation of a problem, and knowledgeable campus personnel developed an intervention under the umbrella of their employment position. In addition, campus prevention interventionists may not have had the resources to conduct the type of evidence-based evaluations required by NREPP. Further, historically, federal and state health promotion and prevention grant competitions gave higher priority to prevention interventions for children and adolescents. An exception is the Garrett Lee Smith Memorial Act (GLSMA), which in 2004 authorized funding for campus suicide prevention programs. The GLSMA, administered by SAMHSA, was the first to fund programs for youth suicide prevention. The reauthorization of GLSMA, with expanded coverage for campus mental health services, was introduced in Congress in 2013, and awaits final passage (see https://www.govtrack.us/

congress/bills/113/s116 for the status of the bill). The importance of suicide prevention on college campuses is addressed later in this chapter, as suicide is a leading cause of death among young adults, and GLSMA offers an opportunity for colleges and universities to fund suicide prevention.

In this section, three specific NREPP recognized prevention programs addressing important topics on college campuses are summarized: a universal prevention program of health promotion, a campuswide drug and alcohol prevention initiative, and a selective prevention program for college students at risk for depression. Because depression places college students at risk for suicide, the chapter concludes with a discussion of the importance of suicide prevention on campuses and an example of a suicide prevention training program for resident advisors.

InShape

InShape is a brief universal campus prevention program to reduce drug abuse and promote positive physical and mental health. InShape is based on a behavior image model that uses one 30-minute session to motivate students to change health behaviors to meet their future image of self. The program specifically targets physical activity, eating habits, managing stress, getting enough sleep, and avoiding drugs and alcohol. InShape includes a self-administered assessment measuring health habits and self-image before an in-person consultation. During the brief individual consultation, students receive feedback about their self-assessment and develop a plan for achieving their goals. Werch et al. (2008) studied 303 students who received the intervention and compared them with a group of control students. Students who received InShape improved on several indicators, including reduced alcohol and marijuana use, improved sleep, and improvement on other health-related quality of life indicators. However, the intervention and control groups did not differ on cigarette use, exercise, and nutritional habits. Motivational interviewing is a component of the intervention, and it is brief. However, additional evaluations of the intervention are necessary to more thoroughly assess its effectiveness on student health and well-being.

Challenging College Alcohol Abuse

Challenging College Alcohol Abuse (CCAA) is a campuswide universal prevention program. CCAA has been implemented at the University of Arizona to reduce high-risk alcohol use. The program is modeled on work conducted at Northern Illinois University to reduce drinking on campus. CCAA is based on principles to establish healthy social norms and managing the campus environment pertaining to alcohol use (Glider et al., 2001; Johannessen, Glider, Collins, Hueston, & DeJong, 2001). CCAA is an ecological and systemic program that incorporates social learning theory to (a) educate the entire campus community about risks related to alcohol abuse, (b) encourage restraint and careful monitoring of alcohol use on and off campus, and (c) use campus newspaper campaigns to educate about alcohol use and abuse. The overarching goals of CCAA are to change student perceptions about campus social norms related to alcohol use and to educate all members of the university community about risks associated with alcohol use.

CCAA focuses on the entire campus community to advocate for the prevention of alcohol use and abuse. Thus, it is considered a universal prevention program and applicable for all students, staff, and faculty. The program offers advantages, as it is systemic to the campus community and not only to those at risk for alcohol use and abuse. College students are at or below legal drinking age, and it is imperative that alcohol prevention efforts address students in both age groups. In a preliminary study, Glider et al. (2001) reported that student binge drinking rates decreased by 29% in a 3-year period during implementation of CCAA.

In a study related to CCAA, West and Graham (2005) surveyed all accredited colleges and universities in the state of Virginia to learn about substance abuse prevention activities. The researchers found that although 80% of the colleges and universities maintained officially sponsored substance abuse programs, the most common types of programs were those that have been found to have low efficacy, for example, drug awareness campaigns and campus policies. Although the survey was conducted in only one state, similar research may help to strengthen prevention efforts in other geographical regions. For example, West and Graham found few systemic prevention interventions, such as those promoted by CCAA, that addressed campus social norms about drinking and the marketing of alcohol on campus. Systemic campus interventions are likely to yield more impact, but evaluation data about their impact is lacking.

Penn Resilience Training for College Students

Penn Resilience Training for College Students (PRTCS) is listed as a selective prevention intervention by NREPP. PRTCS is based on cognitive behavior theory (e.g., Beck, 1976) for college students at risk for depression. Cognitive behavior skills are taught through a workshop format that includes instruction about the relationship between thoughts, feelings, and behaviors, and how participants can identify and reduce negative automatic thoughts that contribute to depressed feelings. Students also receive training in assertiveness skills, relaxation techniques, and interpersonal skills. PRTCS is an important prevention intervention for college students because depression places people at risk for suicide, and suicide is a leading cause of death among young adults.

Seligman, Schulman, DeRubeis, and Hollon (1999) reported that college students at high risk for depression who participated in an early version of PRTCS reported fewer moderate depression episodes, and fewer episodes of moderate generalized anxiety throughout 3 years of follow up. In addition, students reported improvements in their explanatory style, hopelessness, dysfunctional attitudes, and physical health. Although improvements remained at 3-year follow-up, they had diminished from their postworkshop levels.

Several years later, Seligman et al. (2007) replicated the early PRTCS study, adding supplementary web-based materials and e-mail coaching messages to strengthen the long-term effects of PRTCS. All college freshmen were invited to participate and were eligible based on their risk for depression as assessed by the Beck Depression Inventory (BDI; Beck, Ward, Mendelson, Mock, & Erbaugh, 1961). Two hundred and forty students met criteria and were randomized into treatment and control groups. Students in both conditions completed measures of depression, anxiety, and life satisfaction at the beginning of the study. PRTCS students participated in twice weekly, 1-hour group meetings for 8 weeks. Similar to the earlier study (Seligman et al., 1999), workshop topics included information and skill development based on cognitive behavior theory. After the workshop, participants had access to web-based supplemental materials and received regular e-mail messages from their workshop coaches. The web-based supplements included materials to review and reinforce information and skills learned during the intervention workshop. E-mail messages were systematically timed, approximately one per month over 6 months, and sent by workshop trainers to offer reinforcement and coaching of the information and skills originally learned. Participants in both groups completed posttreatment assessments, and researchers planned to follow the students for 3 years after the PRTCS intervention.

Results of the Seligman et al. (2007) prevention intervention showed that at the end of the workshop, students in the PRTCS group reported significantly fewer depressive and anxiety symptoms and significantly greater life satisfaction, happiness, and optimism, compared with students in the control group. These results persisted at 6-month follow-up. However, at 6-month follow-up, episodes of depression and anxiety did not differ between treatment and control groups. Analyses showed that students' explanatory style of optimism mediated the reduction in depressive and anxiety symptoms and increased satisfaction and happiness, but optimism did not lead to a decrease in depressive or anxious episodes. Surprisingly, few students used the web-based materials, and rarely did students consult with coaches via e-mail. However, electronic and social media are more readily available now than when the study began, and therefore it remains to be seen if technology will strengthen the long-term impact of PRTCS in the future.

Penn Resiliency Training has not been limited to college students. It has also been adapted for use with other groups, such as military personnel (Reivich, Seligman, & McBride, 2011) and youth (Brunwasser, Giliham, & Kim, 2009). For example, Brunwasser et al. conducted a meta-analysis based on 17 controlled studies with nearly 2,500 youth. They reported modest reductions in depressive symptoms over 12 months for youth who received the training when compared with youth who did not receive an intervention. However, there were no differences between youth who received the training and the youth who received an active control intervention. Also, there were no significant differences between experimental and control conditions on diagnosis of depression. Although the authors showed that Penn Resiliency Training provided modest symptom reduction with youth, additional study is needed to assess the intervention's effectiveness and applicability as a universal prevention intervention for depression, especially when compared with other models of mental health promotion.

Suicide Prevention and College Campuses

Suicide is a major public health concern. The CDC (2012) lists suicide as the third leading cause of death of adolescents and young adults, ages 15 to 24 years, accounting for 20% of all deaths annually in this age group. Suicide is the 10th leading cause of death in all age groups. Sari, de Castro, Newman, and Mills (2008) argued that suicide prevention programs are cost-effective and prevent tragic and premature death, which in turn benefits society. The CDC also reports that for every suicide of adolescents and young adults from 15 to 24 years old, there are 100 to 200 attempts. Despite alarming statistics on successful and unsuccessful suicide events among 15- to 24-year-olds, there is a lack of suicide prevention programs on college and university campuses, and more are needed (Westefeld et al., 2005). University and college counseling services provide for student emergencies and crisis situations through walk-in counseling appointments and after-hour crisis hotlines, but these services are usually accessed after students are in crisis. Although colleges offer prevention programs to reduce stress, anxiety, and depression, suicide prevention programs per se are not offered frequently on college campuses, especially compared with suicide prevention programs offered in high schools.

Pasco, Wallack, Sartin, and Dayton (2012) examined the effectiveness of training with college residence hall advisers to identify students in crisis, especially students at risk for suicide. The authors compared 1.5 hours of didactic training with 3.0 hours of training that included didactic education plus experiential activities that emphasize communication skills training and practice of the skills. Didactic training included information about suicide prevalence rates, warning signs, and strategies for intervening with students who they suspect may have suicidal ideation. Resident advisers in both training groups completed two measures that assessed their responses to potential crisis and suicidal situations and their self-efficacy related to their skills and knowledge intervening in crisis and potential suicidal situations. Following the training, both groups of resident advisers showed improved scores on the two measures compared with baseline measures. However, the group that received the didactic plus experiential training showed greater improvement on the measures of responding to a crisis and suicide situation and their self-efficacy related to the situation. This example of a campus suicide prevention intervention addresses an important need through psychoeducational training of residence hall advisors who are in positions to be early responders to students at risk for suicide. The evaluation of this short-term training demonstrates the value of providing experiential skills practice training with educational information to strengthen an intervention for suicide prevention.

Suicide prevention programs on college campuses can take different forms. Universal suicide prevention can provide information, through in person presentations and electronic and social media, to the entire campus community about the incidence of suicide, warning signs, risk factors, cultural considerations, and campus mental health resources for students at risk for suicide. Peer and paraprofessional suicide prevention programs, as shown with the residence advisor training above, are beneficial as trained peers can educate other students about suicide, identify students who may be at risk for suicide, make necessary referrals to professionals, and provide support until professionals become involved. Campus employees (e.g., faculty, advisers, housing personnel) may suspect or learn about a student's suicidal ideation in different ways such as through class assignments, advising meetings, changes in student's behavior or dress, and through reports from others. It is important that colleges and universities develop comprehensive suicide prevention programs that inform students and employees about the potential for suicide in young adults and campus resources that can be accessed for assistance.

SUMMARY

Only a small sample of the many prevention programs offered during the preK–16 years of schooling are presented in this chapter. Several of the programs summarized have been reviewed by NREPP, whereas others have been recognized by other organizations. However, more research is needed to demonstrate program effectiveness, especially prevention interventions implemented with high school and postsecondary school students. There are more elementary-school evidenced-based prevention programs, compared with high school and college prevention programs, likely because of the availability of grant funds to support prevention interventions for children, especially children from low-income communities. Although some of the programs report longer term follow-up, most do not, and therefore their effectiveness in promoting lasting behavior changes are not clear. Further, much of the empirical data relies on self-report measures. Some of the programs reviewed describe a theoretical framework, and others are less clear. Nevertheless, this chapter has highlighted a range of school-based prevention programs and activities designed to prevent and/or reduce incidents of problem behaviors and emotions, and enhance health and well-being.

7

PREVENTION APPLICATIONS IN COMMUNITY AND MEDICAL SETTINGS

PREVENTION IN COMMUNITY SETTINGS

Community prevention interventions have been implemented across different community contexts, population groups, and topics. Topic areas include adolescent suicide prevention (Parker et al., 2009), substance abuse prevention (Fagan, Hanson, Hawkins, & Arthur, 2008; Saxe et al., 2006), prevention of depression and anxiety in youth and young adults (Christensen, Pallister, Smale, Hickie, & Calear, 2010; Garber et al., 2009), rape and domestic violence prevention (Townsend & Campbell, 2008; Yick & Oomen-Early, 2009), youth violence prevention (Umemoto et al., 2009; Zeldin, 2004), promotion of health and wellness (E. O. Lee, 2007; Peters, Petrunka, & Arnold, 2003; Reijneveld, Westhoff, & Hopman-Rock, 2003), depression in older adults and suicide prevention for older adults (Blazer, 2002; Oyama, Koida, & Kudo, 2004), and HIV/AIDS prevention (Kaponda et al., 2007; Takahashi, Candelario, Young, & Mediano, 2007).

DOI: 10.1037/14442-007
Prevention Psychology: Enhancing Personal and Social Well-Being, by J. L. Romano
Copyright © 2015 by the American Psychological Association. All rights reserved.

Examples of community-based prevention programs are summarized in this section of the chapter. These examples were selected for inclusion because of the populations and communities they serve, the topics of the interventions, or evidence supporting their efficacy. Sections of the chapter also summarize comprehensive reviews of depression and anxiety community-based prevention interventions with adolescents and older adults. Prevention interventions presented range from prevention topics that address problem areas at different life stages, from childhood youth to older adults.

Better Beginnings, Better Futures

Better Beginnings, Better Futures (BBBF) is a comprehensive universal prevention program for primary school children and their families. Its goals are to prevent childhood emotional and behavioral problems, to promote overall positive development of children, and to strengthen neighborhood and family characteristics in Ontario, Canada (Peters et al., 2003). BBBF is supported by theoretical concepts from positive youth development, systemic community enrichment, and policy initiatives to promote the healthy development of children and youth. The program was first introduced in Canada in 1990. BBBF is a long-term prevention and research demonstration to assess the effectiveness of prevention as policy for children, from preschool through early elementary school (Peters at al., 2003). Communities with lower socioeconomic characteristics were funded to implement BBBF. However, all members of the community could participate in the program.

Each community selected for BBBF was funded to reduce emotional and behavioral problems of children, to strengthen families and community, to develop local organizational support for children's programming, to encourage parents and stakeholders to engage in program development and implementation, and to establish partnerships with schools and service providers across the community. The communities that were funded were to design a prevention model that would be most effective for their own purposes. Therefore, BBBF is not a one-size-fits-all program, but instead offers a set of goals and objectives around which communities develop their own specific programs and activities to best meet the overall goals of the BBBF prevention project.

Peters et al. (2003) reported on three sites in Ontario, Canada, that implemented the community-based research on BBBF's effectiveness with children and their families who were first recruited in 1993 when the children were in prekindergarten. The children and families were followed for 5 years. Although the programs differed somewhat across the three sites evaluated, they all included a mix of school-based programs and before- and after-school programs for children and parents. Examples included classroom enrichment sessions, program activities for children and families during holidays and school vacations, multicultural programs, home visits, and welcome visits to new families. Community development activities were especially prevalent in one of the sites, which included the development of community gardens and environmental enhancement.

BBBF was evaluated in different ways, including measures to assess children's mental health and development, parent and family functioning, and community characteristics. In addition, analyses of the project's development and economic impact were conducted.

Data were gathered from the three sites through quantitative and qualitative methods, over a 5-year period. The results based on teacher and parent ratings showed primarily decreases in children's emotional and behavioral problems and increases in children's social functioning, although children's cognitive functioning did not show patterns of improvement. However, in one site there was a large decrease in the number of students identified for special education services. Improvements were found on several other indicators of child and parent health. For example, in one site a significant pattern of reduced parental smoking and alcohol use was found. No consistent patterns of parent and family functioning were found among the three sites studied. However, there was some increased satisfaction with the quality of local neighborhoods and schools. Generally, the results from the three sites showed increases in positive indicators, although the two sites that used primarily school-based programming showed greater improvement on several indicators, compared with the one site that used fewer school-based activities and more community-based programs.

This comprehensive universal community prevention program has shown positive results, and it is cost-effective to implement (Peters et al., 2003). BBBF offers a unique model of bringing together stakeholders from across a given community to help foster healthy children, families, and neighborhoods. Although community-based prevention initiatives such as BBBF pose many complexities in development, implementation, and evaluation, the results from this evaluation of three sites that implemented BBBF show that the program offers much promise as a model for community-based prevention to enrich the lives of children, youth, and their parents and guardians.

An extended follow-up of children and families who began participating in BBBF in 1993 was conducted when the children were in Grades 3 (8–9 years), 6 (11–12 years), and 9 (14–15 years), comparing BBBF children, families, and communities with communities matched on sociodemographic characteristics (Peters et al., 2010). The follow-up study showed improvements in social and school functioning in Grades 6 and 9, and children and adolescents experienced fewer emotional problems in all three grades. Parents reported increased social support and improved marital satisfaction and family functioning. In addition, positive neighborhood effects were found.

An economic analysis of BBBF participation at Grade 9 showed BBBF to be cost-effective. These extended follow-up data provide additional evidence of the viability and cost-effectiveness of a comprehensive community-based universal prevention program to promote the development of children and families, several years after implementation.

Review of Community-Based Anxiety and Depression Prevention Interventions for Youth

Christensen et al. (2010) conducted a review of community-based anxiety and depression prevention interventions for youth, ages 11 to 25. The research reviewed included studies that were specifically focused on the prevention of depression and anxiety, as well as studies to prevent other problems, such as poor parenting and diabetes, but these studies also assessed the effect of the prevention interventions on depression and anxiety as a secondary outcome. Community settings were defined as health and social care organizations, postsecondary educational settings, family homes, and specialized educational settings outside of regular elementary and secondary schools. Prevention interventions included programs and activities that were categorized as universal, selective, and indicated prevention. Christensen et al. identified 18 anxiety and 26 depression studies.

Of the 18 anxiety studies reviewed, 11 were universal, six were selective, and one was a joint selective/indicated intervention. Approximately 60% of the universal and selective studies yielded positive outcomes, with cognitive behavioral theory as the primary theoretical framework and the emphasis of the intervention activities. Other types of interventions, such as exercise, stress management, and relaxation training with self-esteem enhancement, yielded mixed results. Most of the anxiety prevention programs were conducted in a university or college setting with older teens and young adults, and they were either individual or group interventions. Some of the comparison groups used an automated or computerized program intervention, and three of five of these programs yielded positive results.

Of the 26 depression prevention studies, five were universal, 16 selective, and three indicated. In these studies, cognitive behavioral approaches were used most often in the prevention intervention (46%), and 11 of the 12 cognitive behavioral interventions yielded at least one positive result. Other interventions yielded different outcomes. For example, all three exercise programs yielded at least one positive outcome, but only one of three stress and coping training programs yielded positive results. Other programs that investigated parenting skills training and social support for teens did not affect levels of depression. Similar to the anxiety prevention research, most of the studies were conducted in university settings, and other settings included community and youth social service organizations and alternative schools. Individual and group formats were used to deliver the interventions.

About 60% of the anxiety programs and 63% of the depression prevention programs yielded positive results (Christensen et al., 2010). In the anxiety trials, universal and selective interventions were equally successful, and in the depression studies, universal and indicated studies yielded positive outcomes compared with selective programs. Cognitive behavioral approaches were the most common intervention for both anxiety and depression, and exercise programs showed some effectiveness for depression but less so for anxiety. There was insufficient evidence to support other types of interventions that were used. Computerized interventions yielded some positive results for anxiety and depression, but it is unclear what factors contributed to the success of these interventions.

Christensen et al. (2010) reported that the results of their review showed similar outcomes to other studies conducted in schools. The researchers pointed out the advantages of conducting reviews of this nature. For example, anxiety and depressions interventions that primarily focused on prevention of these problems yielded more positive outcomes, compared with other interventions in which reduction of anxiety and/or depression was a secondary outcome. The review also showed that cognitive behavioral theory is the primary theoretical framework used in the prevention interventions, and there were few intervention differences between universal, selective, and indicated prevention applications. This review also found that community-based depression programs were more common, compared with anxiety programs, and anxiety programs were more common in university settings. Depression prevention programs also attracted a wider range of participants.

In terms of disadvantages of this type of review, Christensen et al. (2010) pointed out that given the range of study variables, populations, and interventions reviewed, it is difficult to identify and compare the most salient components of prevention interventions for anxiety and depression. In addition, categorization of different types of prevention interventions into universal, selective, or indicated programs is difficult if information about recruitment strategies, prior treatment, and diagnostic outcomes are not reported.

Because many of these prevention programs were delivered in university and college settings, they are not strictly community-based. However, the information gathered from Christensen et al.'s (2010) review is useful to advance prevention research and applications. The review demonstrated the use of computer-based prevention programs, which have the potential to reach large numbers of people, especially technology-savvy youth. It is likely that prevention interventions will be greatly enhanced in the years ahead as technology and social media become more sophisticated and more available to larger segments of the population. However, regardless of the mode of delivery, community-based anxiety and depression prevention programs, especially those that target young adults outside of educational institutions, are needed, as is additional research about the most salient and efficacious components of such programs.

Community-Based Prevention for Older Adults

Older adults experience significant health risks, and as the population of older adults increases in the years ahead, the number of risks and problems for this population will also increase. Therefore, developing and implementing prevention activities and programs for this population is taking on greater importance (Konnert, Gatz, & Hertzsprung Meyen, 1999; Vacha-Haase, 2012).

The rapidly increasing population of older adults in the United States and in other countries requires that prevention scholars and practitioners give attention to the application of prevention with this age group. The U.S. Administration on Aging (n.d.) reported that in 2009, 39.6 million, or about 13% of the U.S. population, were 65 years of age and older. This number is projected to grow substantially by 2030 to more than 72 million, or 19% of the population, as life expectancy increases. Thus, increased efforts, especially with prevention approaches, are needed to support older adults living in their own homes and communities and to improve their quality of life.

In recognition of the importance of improving and increasing the coordination of community services for older adults, the U.S. Department of Health and Human Services established a new agency in 2012, the Administration for Community Living (see http://www.acl.gov), which now includes the Administration on Aging, Office of Disabilities, and the Administration of Developmental Disabilities. The goals of the new agency are to increase community supports for older adults and people with disabilities in order to strengthen health care services and improve quality of life so that people can live in their own communities as long as possible. Prevention of problems and health promotion initiatives are major contributors to strengthening the overall health and well-being of older adults in their communities.

Many opportunities exist to improve the health and well-being of seniors through prevention and health promotion activities. These include programs for older adults who need assistance with adhering to medical recommendations (Murdaugh & Insel, 2009; Resnick, Galik, Nahm, Shaughnessy, & Michael, 2009), programs to prevent depression in later life (Blazer, 2002), and suicide prevention programs (Fiske & Arbore, 2000/2001; Pearson, 2000/2001). In this section, community-based prevention and health-enhancing projects for seniors are reviewed.

Health Promotion in Senior Populations

Prevention has a major role to play in health promotion for older adults, and prevention specialists have much to offer (Chapman, 2007; Goetzel et al., 2007). Health promotion may include, for example, programs that facilitate involvement of seniors in the education of youth through mentorship and tutoring programs (e.g., Holmes, 2009), opportunities to socialize with others, and participation in physical exercise programs (Reijneveld, Westhoff, & Hopman-Rock, 2003). Older adults can also use their skills to contribute to community businesses and community services (Holmes, 2009). Because depression is a major risk factor for older adults, opportunities to participate in community activities to combat loneliness, develop relationships, and strengthen self-efficacy (Blazer, 2002) can promote the health and well-being of seniors in communities. However, the interventions must be developed, implemented, and evaluated to assess their effectiveness and their impact.

Prevention of Depression and Suicide in Older Adults

There is an extensive literature on depression and suicide in adults 65 years of age and older (Alexopoulos, 2005; Pearson, 2000/2001). Alexopoulos (2005) summarized the literature that supports the importance of prevention interventions for depression in older adults, citing several types of interventions, often based on a behavioral theoretical framework, that can be helpful, including relaxation training, cognitive restructuring, and behavioral management strategies to improve nutrition and physical exercise. The prevention and management of depression in older adults are important, as depression is a major risk factor for suicide. The National Institute of Mental Health (2009) reported that suicide is disproportionately more common in older adults compared with other age groups, and seniors 75 years and older have the highest rates of suicide in most industrialized countries (Waern, Rubenowitz, & Wilhelmson, 2003).

The relationship between negative life events and depression in older adults was studied by Kraaij, Arensman, and Spinhoven (2002). In their meta-analysis of 25 studies, depression was associated with almost all negative life events, and the cumulative effect of these events together with daily hassles had the strongest relationship to depression. Thus, a selective or indicated prevention intervention for depression in this age group might be an intervention for seniors who have experienced several negative life events within a short period of time. The Kraaij et al. meta-analysis did not provide data on negative life events occurring earlier in the life of the older adults. Interestingly, in their analysis, sudden and unexpected life events were not related to depression.

The relationship of depression to suicide was studied in a community sample of people 75 years and older in Sweden (Waern et al., 2003). This primarily qualitative study found that family conflict, physical illness, minor and major depression, and loneliness were associated with suicide in this age group. Economic problems contributed to suicide in a younger comparison group, ages 65 to 74, but not in the older group. Also, members of the older group who were depressed were less likely to receive treatment for depression than were members of the younger group. This study reinforces the importance of community-based prevention interventions for seniors across the prevention spectrum of interventions, that is, universal, selective, and indicated prevention interventions, and with all age groups of older adults.

Pearson and Brown (2000) reported that age and gender are strong predictors of suicide. For example, men 75 years and older living in industrialized countries have much higher rates of suicide compared with adolescents. Therefore, suicide among older adults is a major public health problem that merits much more attention, especially because suicide is a preventable event. Pearson and Brown stated that one of the best preventive suicide interventions for older adults is treating depression, understanding that treating depression in this age group is challenging. For example, older adults and family members might be inclined to attribute depression to the aging process; another challenge would be the cultural stigma associated with depression. Therefore, universal education programs about depression and suicide in older adults are important to inform older adults, their family, and caregivers about the symptoms and risks associated with depression and suicide in this age group. They should also be educated about referral resources for older adults who are depressed and be provided information about funding for treatment of older adults who are at risk for depression and suicide.

PREVENTION IN MEDICAL SETTINGS

Compared with other practice settings, the application of psychology in medical settings has a more recent history, and even more so in primary prevention (S. B. Johnson & Millstein, 2003). However, in recent years, psychologists have strongly advocated extending the profession's research and interventions to improve the overall health of the nation (DeLeon, Giesting, & Kenkel, 2003; Garcia-Shelton, 2006). As Tovian (2004) wrote, "Health psychologists should promote and emphasize their expertise in the prevention of numerous medical conditions and the important contribution they can make to reducing overall medical costs" (p. 140). This sentiment has been echoed by others, recognizing the importance of psychology applying prevention within medical settings to support health promotion and disease prevention and to reduce overall medical costs (Brown et al., 2002). The importance of psychology's role in health settings was given added impetus when the American Psychological

Association added the word *health* to the association's mission statement in 2001 (Garcia-Shelton, 2006).

S. B. Johnson and Millstein (2003) wrote about the importance of applying prevention interventions in health care settings, especially given the high percentage of children and adolescents who visit health care facilities each year and the amount of trust that adults place in health care professionals. The amount of contact with health care professionals and the value placed on quality health care make these settings excellent venues in which to implement prevention activities, interventions, and research. However, S. B. Johnson and Millstein identified several challenges and barriers associated with psychologists applying prevention in health care settings. These include the extensive focus in health care on healing and interventions after a problem has been diagnosed and the lack of financial support for prevention. In addition, several barriers to conducting rigorous research and evaluations in health care settings exist, including the lack of trained research personnel in many health settings and methodological challenges, such as a limited number of research participants and the problems associated with gathering longer term follow-up data to evaluate prevention interventions.

In her 2010 American Psychological Association Presidential Address, Carol Goodheart articulated the need for a stronger presence of psychologists in primary health care settings, as psychological services can be extremely valuable to patients and the overall health enterprise (Goodheart, 2011). Goodheart cited data showing that fewer than half of the people in the United States in need of mental health services receive them (Kessler et al., 2005) and that two thirds of primary care physicians report being unable to obtain outpatient mental health services for their patients (Cunningham, 2009). To correct these deficiencies and to effect greater and improved use of psychological services for prevention, treatment, and disease management, Goodheart argued for a system of integrated health care that includes primary medical care and psychological services. Such a coordinated system, according to Goodheart, would improve patient care and access, and provide more cost-effective health outcomes.

As one example of coordinated care, McDaniel and Fogarty (2009) proposed the Patient-Centered Medical Home (PCMH), which is a model of integrated primary medical care that includes several medical specialties, such as internal medicine, family practice, and pediatrics. Although psychologists are not included in the current PCMH model, the authors argued for the inclusion of primary care psychologists in the model. Psychologists can be especially beneficial in providing prevention services across the life span through psychoeducational programs and individual and small-group interventions for individuals and families. As team members, psychologists can also be instrumental in advocating for professional self-care of team members and making referrals, as needed, to other mental health and psychological treatment agencies and specialties.

The Netherlands has used a health care system that includes primary care psychologists for more than 30 years (Derksen, 2009). This integrated health care model has contributed to improved services, including prevention activities and interventions, that have contributed to cost benefits for patients, as well as greater cost-effectiveness throughout the health care system.

Several applications of prevention interventions and research in medical settings are summarized next. Unlike interventions in educational settings, prevention interventions specific to medical settings are not generally cited in the National Registry of Evidence Based Programs and Practices. Therefore, the examples of prevention interventions in this chapter were selected for their diversity of health problems, ages of participants, and uniqueness. In addition to specific prevention interventions, reviews of a meta-analysis of the impact of online public health campaigns and working with youth in primary health care settings are summarized.

The interventions reviewed include universal, selective, indicated, and tertiary interventions. Many prevention interventions in medical settings are selected, indicated, and tertiary. This is not surprising, given that patients, medical personnel, and reimbursement structures are much more focused on identifying and correcting existing health problems, compared with preventing health problems through primary or universal programs. However, as evident in this review, physically based medical problems often have comorbid components, such as anxiety and depression, that can compromise the treatment of a newly diagnosed or existing medical condition. In addition, lifestyle patterns and behaviors such as cigarette use, diet and nutrition, and physical exercise can contribute to physical health problems, especially for people at risk for medical problems. Therefore, it is important that the medical professions also actively intervene with prevention interventions that address these risk behaviors.

Prevention Interventions With Medically Referred Patients

Depression is a common comorbid condition of patients undergoing treatment for serious medical conditions such as cancer, HIV, and arthritis (Williams, DiMatteo, & Haskard, 2009). To reduce depression in cancer patients, Hopko et al. (2008) applied cognitive behavior therapy (CBT) to cancer patients with clinical depression, noting that although depression is common among cancer patients, few studies have assessed the outcomes of psychological interventions with cancer patients who are depressed. Hopko et al. conducted their study with 13 patients (11 women, two men) with different types of cancer, who were also diagnosed with clinical depression.

The patients were assessed for depression, anxiety, quality of life, and social support. Following pretreatment assessments, participants completed 9 weeks of individual CBT for depression with psychology trainees. The nine sessions included psychoeducation, goal setting, and behavioral activation therapy, defined as attempting to "increase overt behaviors that bring patients into contact with reinforcing environmental contingencies and corresponding improvements in thoughts, mood, and overall quality of life" (Hopko et al., 2008, p. 130).

Results from the study showed significant improvement across most of the measures from pre- to posttreatment. Depression and anxiety symptoms and most areas of personal functioning showed improvement at posttreatment, although perceived social support and bodily pain did not change. Patients reported being very satisfied with the intervention at posttreatment. Assessments were repeated 3 months following the intervention, and with one exception, all measures remained significant, demonstrating sustained improvement in depressive symptoms and level of functioning. Only anxiety symptoms did not remain significantly improved at follow-up.

The results of this study suggest that a brief 9-week psychological intervention, based on CBT, can lead to improvements in depressive and anxiety symptoms, overall functioning, and quality of life for individuals with dual diagnoses of cancer and depression. Because patients were already diagnosed with depression as a condition for participating in the study, in terms of the spectrum of prevention interventions, this intervention would be categorized as tertiary prevention within the classification proposed by Caplan (1964). However, the psychological intervention helped to strengthen the mental health functioning of patients who were depressed, while preventing more severe psychological dysfunction, and it therefore merits consideration as a prevention intervention. Despite positive results, the study is limited by a small sample and the lacked of a control or comparison group.

In a study of couples coping with metastatic breast cancer (MBC), Badr, Carmack, Kashy, Cristofanilli, and Revenson (2010) examined each couple's dyadic stress and coping associated with the diagnosis. Although this is not an intervention study, the research provides a framework that may inform future prevention interventions with this population. *Dyadic stress* refers to stress that a woman with MBC and her partner share that is related to her illness, including end-of-life issues and ongoing medical care. *Dyadic coping* refers to mutuality and interdependence in the couple's coping responses to MBC as a life-threatening illness. Badr et al. used the systemic-transactional model (STM) as the theoretical framework for dyadic coping, examining how couples respond individually and jointly to stressors. Adapted from Lazarus and Folkman's (1984) transactional model of stress, which uses individually centered coping, STM uses a model of coping at the individual and couple levels (Bodenmann, 2005). At the individual level, partner responses to coping are either supportive or not supportive, whereas coping at the couple level is either positive (i.e., couples working as a team to problem solve, relaxing, sharing, and expressing solidarity) or negative (i.e., avoiding or withdrawing). Badr et al. hypothesized that positive dyadic coping is associated with less illness-related stress and better adjustment as a couple.

Participants in the Badr et al. (2010) study were women who had received an MBC diagnosis and were initiating treatment. The women were in relationship with a male partner for at least 1 year, were relatively pain free, were ambulatory and able to perform self-care, and were fluent in English. At baseline, 191 couples (out of 367 female MBC patients who were originally approached by the researchers) completed the assessment battery, which included measures of cancer-related stress communication (Bodenmann, 1997), a life-events scale (Horowitz, Wilner, & Alvarez, 1979), and a measure of marital distress (Hunsley, Best, Lefebvre, & Vito, 2001). At 3- and 6-month follow-up, 122 and 110 couples, respectively, repeated the assessments. Many reasons contributed to dropouts at follow-up, including increases in the severity of the disease, incomplete surveys, and death of some participants.

Results showed that over the 6-month assessment period, cancer-related distress and marital distress remained relatively stable. However, partners who used a positive dyadic coping style were more likely to experience better marital adjustment, whereas partners who used a negative dyadic coping style experienced more cancer-related distress and marital distress. Individually, women with MBC communicated more stress to their partners, whereas their partners communicated stress less frequently, and women found their partners to be more supportive whereas partners rated the women less supportive. It is interesting to note that women and partners experienced coping styles in different ways. Positive coping was associated with an increase in distress for women, whereas their partners had a slight decrease in distress. Negative coping led to increased distress in both women and partners, but partners experienced distress to a higher degree.

This study provides an interesting examination of stress and coping among couples when one member of the dyad is faced with a life-threatening illness. However, because this was not an intervention study, it remains to be seen how an actual intervention might improve a couple's stress and coping responses, and communication style after an MBC diagnosis. The results of the study may demonstrate individual and couple patterns that had already been deeply engrained in the couple's relationship, rather than reflecting changes as a result of an MBC diagnosis (Badr et al., 2010). Therefore, in terms of prevention, this study suggests the potential for a prevention intervention to reduce individual and couple stress, and improve coping and couple communication after a diagnosis of MBC, or other life-threatening illness.

In another study with women receiving treatment for breast cancer, Montgomery et al. (2009) investigated the effects of CBT and hypnosis on women's levels of fatigue while undergoing radiation therapy. Fatigue is one of the main side effects of radiation therapy, and it can be catastrophic when combined with emotional distress and expectancies of fatigue (e.g., Montgomery & Bovbjerg, 2001; Valentine & Meyers, 2001). Research has shown that CBT is effective in reducing distress and managing symptoms of medical treatments for cancer (Kangas, Bovbjerg, & Montgomery, 2008; Redd, Montgomery, & DuHamel, 2001). Hypnosis has also been found to control the side effects of cancer treatments, in particular, fatigue in breast cancer surgery patients (Montgomery et al., 2007). Therefore, Montgomery et al. (2009) used a combination of CBT and hypnosis (CBTH) and assessed its effectiveness in reducing fatigue in patients undergoing radiation treatment for breast cancer.

Forty-two women who were scheduled to begin radiation therapy were randomized into the treatment group ($n = 22$) or the control group ($n = 20$). Participants in both groups completed daily and weekly fatigue measures. Before beginning radiation, all participants completed a demographic survey and a measure of neuroticism (Costa & McCrae, 1992). Neuroticism has been associated with higher levels of fatigue in cancer patients (Michielsen, Van der Steeg, Roukema, & De Vries, 2007). Women in the treatment group were seen by one of two trained staff before each radiation session. In Weeks 1 and 2, participants were educated in 15-minute sessions on hypnosis and CBT, and they were given a CD player and hypnosis CD to use at home. In Weeks 3 through 8, participants were given a CBT workbook and asked to complete two worksheets each week. Participants met twice weekly with an interventionist staff member for 15 minutes to review the worksheets. Control group participants received standard medical care without additional interventions.

The results of the study found that the treatment group showed only a modest increase in weekly fatigue, whereas the control group had significant increases in fatigue. Similarly, daily fatigue and muscle weakness of the control group were also more pronounced compared with the treatment condition.

Montgomery et al. (2009) demonstrated that CBTH is effective in reducing fatigue and muscle weakness associated with radiation therapy for breast cancer patients. The authors pointed to one significant limitation. The patients in the treatment group received significantly more professional attention than those in the control group, and this could have accounted for some of the differences. In addition, patients were aware of their treatment condition, which may have biased their reporting. The researchers did not attempt to determine the most salient components of the intervention, and, therefore, it is not known whether treatment effects were due to CBT, hypnosis, or the combination of the two. A future study with multiple groups receiving different components could help determine the most effective treatment components. Nevertheless, despite some limitations in the study related to the extent to which patients followed through on homework assignments, CBTH provides a prevention intervention for this population that merits further study.

Caldwell et al. (2003) examined the effects of group therapy on sexual functioning of gynecological cancer survivors. Women who are treated for gynecological cancer may experience significant sexual problems following treatment (R. Harris, Good, & Pollack, 1982; Wenzel et al., 2002). Nineteen women participated in 12 weekly group therapy sessions and completed baseline and follow-up assessments of sexual functioning (Clayton, McGarvey, & Clavet, 1996) and mood (McNair, Lorr, & Droppleman, 1992). Topics of the weekly group therapy sessions, conducted in groups of three to five women by a clinical psychologist, included communicating with sexual partners, loss of ability to have children, mutation of sexual body parts, and residual effects of chemotherapy on sexual desire and functioning. Each therapy session also included process components of trust, expression of emotion, encouraging pleasurable experiences, and exploring old sexual scripts and creating new ones.

The results of the study showed that women significantly increased their sexual functioning at the end of the intervention. However, although sexual functioning scores improved at 3-month follow-up from baseline, they were no longer significantly different from baseline measures. Similarly, for the measure of mood, significant improvements were found at postintervention, but they were not sustained at 3-month follow-up.

The results of this study showed that there was some improvement in sexual functioning, at least in the short term, for women recovering from gynecological cancer. In the long term, women reported participating more frequently in sexual activity after the group therapy intervention, but gains in mood, sexual arousal, and overall sexual functioning were not sustained. The study has several limitations, including small sample size and a lack of a comparison group. However, Caldwell et al. (2003) suggested that multidisciplinary treatment, including psychological interventions, may be beneficial for women with gynecological cancer. Additional studies that use more robust experimental designs are needed to further examine the role of group and individual psychotherapy in helping women with gynecological cancer to improve their sexual and overall functioning, and thus prevent emotional difficulties and enhance overall well-being.

Patients with coronary heart disease (CHD) were the focus of a study by Pischke, Scherwitz, Weidner, and Ornish (2008). In addition to the contribution of lifestyle behaviors (e.g., smoking, nutrition, exercise) to CHD, psychosocial factors, including stress, hostility, depression, and anxiety, have been identified as CHD risk factors (Chaput et al., 2002; Hemingway & Marmot,

1999; Kuper, Marmot, & Hemingway, 2002). Although many studies have examined how lifestyle changes influence CHD, little is known about their effects on psychological well-being of CHD patients. Therefore, Pischke et al. evaluated the effects of lifestyle changes on psychological well-being and sought to determine whether there are associations between lifestyle changes and cardiac variables in CHD patients over a 5-year period.

Male and female CHD patients were recruited and randomized to intervention ($n = 28$) or control ($n = 20$) groups. Both groups consisted mostly of men, with 96% and 80% of the patients being men in the intervention and control groups, respectively. Patients in both groups were similar in age (in their late 50s), education (at least some post–high school education), and marital status (married or living with someone). All participants completed baseline psychosocial questionnaires assessing general health, social support, anger, and time urgency. Participants in the intervention group completed a 1-week intensive residential retreat to introduce healthy lifestyle behaviors, such as getting proper nutrition, appropriate exercise, stress management, and social support activities. Following the retreat, participants were asked to maintain these new lifestyle behaviors and also to attend 1-hour group sessions twice a week for 1 year. Participants also had the option to continue in a self-directed group after 1 year. Psychosocial questionnaires were completed after the 1-year intervention and again 5 years later. Participants in the control group completed only the questionnaires.

The results showed that psychosocial distress can improve, at least in the short term, as a result of lifestyle changes. After 1 year, significant positive changes were found in psychological distress and insomnia for experimental group participants, compared with the control group. However, significant changes were not maintained at 5-year follow-up. At 5-year follow-up, a trend toward improvement in hostility was maintained for the experimental group compared with the control group. When intervention patients were divided according to program adherence, however, those in the higher adherence group showed significantly greater reductions in psychological distress from baseline at 1- and 5-year follow-ups. Improvements in stress management were also shown to be associated with cardiovascular health, even after controlling for improvements in diet. The study suggests the importance of targeting multiple lifestyle behaviors and psychological variables to reduce the impact of CHD, and the importance of follow-up booster sessions to enhance the long-term effectiveness of behavioral changes.

Translating Research to Clinical Practice

To test the feasibility of translating an empirically supported diabetes prevention program into a hospital-based weight loss program, Pagoto, Kantor,

Bodenlos, Gitkind, and Ma (2008) used diffusion of innovations theory (DIT; E. M. Rogers, 2003) to adopt the research program into real-world practice. DIT has been used as a model to disseminate health care services (Backer & Rogers, 1998). Pagoto et al. wrote that although controlled empirical studies have demonstrated the efficacy of weight loss interventions, the success of the translation of these interventions into clinical settings has received much less attention. DIT uses a five-stage process for the decision maker in determining the feasibility of adopting and implementing an innovation. DIT stages are knowledge, persuasion, decision, implementation, and confirmation. DIT was used as the framework to modify the Diabetes Prevention Program (DPP) Lifestyle Intervention (DPP Research Group, 2002) into a hospital-based weight loss clinic.

Pagoto et al. (2008) described the five-stage process in adapting DPP for implementation in a hospital clinic. First, hospital decision-makers became knowledgeable about DPP and professional practice guidelines for weight-loss programs. They also examined the feasibility of adapting DPP to the clinic. Second, during the persuasion and decision stages, hospital personnel examined the suitability of DPP for their setting and made a deliberate decision to adopt the program. Third, the program was implemented, with several modifications to adjust to the hospital setting. Fourth, during the confirmation stage, DPP was integrated into the regular routine of the clinic, benefits were assessed, and promoted. DPP has been in existence in the hospital since 2004. To participate in the program, patients were given medical and behavioral medicine evaluations, including a medical intake evaluation with a physician and a behavioral medicine intake with a health psychologist.

To evaluate the benefits of the program, and after 18 months of integrating the program into routine practice, the researchers assessed 118 patients who completed the core phase. Average weight loss after 16 weeks in the program was 5.57 kg, and 49% of the patients achieved clinically significant weight loss. In comparison with the original DPP research program outcomes, weight-loss clinic patients did not achieve the same levels of weight loss. In addition, comorbid conditions (e.g., Type 2 diabetes, depression) were much higher in the clinic sample compared with the original DPP research sample. However, patients without comorbid conditions achieved weight loss similarly to the original DPP research sample. A patient satisfaction survey indicated that patients learned much from the program, and although 90% were satisfied with the program, only 56% were satisfied with their weight loss. The results from this implementation study suggest that it is possible to translate clinical research findings into a hospital-based community setting using DIT as a framework. Although clinic patients did not achieve the level of weight loss found in the original DPP research study, clinic clients had more comorbid conditions, and many patients did attain weight loss at clinically significant levels

(Pagoto et al., 2008). Further study of the intervention is necessary to assess if patient weight loss was maintained over a longer period. Also, it is important to compare DPP with other clinically based weight loss programs. This study is important because it attempted to replicate the results from a research study in a clinical setting. Although the clinical setting did not achieve the same results as the research project, the clinical study achieved positive results, and more important, addressed challenges associated with translating research study results to clinical practice in health care settings.

Diabetes mellitus has reached epidemic proportions in recent decades (Mokdad et al., 2001). Although diabetes education stresses reducing weight and glucose levels, it does not often describe how to achieve lifestyle changes necessary to prevent diabetes-related health complications (Stetson, Carrico, Beacham, Ziegler, & Mokshagundam, 2006). Therefore, Stetson et al. (2006) designed a behavior change intervention that included six weekly 90-minute group sessions designed to address barriers to self-care, reducing dichotomous thinking about diabetes, and enhancing self-regulation. Twenty participants were enrolled in three sequential cohorts. They were given pretests that included measures of health-relevant indicators (e.g., blood tests, weight), physical activity, eating behaviors, and stress management. Patients were also asked to write personal goals to improve health habits. Sixteen of the 20 participants completed postintervention assessments.

Results from the study indicated that after the intervention, changes were not found in eating behaviors, physical activity, stress/mood management strategies, weight, blood pressure, or reported daily blood-glucose tests. Although goal setting results showed that from pre- to postintervention participants became more specific in their goal setting, the results did not reach statistical significance. Despite a lack of significant findings or changes in behavior on the assessments, participants were highly satisfied with the program. Stetson et al. (2006) concluded that the brief intervention was valued by participants and may facilitate positive health changes in the future. They emphasized that psychologists can play an important role in bringing about health-related client behavioral changes in clinical health settings. Thus, a program such as this has the potential to prevent additional complications from diabetes and to enhance overall health outcomes, thus serving as a selective or indicated prevention intervention.

Autism Spectrum Disorders

Early detection and treatment of autism spectrum disorders (ASD) has the potential to improve outcomes for children who receive this diagnosis (Dawson et al., 2007). Pierce et al. (2011) set out to determine the feasibility of a universal prevention program designed to screen all children for ASD, language delay, and developmental delay at their 1-year checkup. Using an established network of pediatricians in San Diego County, Pierce et al. had the children screened with the Communication and Symbolic Behavior Scales Developmental Profile Infant–Toddler Checklist (Wetherby, Brosnan-Maddox, Peace, & Newton, 2008), which was completed by parents, scored by medical personnel, and reviewed by the pediatrician. All 1-year-olds who did not pass the screening were referred for further evaluation and testing. Those who received further testing were followed every 6 months until they reached 36 months of age.

Over the course of the study, 10,479 children were screened. Of those screened, 1,318 children failed the test, and 346 were referred for additional developmental testing. Of those referred, 208 enrolled for further testing and 184 children had at least two visits for developmental evaluation. These 184 children were the focus of the study, along with 41 randomly selected children from a control group. At the time of the publication, all children had been followed at least until 24 months of age. Results showed that 37 infants with ASD were identified, and five children initially identified with ASD no longer met criteria at follow-up, for a total of 32 children receiving a final diagnosis of ASD. Regarding other developmental diagnoses, 56 were identified with a learning disability, nine were developmentally delayed, and 36 were categorized as having some "other" diagnosis. Forty-six children were considered "false positives" and did not reveal any developmental abnormality upon further evaluation (Pierce et al., 2011).

The study demonstrated that a screening program for ASD increases early detection and diagnosis of ASD and other developmental disorders. Because only 22% of pediatricians were screening for these disorders at 1 year before initiation of this program, this reflects an improvement in the screening of ASD at an early age, particularly as ASD screenings typically start at 18 months (Pierce et al., 2011). One question about the screening program is the discrepancy between the number of children who failed the screening test ($n = 1,318$) compared with the number of children who were referred for additional testing ($n = 346$), and the number who were tracked for at least two visits ($n = 184$). The authors suggested that pediatricians may have lacked follow-through, referred some children to different organizations, or felt that the child did not need additional evaluation. Further evaluation is needed to better understand why pediatricians referred only a fraction of children who failed the screening and whether this is noncompliance or based on clinical judgment. However, overall this universal prevention program shows much promise for identifying children with ASD at an early age. In addition, Pierce et al. (2011) reported that 92% of the participating pediatricians completed a satisfaction survey on the screening program and 96% indicated that the program improved their practice. This information from pediatricians is an important outcome of the program.

Remission in Geriatric Patients Who Are Depressed

Depression is a major health problem for many older patients, and patients who are depressed are more at risk for suicide. Therefore, remission in older patients who are depressed is an important goal in their treatment (Alexopoulos et al., 2005). Alexopoulos et al. (2005) set out to investigate whether a case management model of care for primary care patients who are depressed is preferable to usual care in terms of time to first remission.

The case management model of care data analyzed in this study is part of a larger data set collected through the Prevention of Suicide in Primary Care Elderly: Collaborative Trial (PROSPECT; Bruce et al., 2004). In the earlier trial, Bruce et al. (2004) reported that older adults who are depressed and who received a case management approach to care had fewer depressive symptoms and greater remission rates over a 12-month period, compared with older patients receiving usual care. Case managers in this model monitored psychopathology and side effects of medications, provided recommendations to primary care physicians, and helped patients adhere to treatment recommendations. They also provided follow-up care as necessary, but the physician was responsible for patients' care.

Alexopoulos et al. (2005) focused on time to first remission of depression and depression severity. The study hypothesized that patients receiving PROSPECT case management care, compared with patients receiving care as usual, would achieve first remission rates more rapidly, whereas patients with more complex clinical problems (e.g., disabilities) would be less likely to achieve remission as rapidly. The researchers also hoped to identify risk factors related to nonremission for patients for whom case management was more effective than usual care.

The final analyses of the data were conducted with 215 older adults who had met criteria for major depression and had been evaluated at 4-month follow-up. The major finding of this study was that the case management care intervention of older patients who are depressed facilitated remission of depression and remission occurred earlier, compared with patients receiving usual care. However, other results were more nuanced between the two groups. For example, during the early stages of the study, patients with higher levels of hopelessness in the case management group had better rates of remission, compared with usual care patients, but these differences were not maintained during the entire 18 months of the study; older adults who were depressed and had several comorbid disorders did not realize improved remission rates regardless of type of care. Nevertheless, the PROSPECT case management approach to primary care offers several benefits as a treatment approach for older patients who are depressed, and this type of care may be more cost-effective and more readily available to patients who are depressed. Increasing remission rates of depression in older adults, and preventing relapse of depression, are important goals in the treatment and prevention of depression of older adults in primary health care settings.

Public Health Campaigns

Cugelman, Thelwall, and Dawes (2011) conducted a meta-analysis to assess online public health campaigns to encourage positive health behavior change. This type of universal study at the macrolevel of interventions is important to measure the impact of universal prevention interventions. Online universal prevention interventions offer advantages of using rapidly increasing, sophisticated, and portable technology, as well as being cost-effective. The study is unique because although Internet campaigns have encouraged people to alter lifestyle behaviors, such as increasing physical exercise and stopping smoking, there are few guidelines to develop such interventions, and those that are developed often lack impact data. The study also attempted to increase understanding of the relationships between the interventions, study adherence, and behavioral outcomes.

Although a systematic search yielded 1,271 abstracts and articles as possible studies to be included in their meta-analysis, only 31 met inclusion criteria (Cugelman et al., 2011). In total, 29 articles describing 30 interventions that were included in the primary meta-analysis, and two additional studies, qualified for the adherence analysis. Using a random effects model, the first analysis estimated the overall effect size, including groupings by control conditions and time factors. The second analysis assessed the impact of psychological design features that were coded with taxonomies from evidence-based behavioral medicine, persuasive technology, and other behavioral influence fields. These separate systems were integrated into a framework called the communication-based influence components model. Finally, the third analysis assessed the relationships between intervention adherence and behavioral outcomes.

The overall impact of online interventions across all studies was statistically significant. The largest impact with a moderate level of efficacy was achieved from online interventions when compared with wait-lists and placebos. The next largest impact was comparison with less sophisticated online interventions. No significant differences were found when advanced online interventions were compared with sophisticated print interventions, although online interventions are more cost-effective and have the potential to reach more people. Time was a critical factor, as shorter interventions generally achieved larger impacts and greater adherence. Most interventions drew from the transtheoretical model of behavior change (Prochaska et al., 2009). Interventions were goal oriented, used numerous influence components showing the consequences of behavior, assisted users to reach goals, and provided normative pressure. Results found correlations between the number of influence components and intervention efficacy and between intervention adherence and behavioral outcomes.

These findings demonstrate that online interventions have the capacity to influence voluntary behaviors, such as those routinely targeted through public health campaigns. Given the access and low cost of online technologies, it behooves behavioral scientists to work with other professionals to increase public health campaigns that blend personalized social network technological systems with mass-media approaches. Such a combination of approaches may help individuals achieve personal goals to improve the quality of their lives, and thus contribute to an overall healthier society with reduced medical costs.

Youth and Health-Based Prevention

In another unique application of a health-setting-based prevention intervention, Taveras et al. (2007) surveyed 324 youth, ages 10 to 18 (mean age, 13.7), who had had a physical exam during the past year. Seventy-six percent of the youth were either Black or Hispanic. The survey asked the participants about topics that health care professionals discussed with them during their last physical examination. Youth reported that they infrequently received prevention counseling related to topics that contribute to being overweight, such as diet and amount of television viewing. Also, the researchers found that youth whose mothers' had lower levels of education were less likely to receive prevention counseling related to being overweight. They also found that younger respondents reported greater motivation to change TV viewing habits if recommended by a health professional. This study suggests the importance of discussing lifestyle behaviors with youth and parents during routine physical exams conducted by health professionals.

SUMMARY

This chapter provided examples of prevention programs and activities delivered in community and medical settings. Like those summarized in the previous chapter, the prevention interventions just described have diverse applications in community and medical settings. The numbers of prevention programs in these settings are growing, but these numbers lag behind those of prevention programs undertaken in educational settings, which have a longer history of offering them. Nevertheless, communities are developing and implementing prevention interventions across the life cycle. A useful resource for communities desiring to develop prevention interventions is

Focus on Prevention by the Substance Abuse and Mental Health Services Administration (2010). This action-oriented publication provides guidelines, processes, and resources for communities interesting in developing or strengthening their community prevention activities.

In medical settings, the opportunities for psychologists and other mental health professionals are varied and will likely increase in the future, especially given their expertise in promoting positive behavioral change to enhance health and well-being. The range of the interventions and research discussed in this chapter demonstrates some of the opportunities. Most of the psychologically based interventions have been implemented with individuals who were already diagnosed with medical conditions. However, prevention interventions have been developed as complementary to standard medical procedures to help manage the impact of disease symptoms and psychological stress. Selective and indicated prevention activities are more common than universal prevention interventions in medical settings. Psychologists and mental health professionals are exceptionally suited to engage in prevention work in medical settings.

Lifestyle behaviors are a major contributor to the onset of the major physical health problems in industrialized nations. Primary health care services are often the first place that people seek professional advice and treatment about a potential problem or the beginning of a problem. Primary health care is also where patients receive periodic physical exams and health screenings. During these visits, medical professionals can identify potential future health problems due to patients' smoking, using drugs, engaging in unsafe sex, being overweight, and so on. Screening for these behaviors is a first step to help patients identify their risk. Psychologists and other mental health professionals can assist in the design of intake surveys, the collection of patient information, and how the information might be used in conversations about risk and protective factors.

Psychologists and other mental health professionals are skilled in helping people make behavioral changes. However, appropriate opportunities must exist for psychological practitioners to intervene with patients in medical settings. Prevention work with patients can be accomplished through group interventions. Psychologists and mental health professionals leading these groups with another health care professional may increase the efficacy of the groups. A group intervention is cost-effective and may be more attractive to patients, compared with individual sessions.

As reported in this chapter, depression is a common comorbid condition of cancer and other life-threatening illnesses. Serious illness can also disrupt patient relationships and family dynamics. Medical personnel, understanding the potential for comorbid psychological conditions after diagnosis, can screen patients for depression, anxiety, and other mental health problems and can recommend referrals for mental health counseling as needed.

Other areas in which mental health professionals can make an impact with prevention applications in medical settings include in-service training with medical staff about the emotional and familial issues that often accompany medical diagnoses. Mental health professionals can also assist medical staff with personal issues related to topics such as work stress, burnout, and developing and maintaining strategies for self-care. These areas are especially important in medical settings that treat patients with serious health problems. Finally, psychologists and other mental health professionals can assist in developing media publications and electronic messages that encourage patients to attend to prevention behaviors, for example, flu shots, proper nutrition, infant vaccinations, and so on. These materials and messages must be culturally sensitive and attend to cultural and ethnic differences in the community. Therefore, adapting materials and messages to specific community population groups will likely enhance the impact of materials and strengthen communication.

Psychologists and other mental health professionals are likely to play larger roles in improving the overall health of the population in the future. This chapter presented a diversity of opportunities in community and health care settings. However, challenges related to funding and insurance reimbursements for preventive activities in primary medical settings will need to be addressed and mitigated to fully realize the important contributions that psychology can make to enhance health and well-being through preventive interventions.

8

RECOMMENDATIONS FOR DEVELOPING, IMPLEMENTING, AND EVALUATING PREVENTION INTERVENTIONS

The American Psychological Association (APA, 2014) "Guidelines for Prevention in Psychology" (see Appendix A) present aspirational goals for the development and implementation of prevention interventions. Among the "Prevention Guidelines" are those that recommend that psychologists develop and implement prevention interventions that are theory- and evidence-based, are culturally relevant, attend to ethical issues in the design and implementation of prevention, address prevention of problem behaviors, and promote health-enhancing behaviors. In addition to addressing prevention at the individual and personal levels, the "Prevention Guidelines" recommend that prevention psychologists apply prevention knowledge and skills to broader social conditions and use data and knowledge to inform public policy decisions.

Although the APA (2014) "Prevention Guidelines" provide a broad foundation on which to develop and implement prevention interventions, this chapter offers specific recommendations for development, implementation,

DOI: 10.1037/14442-008
Prevention Psychology: Enhancing Personal and Social Well-Being, by J. L. Romano
Copyright © 2015 by the American Psychological Association. All rights reserved.

and evaluation at different stages. The development and implementation of prevention interventions can be challenging (Embry, 2004; Julian, Ross, & Partridge, 2008), but the challenges can be mitigated and the interventions strengthened by attending to activities and processes at different stages of prevention initiatives. Both the "Prevention Guidelines" and the more specific recommendations in this chapter apply, regardless of the setting or population of a prevention initiative.

Therefore, this chapter recommends activities to be conducted by prevention specialists at early, intermediate, and later stages of a prevention intervention. In addition, the chapter attends to three topics important to prevention program implementation and evaluation: assessment of prevention program fidelity across 16 community-based programs, lessons learned from the transfer of a university-based prevention program to the community, and considerations of prevention activities in medical settings. These topics are instructional for prevention specialists, as they highlight dimensions of program implementation fidelity, challenges associated with the transfer of a university-based program to a community agency, and prevention activities for psychologists and other mental health professionals in medical settings, settings that have much potential for the practice of prevention psychology.

EARLY STAGE

Form an Advisory Group

The first step in developing a prevention intervention is to assemble a group of major stakeholders, as an advisory group, from the institution or community that will ultimately implement the intervention. Ideally, this group is represented by different constituents and represents the demographic characteristics of the institution or community. In a community setting, major stakeholders might include community institutions and services from law enforcement, education, medical and social service agencies, government and policymaking bodies, faith communities, and the business community. The advisory group should also be representative of the diversity within the community that is relevant to the prevention intervention (e.g., age, socio-economic status, race/ethnicity, and sexual orientation). An advisory group will serve its purpose well if it is inclusive and represents differing opinions and perspectives. Once formed, the group may choose to develop a more formal needs assessment to better meet the prevention need. The advisory group can serve as a standing committee to provide guidance and be regularly consulted about program development, implementation, and evaluation.

Assess Community Needs

What problems most need to be prevented, or what behaviors most need to be promoted? A comprehensive needs assessment should measure individual and community or institutional needs that are risks in light of the identified problem or problems as well as behaviors that serve as protections against the problem. Too often the emphasis in prevention revolves around preventing problems, but protections that help to mitigate problems are equally important. The Search Institute's list of developmental assets and deficits are examples of community characteristics that may either contribute to problems in a community or offer protections to a community (Benson, 2006). Examples of community protections against problem behaviors for children and adolescents might include (a) increased levels of communitywide enforcements to reduce the sale of alcohol to minors; (b) extension of recreational building hours in community centers and other structures, especially during the summer, to engage youth in structured or unstructured play and sports activities; (c) increased physical exercise opportunities and health nutrition classes for adults and seniors living in the community; and (d) parenting classes for expectant and new parents. For example, in a school setting, a building-wide message might promote respectful behaviors by students and staff. Similarly, in medical settings, materials that promote prevention of illness should be readily available, and in languages that are representative of the community.

Consult With Experts and Access Relevant Resources

During the prevention intervention development phase, stakeholders may wish to consult with prevention experts at universities and colleges, school districts, and government agencies. Given the increased attention to prevention during the recent decades, it is likely that others have developed and are further along with a similar prevention application. In addition, it is recommended that prevention specialists be aware of relevant resources to assist them in designing a prevention intervention. Appendix B lists resources that can be readily accessed to inform the prevention specialist. Many of these resources were generated by U.S. government agencies to strengthen prevention initiatives. For example, the National Registry of Evidence-Based Prevention Programs, cited several times throughout this book, is an excellent resource for prevention interventions that may meet school and community needs. In addition, *Focus on Prevention* (Substance Abuse and Mental Health Services Administration, 2010) is an excellent resource and practical guide for developing and implementing alcohol, tobacco, and illicit drug use prevention programs, although the recommendations therein also apply to other problem behaviors. *Focus on Prevention*, published by the U.S. Department of Health and Human Services, offers comprehensive guidance and a strategic prevention framework (see Figure 8.1), with an overarching theme of sustainability and cultural competence across areas such as capacity, assessment, and evaluation for communities and institutions in the development of prevention initiatives. Therefore, it is recommended that prevention specialists become familiar with materials, resources, and other's experiences in preventing similar problems or promoting similar behaviors. Organizations, such as government agencies and universities, may welcome the opportunity to collaborate with a community or school to develop and implement a prevention program. Such a partnership offers value because it brings different types and levels

Figure 8.1. Strategic prevention framework. From *Focus on Prevention* (p. 14), by Substance Abuse and Mental Health Services Administration, 2010, Rockville, MD: Author. In the public domain.

of expertise to the problem, and the collaboration may enhance funding opportunities to support and sustain a prevention initiative.

Consider Theoretical Frameworks for Prevention

As recommended in Chapter 2 of this volume, it is important that prevention interventions be anchored in one or more theoretical frameworks that support the activities being implemented. A theoretical foundation supporting the intervention will assist in the interpretation of process, outcome, and impact data collected about the intervention. The theoretical framework will also assist developers in making needed adjustments to an intervention based on data collected, and therefore, help to sustain modifications to the original intervention.

Choose Prevention Activities

Prevention specialists should develop a plan to sustain the intervention over a multiyear period, taking into account the needs and resources of the community or institution. Prevention interventions are more likely to be sustained after the initial enthusiasm lessens if plans are in place to institutionalize and sustain the interventions within a community or institution for as long as the need exists. Appendix B lists resources that identify possible prevention activities, depending on the nature of the prevention intervention.

Select Evaluation Criteria

The prevention specialist should determine the types of assessments and data collection strategies that will be needed and used. Once the specialist has identified evaluation assessments, they should be explained to the advisory group. The measures should assess, as much as possible, process information about the intervention (e.g., number of participants, attendance, program fidelity), outcome data (e.g., change in participant attitudes and behaviors), and impact data (e.g., systemic changes that have been demonstrated within an institution: e.g., school, workplace, or community). For example, schools may report a positive change in the incidents of bullying, and communities may demonstrate a reduction in juvenile crime. *Focus on Prevention* (Substance Abuse and Mental Health Services Administration, 2010) gives guidance on evaluation strategies, including using both qualitative and quantitative assessments, attending to the cost-effectiveness of an evaluation plan, and keeping the prevention advisory group of stakeholders apprised about evaluation decisions and evaluation data.

INTERMEDIATE STAGE

Plan Implementation and Evaluation

Once a set of prevention goals, objectives, activities, and evaluation measures has been selected, the prevention specialist (in consultation with the advisory group) develops plans to recruit participants, select implementation strategies, and delineate an evaluation plan. In this stage of the process, it is also important to identify major organizations and/or individuals that will have primary responsibility for implementation. The prevention initiative is now ready for implementation.

Data Collection

Depending on the evaluation plan, individual, community, and institutional data may be collected before the start of prevention intervention and at various points during and after implementation. Quantitative and qualitative process and outcome data will provide important information to stakeholders as they review and evaluate the initiative. Eventually, the community or institution will assess the impact of the intervention, but it may take some time to fully measure the impact on a community or institution such as a school or workplace.

Data should answer questions such as the following: (a) What is working well? (b) What implementation problems are encountered? (c) What changes, if any, should be made? (d) How is program fidelity maintained? and (e) What are the strengths and challenges of program leadership and organization? Collecting evaluation data throughout the prevention intervention will help stakeholders make future decisions about the prevention initiative, especially planning for a sustained prevention intervention over the long term. Evaluation data, even preliminary data, should regularly be shared with stakeholders, and necessary adjustments made to the prevention initiative.

LATER STAGE

Make Adjustments as Needed

Once a sufficient amount of data about the prevention intervention has been collected, stakeholders and the advisory group can begin planning for needed changes to enhance the intervention, if it is to be sustained. During this stage, the advisory group and other stakeholders make decisions about the continuation of the intervention and suggest ways that it can be strengthened. Suggestions might be made in terms of intervention activities, whether intervention fidelity was upheld, leadership for the intervention, intervention personnel, data that are important to collect that were not initially collected, and future funding for the initiative. It is highly likely that the topics of prevention that are currently important to communities and institutions will also be important in the future. Therefore, if at all possible, prevention initiatives should be planned for multiple implementations over longer periods, rather than a one-time, short-term intervention.

FIDELITY OF PREVENTION INTERVENTIONS

Prevention program fidelity is important to consider during implementation. Fagan et al. (2008) studied program implementation fidelity of 16 different prevention programs in 12 communities. The authors examined implementation fidelity of communities that participated in the Community Youth Development Study and Communities That Care (CTC) initiative. Fagan et al. reported that few studies assessed all four dimensions of implementation fidelity: (a) adherence, (b) dosage, (c) quality of delivery, and (d) participant responsiveness. Adherence and dosage (i.e., the extent to which prevention activities are delivered as recommended) are most often measured. However, the quality of delivery of prevention activities and response of participants to an intervention are less often measured. Fagan et al. stressed the importance of assessing all four dimensions of fidelity to adequately measure the effectiveness of a prevention intervention.

In the Fagan et al. (2008) study, implementation data were collected over a 2-year period from communities that participated in CTC (Hawkins & Catalano, 1992). CTC is a community-owned and community-operated system to prevent problems such as substance abuse, delinquency, and violence. The 12 CTC communities implemented different types of prevention interventions, including after-school tutoring and mentoring programs, parent training programs, and school-based drug prevention curricula, as well as addressing schoolwide systemic changes.

The CTC system includes several components: assessing community readiness to participate in a prevention intervention, developing a community coalition, assessing prevention needs, selecting evidence-based prevention policies and practices, implementing the prevention initiative, and monitoring fidelity and impact. The CTC fidelity monitoring system is designed to be easily understood and used by members of the community.

The four dimensions of fidelity implementation across the communities were measured. Adherence and dosage rates were very high across the 2 years of program implementation. However, dosage rates of the school-based components were lower than the parent training and after-school prevention activities. The quality of delivery and participant responsiveness were also high across the implementation period, with average scores over 4.0 on a 5-point scale across each fidelity dimension. As might be expected, program attendance was higher for the in-school activities than for the after-school activities and parent training sessions.

Fagan et al. (2008) reported that despite high levels of implementation fidelity, several challenges were faced during implementation of the prevention activities. The biggest challenges were lack of time to deliver required material and lack of participant responsiveness. However, these challenges declined during the second year of the study, suggesting that staff became more skilled as they implemented the activities. Despite the high levels of program fidelity, four programs were not maintained into the third year. Three of these programs were either after-school or parent training, and they were discontinued because of difficulties recruiting participants. The fourth program was a schoolwide one in which schools were to conduct a needs assessment and develop interventions and action plans to address schoolwide problems.

Although previous research cited by Fagan et al. (2008) showed mixed reviews of fidelity implementation when implementing prevention activities in communities, this was not the case in their fidelity study. Fagan et al. found that all four dimensions of fidelity were high across prevention activities that were replicated in the selected communities. Further, the measures of fidelity increased and challenges decreased over the 2 years of the study. Thus, on the basis of the results of this study, communities can successfully replicate prevention activities with high implementation fidelity. Although communities will face challenges when doing so, Fagan et al.'s findings bode well for communities that wish to replicate high-cost demonstration projects and maintain high levels of implementation fidelity.

TRANSFERRING UNIVERSITY RESEARCH TO A COMMUNITY AGENCY

Prevention programs are sometimes initiated at a university with external funding, with the goal of transferring the program to a community setting, where it will be sustained. The example below describes such a transfer, which can be instructive for others desiring to transfer a university-based research prevention intervention to an applied setting in the community.

Baptiste et al. (2007) described a process of transferring a university research-based HIV/AIDS prevention program to a community agency. The

Collaborative HIV/AIDS Adolescent Mental Health Project (CHAMP) is a university-led (University of Illinois at Chicago) research project that focuses on factors related to HIV/AIDS risks of youth living in high-prevalence urban areas, with the goal of developing and implementing prevention interventions to protect youth against HIV. Eventual community implementation of HIV/AIDS prevention interventions was a key element of CHAMP, but it was also understood that transferring research and scientific knowledge from university settings to community intervention settings does not necessarily happen naturally or with ease. Therefore, the transfer of CHAMP to a community agency (Habilitative Systems Incorporated; HSI) is instructive. HSI is a Chicago-based human development agency offering an array of services across the city; goals of their client services include alleviating suffering and promoting independence and responsible behavior.

Baptiste et al. (2007) acknowledged an extensive literature on the transfer of university-based research to community settings, and they briefly summarized principles that guided their work in transferring CHAMP to HSI. These principles include (a) good fit between the academic project and community agency, (b) early and extended planning with the community agency, (c) continued monitoring and evaluation of the transferred community intervention, and (d) balance maintained between program fidelity and adaptations necessary to implement the program in the community.

Transfer of CHAMP to HSI was a long-term process, 6 years, with more concrete and specific discussions about the transfer occurring in the third year (Baptiste et al., 2007). The transfer process was labor intensive and involved major and minor conflicts among staff. Baptiste et al. (2007) identified several specific challenges: (a) balancing a collaborative process with outcome goals (community members, at times, feeling less powerful than university personnel); (b) difficulties transferring the scientific basis of CHAMP to HSI (e.g., evaluation designs, program fidelity, dissemination of outcomes and results); (c) training and mentoring community leaders at the university away from HSI, creating challenges related to different organizational cultures and employee expectations and aspirations; and (d) transfer of CHAMP created multiple logistical issues, such as maintaining continuity with staff turnovers and changing priorities of HSI and CHAMP.

Baptiste et al. (2007) offered several recommendations as a result of the long and labor-intensive process of transferring CHAMP from a university-led research program to a community agency for implementation. First, it would have been preferable to involve HSI from the very beginning of the CHAMP project, rather than several years after CHAMP was started. Second, in retrospect, it would have been helpful to be more deliberative in monitoring and collecting data about the transfer process itself, instead of relying on retrospective data and documents. Third, maintaining long-term sustainability of the program at HSI will require additional funding, and these discussions are best started several years before implementing the transfer. Fourth, the role of academic researchers after the community transfer should be discussed during early transfer meetings (rather than later in the transfer process). Fifth, despite the relative success of the transfer, questions remain as to whether a community collaborative, as presented by Baptiste et al., is the best way to deliver HIV/AIDS prevention.

Baptiste et al. (2007) presented a valuable description of the process in transferring a university-led prevention research program to a community agency. Although the focus was HIV/AIDS prevention, the transfer process offers valuable lessons for transfers of other prevention programs from university demonstration projects to implementation in communities.

CONSIDERATIONS FOR MEDICAL SETTING INTERVENTIONS

As shown in the previous chapter, medical settings offer numerous prevention intervention opportunities for mental health professionals, and the opportunities are likely to grow in the future. Lifestyle behaviors, including cigarette smoking, poor diet, and lack of physical exercise, place people at risk for heart disease, cancer, diabetes, and other chronic illnesses, some of which are leading causes of illness and death in the United States and other industrialized countries. Mass media messages that encourage people to stop smoking, eat healthfully, and exercise increase awareness but usually do not educate about how to make necessary behavioral changes. Most people experience difficulty changing long-standing behaviors and habits. Psychologists and mental health professionals are specialists in helping others make behavioral changes, and thus their expertise is very relevant to helping others make recommended lifestyle changes.

Physical exams and health screenings offer opportunities for medical professionals to identify health risks and begin preventive interventions in collaboration with a psychologist or other mental health professional. In addition, primary health care services are often the first place where people seek out professional advice about a potential problem or the beginning of a problem.

Another role for psychologists and other mental health professionals in health care is to assist, in partnership with medical personnel, in the design of intake questionnaires to collect patient information. The information can then be used in conversations with patients about behaviors that place them at risk for problems or can serve as protections against problems. Electronically delivered and scored health and wellness questionnaires, sometimes used by organizations to assist employees in assessing their risk and protective behaviors, can also be used in such conversations. Health and wellness surveys increase awareness and identify areas to change. However, people often need assistance in developing motivation to initiate positive changes and then maintain them over time.

Direct patient referral to mental health practitioners in a medical facility or health care system is ideal, but mental health resources may not be available. Therefore, referrals to mental health professionals outside of the system will need to be made. In this case, having readily available the names of mental health professionals in the community is important. In addition to name, license, educational degrees, and contact information, the referral list should include specific areas of specialization and cultural and non-English language competencies.

Prevention interventions are often provided through group work, such as through universal prevention psychoeducation workshops and selective and indicated support groups on various topics or medical conditions. In medical settings, group leadership that pairs a mental health professional with a health care provider with expertise in the medical condition of concern to the group members will enhance the group, as the group leaders bring specific medical expertise germane to the group. Regardless of the setting, group interventions for prevention are cost-effective and offer advantages in peer support that are lacking with prevention interventions delivered individually.

The social and psychological impact of a medical diagnosis can be debilitating for patients and their loved ones, causing distress, anxiety, and depression. Therefore, selective and indicated prevention interventions are especially important in medical settings to address the psychosocial impact of a serious medical diagnosis. Medical personnel, understanding the potential for comorbid psychological conditions after a serious diagnosis, can screen patients for depression, anxiety, and other mental health and relational problems, and recommend referral for counseling or another psychological intervention as appropriate.

SUMMARY

This chapter highlighted several recommendations and strategies for designing and implementing prevention interventions, including referencing resources that are readily available to assist the prevention specialist. The chapter recommended several strategies in the development and implementation of a prevention intervention, from the early to the later stages of an intervention. In addition, the importance of attending to issues of fidelity in prevention programs was highlighted, with a summary of community-based prevention programs and their attention to program fidelity at different stages of the programs and in different community settings. Also, an example of challenges faced when transferring a university-based research prevention program to a community agency illustrated some of the issues that will need attention when prevention specialists contemplate such a transfer. Finally, suggestions and prevention opportunities for psychologists and other mental health professionals intervening within medical settings were highlighted, because medical settings are projected as emerging settings for psychological practice.

9

PREVENTION ETHICS, EDUCATION, AND FUNDING

This chapter addresses several issues that are important to prevention psychologists and others who work within the prevention specialty. First, I present ethical issues, then I discuss education and training of prevention specialists. Education and training focuses on both preservice and in-service education for those who desire to strengthen their prevention skills. In the final section of the chapter, I address the cost-effectiveness of prevention from institutional and societal perspectives, and I discuss strategies to secure funding for prevention interventions and research.

PREVENTION ETHICS

Ethical considerations in prevention practice and research is not a completely new topic, although until recently there has been a dearth of scholarship that specifically focuses on the ethics of prevention work. In one of

DOI: 10.1037/14442-009
Prevention Psychology: Enhancing Personal and Social Well-Being, by J. L. Romano
Copyright © 2015 by the American Psychological Association. All rights reserved.

the earliest articles on applying ethical standards to primary prevention, Pope (1990) wrote that there is no code of ethics and no enforcement mechanisms to guide prevention specialists. More than 20 years ago, others also raised the issue of the lack of prevention ethics in the training of prevention specialists and in school-based prevention applications (Bond & Albee, 1990; Gensheimer, Ayers, & Roosa, 1993; Trickett, 1992). Although some recent literature, as reviewed in this chapter, has been published about prevention ethics, there is not as yet an officially approved code of ethics for the practice of prevention. However, *The Belmont Report* (National Commission for the Protection of Human Subjects of Biomedical and Behavioral Research, 1979) provides a foundation and context for protecting all research subjects and participants.

In 1979, *The Belmont Report* was issued by the U.S. government (specifically, by the National Commission for the Protection of Human Subjects of Biomedical and Behavioral Research) to address the protection of research subjects who participate in clinical trials (Sims, 2010). The three ethical principles described in *The Belmont Report* are (a) beneficence, (b) justice, and (c) respect, and these principles guide institutional review boards when reviewing research proposals (Shore, 2006). In addition, *The Belmont Report* attends to the application of the principles by addressing issues such as informed consent, voluntariness, and information about risks and benefits of participating in research. The American Psychological Association's (2010) "Ethical Principles of Psychologists and Code of Conduct" is more comprehensive than *The Belmont Report*, as might be expected given that codes of conduct for mental health professionals address more than the ethics of conducting research (e.g., providing counseling and therapy, clinical supervision, teaching of psychology).

Although ethical standards have a lengthy history in the medical and human services professions, and despite published works on prevention ethics more than 20 years ago, important ethical issues as applied to prevention have been dormant until recently. Professional organizations' codes of conduct, such as those published by APA and the American Counseling Association, have applicability to prevention work, but the guidelines do not discuss situations that may occur when conducting prevention research and interventions (Schwartz, Hage, & González, 2013). Fortunately, interest in ethical issues in prevention research and practice is rising (Caskey & Rosenthal, 2005; Mishara & Weisstub, 2005; Schwartz & Hage, 2009; Waldo, Kaczmarek, & Romano, 2004).

Schwartz et al. (2013) recommended a code of ethics for prevention that includes principles related to the planning of interventions, intervention activities, and evaluation of interventions. These sections address components such as using appropriate research methods to evaluate prevention interventions, attending to issues of social justice and inclusivity in prevention work, and adhering to ethical principles of current professional codes of conduct. These principles include beneficence, providing informed consent, and maintaining confidentiality.

Caskey and Rosenthal (2005) addressed the ethical issues involved in research with adolescents on sensitive topics, such as sexual behavior and alcohol and drug use. They stressed the importance of attending to ethical dilemmas that may arise from adolescents' insufficient knowledge about risks to them and their families when giving informed consent, especially when the research involves behavior that is illegal (e.g., alcohol and drug use). Caskey and Rosenthal cautioned that researchers should give special attention to an adolescent's stage of development when designing research protocols to help ensure that adolescents and their parents or guardians are aware of the risks and benefits of participating in research. Informed consent statements should also emphasize that participation is voluntary and refusal to participate will not result in negative consequences.

Lothen-Kline, Howard, Hamburger, Worrell, and Boekeloo (2003) faced the ethical issue of confidentiality when conducting longitudinal prevention research on alcohol use and mental health issues with adolescents. As part of the study, adolescents completed a mood survey that asked them about suicidal ideations during the past 2 weeks. In an initial consent form approved for the study, the researchers stated that confidentiality would be maintained unconditionally, but because of concerns about insufficient protections for adolescents who answered affirmatively to the suicide question, the study was suspended until a revised confidentiality consent statement could be developed and incorporated. Hence, the conditional confidentiality statement used during the second wave of the study informed participants that if abuse or suicidal ideation were indicated on the survey, the researchers would share the information with parents and authorities. The researchers reported that only 1% answered affirmatively to the suicidal ideation question when presented with the conditional confidentiality statement, whereas 9% had answered affirmatively with the unconditional statement. However, overall participation rates were not affected by the different consent forms. This study points out one of the ethical dilemma associated with confidentiality statements when conducting research with adolescents about very sensitive topics: It is important to elicit truthful answers, but it is also important to protect or assist participants if their answers reveal that they are at risk to themselves or others. Lothen-Kline et al. called for more specific ethical guidelines for conducting prevention research with adolescents.

Others have also raised concerns about ethical ambiguities in prevention work in areas as diverse as violence prevention in schools (Hermann & Finn, 2002), research on suicide prevention (Mishara & Weisstub, 2005), and marriage and family counseling (Murray, 2005). Hermann and Finn (2002) raised questions such as when and how to implement duty-to-warn proce-dures if others are in danger of being the recipient of violence, how best to identify students who pose risks to themselves and others, and how best to proceed with violence prevention interventions. Mishara and Weisstub (2005) differentiated between legal and ethical issues in research on sui-cide prevention, especially with respect to vulnerabilities of participants, obtaining informed consent, balancing confidentiality with the need to disclose to others, and the prevention specialist's obligations to intervene. Murray (2005) addressed prevention and ethical issues in marriage and family counseling, including professional competencies needed to engage in prevention work and whether providing clinical and preventive services to counseling clientele causes an unethical dual relationship between ther-apist and client. These ethical issues are relevant to other mental health professions as well.

Ethical principles of prevention research and applications within ethnic communities have also been studied (Jurkovic et al., 2004; Quigley, 2006). Quigley (2006) reviewed abuses that have occurred in public health research with Native American communities and how these can be over-come with community-based participatory research (CBPR). Quigley emphasized that CBPR strengthens research and addresses ethical consid-erations by developing strong community partnerships and community capacity-building and by providing mechanisms that promote community control and empowerment. Thus, CBPR encourages communities to be fully engaged throughout the research process and invested in making research decisions. CBPR helps to build a community's capacity for change and increases the likelihood that the prevention project will be sustained after the initial intervention.

Jurkovic et al. (2004) presented an ecological and ethical perspective in primary prevention with immigrant Latino youth. Their conceptual frame-work encourages prevention specialists to consider contextual issues and filial responsibilities when conducting prevention activities with this population. Latino youth may have family and caregiving responsibilities, as well as envi-ronmental stressors related to discrimination and poverty that interfere with societal and community expectations. Therefore, Jurkovic et al. recommended that prevention specialists attend to cultural and environmental variables that may impact a given population and adjust their research questions and methods accordingly. In this example, qualitative and mixed methods research may be more informative during the development and implementa-tion of a prevention project to strengthen eventual measures of outcomes and impact. Further, elicitation research, as discussed in Chapter 3 of this volume (see the passages on the theory of reasoned action and the theory of planned behavior), may be especially useful with populations to better understand community norms and attitudes that relate to a topic selected for a prevention intervention.

Although parents and guardians must give consent for minors to participate in research, prevention specialists must be ethical in soliciting such consent. In schools, the frequent sites of prevention research and interventions, researchers must receive approval from several sources: school authorities, parents or guardians, the research participants, and the researcher's institution and institutional review board. Some schools and school systems distinguish between active and passive consent. In *active* consent, parents or guardians give signed approval to allow their child to participate. In *passive* consent, after learning about the research project, parents or guardians have the opportunity to raise objections about their child's participation; if no objections are made, the minor can participate. However, for parents or guardians to make an informed decision, they must understand the project and the risks and benefits of their child's participation. The same is true for participants in the research intervention.

Prevention projects can present unique ethical dilemmas, whether interventions are universal, selective, or indicated, or are strategies meant to bring about institutional or societal change. A universal prevention research intervention in a school, or in selected grades in a school, must also follow ethical guidelines. As such, the prevention specialist must allow sufficient planning time for the project to be fully discussed with stakeholders and with parents and guardians. Important information to share and discuss includes the need for and purpose of the intervention; details about the intervention and how students will be involved; risks and benefits to students participating in the project; and how evaluative data about the intervention will be selected, collected, and disseminated. This information will help stakeholders, parents and guardians, and students (as age appropriate) make an informed choice about participation. If parents object to their child participating, then the research and prevention specialist, along with school personnel, will identify ways for those students to participate in alternative school activities, without disadvantages to the student.

As yet, there is no formal set of guidelines or ethical code that guides prevention research and practice, although best practice guidelines and institutional policies exist within specific areas of prevention (Francis, 2003; MacQueen, Karim, & Sugarman, 2003; Taleff & Neal, 2000). Others have supported the need to develop a more comprehensive code of ethics for the prevention specialty (Schwartz et al., 2013). In recent years, prevention researchers and practitioners have produced scholarly works that address the ethical dilemmas they contend with. It is now time for one or more prevention professional organizations to take on the task of developing a set of ethical guidelines and code of conduct for the specialty.

EDUCATION AND TRAINING

For more than half a century, applied psychology has been dominated by a crisis intervention approach to the training of future psychologists, whereas other mental health professions, such as counseling and social work, have enjoyed a more balanced history of infusing components of crisis counseling, social advocacy, and prevention into their curricula (Conyne, 1997; Lewis & Lewis, 1981; Marshall et al., 2011; M. J. Perry, Albee, Bloom, & Gullotta, 1996). In recent years, however, more attention has been given to the need to train prevention researchers and practitioners within psychology (Conyne, Newmeyer, Kenny, Romano, & Matthews, 2008; Eddy, Smith, Brown, & Reid, 2005; Matthews, 2012).

Eddy et al. (2005) surveyed graduate students, early career prevention scientists, and established career prevention scientists about their education and training in 13 prevention content and knowledge areas: (a) basic research, (b) prevention program design, (c) timing of prevention interventions, (d) design of prevention trials, (e) program evaluation, (f) community collaboration, (g) gender and cultural issues, (h) economic analysis, (i) history and context of prevention efforts, (j) scientific collaborations, (k) funding, (l) administrative skills, and (m) ethics. In general, the amount of training, preparation, and knowledge increased with the respondent's level of experience. However, the importance that respondents attached to the different training areas and their desire for additional training in the content areas did not increase. Although established professionals rated themselves highly in the traditional prevention areas, such as prevention research design and evaluation, students and early career professionals rated themselves low in these areas. Education in economic analysis and ethics was lacking for both established and newer prevention scientists, as respondents rated themselves low on their knowledge about these areas, and the majority indicated the importance of and need for further training in these areas. Eddy et al. concluded that there are serious gaps in the prevention training of early and established prevention scientists and recommended increased attention to prevention education and development of prevention competencies during graduate and postgraduate training.

Romano and Hage (2000b) identified eight domains that are important in the training of prevention specialists: (a) skills developing community and multidisciplinary collaborations, (b) knowledge of social and public policy history related to a prevention topic, (c) understanding protective and risk factors as they relate to the prevention topic, (d) skills implementing systemic interventions, (e) understanding current political and social issues about a prevention topic, (f) skills leading psychoeducational groups, (g) skills in conducting prevention research and evaluations, and (h) knowledge about prevention ethics. There is some overlap in these domains with the content areas of Eddy et al. (2005; i.e., collaborations, history, ethics), and some are unique to each set of authors (i.e., economic analysis and gender and culture [Eddy et al., 2005], protective and risk factors and psychoeducational groups [Romano & Hage, 2000b]). Nonetheless, the training content and skill areas provide a useful framework for prevention training at the pre- and postgraduate levels.

In a special issue of the *Journal of Clinical Psychology*, Snyder and Elliott (2005) presented a four-level matrix model for the training of clinical psychologists in the 21st century. The four levels are individual, interpersonal, institutional, and societal–community. Traditional education of clinical psychologists has been primarily about treatment at the individual level, but Snyder and Elliott argued for increased training in the three other dimensions of their model and for the importance of prevention education in clinical psychology training. They advocated for clinical psychologists playing major leadership roles in the prevention of health problems through the development and application of psychological interventions in health promotion and disease prevention. They also recommended that psychology have a prominent voice in the development of public health policies. Furthermore, Snyder and Elliott stressed the importance of didactic and applied prevention training of clinical psychologists, including giving increased attention to human strengths and their place in prevention and health promotion.

There is no one "right" way to educate prevention researchers and practitioners, as training may occur in different ways in graduate school, in formal postdoctoral training, and in continuing education (Hage et al., 2007; Sandler & Chassin, 1993). Conyne et al. (2008) described two different strategies for teaching prevention in graduate school: specialized courses and infusion of prevention content into required core curriculum courses. For example, since 1984, the University of Cincinnati has offered a prevention counseling course that uses didactic approaches to infuse traditional prevention content and contemporary issues into course lectures and discussions (Conyne et al., 2008). Throughout the course, counseling students gain an appreciation of prevention in mental health work. Students work in small groups to examine important prevention issues and to gain real-world experience by evaluating existing prevention programs. To further their development in prevention work, students also conduct a self-assessment of their strengths and education needs.

Conyne et al. (2008) also provided examples of graduate-level prevention education from the counseling programs and counseling psychology programs at Boston College and the University of Minnesota. These examples incorporate prevention education into core curriculum courses. At Boston College, a doctoral-level first-year experience makes use of faculty-created community projects that involve students in prevention activities through participation in multidisciplinary collaborations, systemic prevention interventions, and political and social advocacy. The doctoral program also includes prevention education in core courses and the seminar that accompanies the first-year experience. For example, the core advanced psychopathology seminar incorporates information about risk and protective factors and their importance in mental health promotion, and the research design course includes examples from prevention science.

At the University of Minnesota, prevention education is infused into graduate courses, such as counseling theory, group counseling, and practicum (Conyne et al., 2008). Activities related to prevention include required readings, assignments in counseling practicum, and student presentations. At Minnesota, the inclusion of prevention education in specific courses is heavily dependent on the instructor's skills, interests, and commitment to bringing the content into the course. Other course and infusion examples have been reported (e.g., Penn State University; Matthews & Skowron, 2004). At some institutions, students may enroll in prevention courses in departments other than their home department.

In addition to the above models, universities have developed more comprehensive prevention education opportunities. The University of Wisconsin offers an interdisciplinary graduate minor in prevention science (see http://www.preventionscience.wisc.edu/). The minor is offered collaboratively in several departments and focuses on social problems of at-risk populations across the life span. The University of Minnesota also offers a graduate minor in prevention. The minor is an interdisciplinary certificate program comprising 11 academic units and six colleges. The academic units include psychology, education, health sciences, and public policy, as well as research centers and diverse specialty areas, such as behavioral genetics and neurobehavioral development (see http://www.preventionscience.umn.edu). Recently, the University of Oregon developed a prevention science specialty in its master's program in counseling, family, and human services (see https://education.uoregon.edu/program/prevention-science). These examples of graduate education in prevention science give students an integrative academic and applied education in prevention, which serves as a foundation for further work in prevention science.

Despite recent examples of formal prevention education at a few universities, the integration of prevention education into the standard graduate curricula of applied psychology has not advanced very rapidly (Matthews, 2012). Therefore, postdegree prevention training is necessary for those who desire to achieve greater competency in prevention work. In-service training can be accomplished in ways similar to how other professional skills are gained after formal schooling. Although postdoctoral internships with a prevention emphasis are available, the opportunities are limited. Therefore, professionals are more likely to gain prevention education and skills through conferences, journals, books, and Internet sources (see Appendix B). In addition, collaborations with prevention specialists from disciplines other than one's own are important sources of education and skill development. These types of collaborations promote learning opportunities as specialists come together to address common prevention topics from the perspective of their own discipline.

There are barriers to formal prevention education. For example, because prevention is an interdisciplinary specialty, there is no consensus about important content areas and how they are taught (Tebes, Kaufman, & Chinman, 2002). In addition, motivation for graduate programs to teach about prevention is low, because prevention is not specifically included as a content area in APA accreditation guidelines and state and territorial licensing board requirements. Although prevention science can apply to some competency domains in APA accreditation guidelines, psychology graduate programs would need to infuse prevention education into relevant APA accreditation domains, such as cultural and individual differences, research methods and evaluation, ethics, and psychopathology and theories. However, core courses in these areas are already full with traditional content, leaving limited opportunities to infuse additional material related to prevention. Another major accrediting body of counseling programs, the Council for Accreditation of Counseling and Related Educational Programs, includes prevention in its standards, but there are no clear guidelines on how best to infuse prevention content into curricula (Matthews & Skowron, 2004).

Economics is another barrier (Koocher, 2005). Prevention services delivered to clients have not been reimbursable by insurance companies in the past, and therefore students and graduate programs have made prevention less of a priority. However, this may be changing, as health preventive services are included in the 2010 U.S. Affordable Health Care Act legislation. Prevention services such as screening and counseling for depression, sexually transmitted infections, and obesity are included in the U.S. health care law. In addition, psychology licensing requirements have not mandated prevention education to become licensed. However, psychology license boards recognize the rapidly changing nature of the profession, and education requirements may change in the future (DeMers, VanHorne, & Rodolfa, 2008). Another barrier to offering formal prevention courses and experiences in graduate education is that the application process for predoctoral psychology internships emphasizes clinical intervention experiences; less emphasis is given to knowledge and skills in prevention. Koocher (2005) identified several additional factors that inhibit a greater focus on prevention in psychology graduate education, including the historical structure of psychology training programs, the medical model of psychological practice, and insurance reimbursement policies.

Collectively, these factors contribute to low faculty interest and low student motivation to acquire prevention education during graduate school.

Therefore, the training of prevention specialists will likely continue to include multiple pathways to acquire competencies in the near future. In current graduate education, infusion of prevention content into core didactic courses and applied experiences is the most promising avenue, as this path will require the fewest institutional resources. However, faculty teaching the courses must have the knowledge, interest, and commitment to include prevention readings, assignments, and discussions in their classes. Online courses and certificate programs are viable options for prevention education. Online in-service prevention training has met with success in areas of substance abuse (McPherson, Cook, Back, Hersch, & Hendrickson, 2006) and suicide prevention (D. M. Stone, Barber, & Potter, 2005). Reports from these examples showed that online training was user friendly and, in the case of the substance abuse training, more engaging to participants, compared with print-based training. These educational experiences would supplement traditional continuing education offered through conferences, workshops, and the professional literature. However, perhaps most significant is that mental health professionals recognize the importance of prevention and feel motivated to gain more education and additional skills in that area.

FUNDING

The economics and funding of prevention can be presented in two ways: (a) the cost-effectiveness of prevention in society and the workplace and (b) the challenges of conducting prevention activities with little or no reimbursement for services provided by mental health professionals employed in clinical settings that attach little importance to prevention.

First, the cost-effectiveness of prevention in society and the workplace has been well documented (T. Miller & Hendrie, 2008; National Research Council and Institute of Medicine, 2009; A. J. Reynolds, Rolnick, Englund, & Temple, 2010; U.S. Department of Health and Human Services, 2003a). Considering cigarette smoking alone, the National Prevention Council (2011) reported U.S. government data showing that cigarette smoking leads to approximately 443,000 deaths in the United States, with costs of $96 billion in medical care and $97 billion in loss of worker productivity each year. The National Prevention Council also reported that where smoking bans are enforced in the workplace, restaurants, and other public places, there has been a decrease in heart attacks of nonsmokers in the 17%-to-19% range.

A Centers for Disease Control and Prevention (CDC) report (U.S. Department of Health and Human Services, 2003a) further delineated spiraling medical costs in the United States, due to an aging population and chronic health conditions. Often, these conditions can be reduced through preventive efforts. For example, the CDC estimated that in 2003, cardiovascular disease and stroke accounted for $351.8 billion in medical costs and lost productivity; in 2002, obesity cost $117 billion, with $61 billion in medical expenses and $56 billion in lost productivity; and diabetes expenditures in 2002 were estimated at $92 billion in medical costs and $40 billion in lost productivity. Collectively and singly, these costs are staggering for the nation, not only in terms of dollar amounts but also in terms of psychological distress and hardship for individuals and families.

The financial benefits of workplace health and wellness programs for both employers and employees have also been documented. A U.S. Department of Health and Human Services (2003b) article on prevention programs in the workplace, titled "Prevention Makes Common 'Cents,'" reported on the cost-effectiveness of workplace prevention programs and their impact on employee health. The report summarized several exemplary health and wellness programs in major U.S. corporations and cited research showing that the median financial benefit for corporations that provide health promotion opportunities for their employees is $3.14 for every $1.00 spent on the program. In a more recent analysis, Goetzel and Ozminkowski (2008) conducted a comprehensive review of worksite health promotion programs. Their review included information about the types of programs offered, employee participation incentives, and the costs and benefits for employer and employee. Generally, cost–benefit analyses of such programs yielded positive results in worker productivity, reduced employee absenteeism, and reduced employer medical costs. Studies cited by Goetzel and Ozminkowski found that health promotion programs in the workplace are worth their investment; they cited cost–benefit studies of such programs during the past 20 years that revealed returns from $1.40 to $10.10 for every dollar invested. Chapman (2005), cited by Goetzel and Ozminkowski, found a 25% to 30% reduction in employer medical costs and employee absenteeism attributable to health promotion programs.

Cost-analysis studies have also reported on the cost-effectiveness of different types of prevention programs. For example, Rosenthal et al. (2009) assessed the costs and benefits of a community-based teen pregnancy prevention program. Their cost analysis showed that the program reduced childbearing by teenage girls, with an economic benefit to society of over $2.6 million.

Swisher, Scherer, and Yin (2004) reviewed seven studies that estimated cost–benefit ratios of community- and school-based prevention programs. The cost–benefit ratios ranged from a savings of $2.00 to $19.64 for each dollar spent, a range attributed to the variety of prevention approaches and cost–benefit analyses used, demonstrating the cost-effectiveness of the programs.

A. J. Reynolds, Temple, White, Ou, and Robertson (2011) conducted a longitudinal study of low-income children who participated in the preschool and elementary school Child–Parent Centers in Chicago to promote their healthy development. The children were followed until they were 26 years of age. In relation to a comparison group of low-income children who received other types of services or traditional in-home care, the costs–benefits of the Child–Parent Centers ranged from $3.97 to $10.83 per dollar spent on the program, with the preschool and early school programs yielding the largest ratios. For society, the financial benefits of the program were increased incomes and tax revenues from participants, and participants' avoidance of involvement with crime and the criminal justice system. The study reinforces the importance of funding for early child development programs—not only do they enhance lives but they are also cost-effective and provide financial benefits to society.

The financial benefits and cost-effectiveness of prevention programs across topics and ages have also been estimated for alcohol abuse prevention (Kraemer, 2007; Spoth, Guyll, & Day, 2002), prevention of depression in older adults (Smit, Ederveen, Cuijpers, Deeg, & Beekman, 2006), correctional interventions to prevent crime and reduce recidivism (Welsh & Farrington, 2000), smoking cessation (Ruger & Emmons, 2008), and the economic impact of a supervised injection facility in Canada as a strategy for preventing HIV infections (Andresen & Boyd, 2010).

Evaluating the cost-effectiveness of a prevention program can be a complex and daunting task for stakeholders. The *Guide to Analyzing the Cost-Effectiveness of Community Public Health Prevention Approaches* (hereinafter, *Guide*) was developed for the U.S. Department of Health and Human Services by a team from Research Triangle Institute International (Honeycutt et al., 2006). The *Guide* provides steps in conducting a cost-effectiveness study for community prevention programs, including planning the study, identifying cost-effectiveness questions, and selecting the appropriate type of cost analysis. In addition, the *Guide* provides information on identifying outcome measures and quantifying the outcomes and costs of the prevention intervention. The information the *Guide* contains is applicable to prevention interventions implemented in settings other than those that are community based. The *Guide* is especially informative for prevention program developers and stakeholders because a cost-effectiveness analysis of prevention programs is usually omitted, except in very general ways, in descriptions and evaluations of prevention interventions.

The second issue related to the economics and funding of prevention concerns psychologists and mental health professionals who practice in clinical settings, where prevention services are generally not reimbursable through health insurance. Although lack of reimbursement has been a major barrier to the delivery of prevention services, this is changing. For example, the 2010

U.S. Affordable Health Care Act identified several areas of preventive services, including assessments and counseling for problems that compromise health, such as obesity, alcohol, depression, interpersonal violence, and sexually transmitted infections. When fully implemented, the law should reduce some of the financial barriers to practitioners who wish to engage in preventive services.

Many mental health practitioners are employed in settings that are not dependent on private or government insurance plans for financial reimbursements, for example, educational institutions, community mental health clinics, and health care settings. These settings have a history of offering prevention services as well as opportunities to engage in prevention without being disadvantaged financially. One recent study conducted in a metropolitan region of the Midwest reported that prevention was identified in all of the mission statements appearing on the 62 community mental health organizations' websites (Hane, 2013). In addition, 60 of the 62 organizations offered prevention programs, and in total 409 prevention programs were offered across the organizations. Thus, opportunities to engage in prevention are available, at least as reported in this study. It would be informative to conduct similar studies in other communities and regions.

SUMMARY

This chapter addressed three issues that are important to consider in the prevention specialty. The mental health professions need to continue to give increased attention and priority to prevention ethics, education, and funding—in training, research, and practice. Although advances have been made in these three areas, more needs to be done in identifying how they can be more fully incorporated into a broader conceptualization of the prevention specialty. In different ways, these three topics are interrelated. If prevention funding becomes more available, training institutions and mental health personnel may be more likely to support prevention education and to engage in prevention work. Prevention ethics is important in courses and curricula that educate about prevention, and ethical practices are required when conducting prevention research and implementing interventions.

10

MAPPING AN AGENDA FOR THE FUTURE OF PREVENTION PSYCHOLOGY

Prevention has a bright future in psychology and other mental health and human development disciplines and professional specialties. This book is rich in resources, and it reviews current literature in prevention research and interventions. As this volume demonstrates, prevention is applicable across the life span and has become an area of specialty in different disciplines and professional specialties. There has also been increased attention to prevention in various U.S. government agencies and in policy (see Appendix B). Professional organizations, including the American Psychological Association, are recognizing the value and potential of prevention (see Appendix A).

Yet, despite advances in prevention research and practice, and increased visibility through professional organizations and public policy initiatives, a number of challenges will need to be addressed. Greater emphasis needs to be placed on prevention in the education of applied mental health professionals, and more attention to prevention is needed in the professional accreditation guidelines and education requirements of professional license boards.

DOI: 10.1037/14442-010
Prevention Psychology: Enhancing Personal and Social Well-Being, by J. L. Romano
Copyright © 2015 by the American Psychological Association. All rights reserved.

And mental health and human development agencies need to provide greater opportunities for reimbursement of prevention services, a challenge that is especially important for mental health practitioners who deliver such services in private practice settings.

Prevention is not a new area of scholarship, as described in the first chapter of this book. However, despite the advances made, especially in the past 50 years, there are several areas for future growth and development, and opportunities for mental health and human development professionals. The remainder of this chapter highlights these areas.

Throughout this book, I have emphasized implementing evidence-supported prevention interventions, and they will continue to be required in the future. There is a plenitude of material, websites, and clearinghouses that prevention specialists can use to identify evidence-supported interventions that may be appropriate for their setting, population, and desired behavior change. Although many of the earlier prevention interventions focused on children and youth during the years of schooling, more interventions have been developed and implemented with other age groups, although these are not as numerous as prevention activities implemented in educational institutions. Prevention and health promotion interventions that can be implemented with adults in communities are important, as are interventions that can be implemented in employment settings. And, of course, prevention and health promotion interventions with older adults will become more important in the 21st century as people live longer and enjoy active lifestyles after retirement.

Regardless of setting, population, and type of intervention, it is important that prevention and health promotion interventions have at least some evidence to support their efficacy and effectiveness and that they are supported by one or more theories or models that can help to explain their outcomes. This book highlighted several models of behavior change in Chapter 3 and mentioned other theoretical frameworks in the descriptions of interventions in Chapters 6 and 7. Psychological applications from positive psychology (see Chapter 4) and social justice (see Chapter 5) are also areas of scholarship that can frame prevention and health promotion interventions.

As even a casual review of this book demonstrates, prevention is a multidisciplinary specialty and is likely to remain so in the future. No one professional discipline or specialty owns prevention and health promotion. They cut across many disciplines, so much so that some institutions have developed graduate minors and specialty areas in prevention (see Chapter 9). Ideally, these types of educational opportunities will exist in greater numbers in the future. Prevention demands that disciplinary experts come together to not only train the next generation of prevention specialists but also to collaborate on development, implementation, research, and evaluations of prevention interventions. Professional collaborations are important because no one discipline has expertise in all of the areas necessary to carry out prevention initiatives. As reported in this book, prevention experts have come from fields such as counseling, economics, education, nursing, psychology, public health, public policy, and social work. In recent years, specialists from behavioral genetics, marketing, neuroscience, and information technology have also contributed to prevention, and their contributions will increase in the future and strengthen the education of future prevention specialists.

Prevention specialists must be aware of, and attentive to, national and organizational priorities that support prevention and health promotion. From programmatic and funding perspectives, priorities are important, whether they pertain to national, state, or local government; private foundations; local employers; or educational institutions. Appendix B lists many government and nongovernment entities that are helpful in locating information and sources of funding. However, more resources are available in addition to those listed in Appendix B, and some of the resources are also listed in the chapters of this book. One example of a major U.S. government agency that reports strategic initiatives relevant to prevention is the Substance Abuse and Mental Health Services Administration (SAMHSA). SAMHSA (2011) listed eight strategic initiatives for the next several years, as follows.

- *Prevention of substance abuse and mental illness:* Community focused and promotes emotional health and prevention of mental illness, substance abuse, and suicide through community coalitions; includes a focus on at risk youth, youth in Tribal communities, and military families.
- *Trauma and justice:* Focuses on reducing violence and trauma by integrating systemic and individual interventions, especially with those who are at risk or already involved with the criminal and juvenile justice system.
- *Military families:* Supports servicemen and -women, active duty, reserves, and veterans, to ensure that behavioral health services are available and that they promote positive outcomes.
- *Recovery support:* Promotes individual, family, and systemic approaches to foster health and resiliency through permanent housing, employment, education, and reduction of discriminatory barriers.
- *Health reform:* Promotes access to preventive, treatment, and recovery services, and reduces health care disparities between people with mental health conditions and those with physical health conditions, and supports coordinated care services for co-occurring conditions.

- *Health information technology:* Promotes full participation of health care providers, including prevention specialists, in health information technology and electronic health records.
- *Data, outcomes, and quality:* Supports integrated strategy of data collection and evaluation to determine impact, inform policy, and improved quality of behavioral health services.
- *Public awareness and support:* Promotes increased public awareness and understanding of mental disorders and substance use disorders and the potential for prevention to reduce their incidence and impact through early detection and treatment. Prevention specialists should periodically consult other government agencies, such as the National Institute of Mental Health, to learn about strategic initiatives and research priorities; state agencies and offices may also develop strategic initiatives related to prevention applications, and they should also be regularly reviewed.

The use of technology in prevention research and interventions is described in several chapters (see, e.g., Chapters 3, 6, and 7). As technology becomes even more widespread, sophisticated, and convenient, technological tools will have a major impact on prevention work. For example, as presented in this book, Internet-based prevention interventions, and supplemental components of interventions, have been implemented with some success. Such interventions offer convenience for participants and have the capacity to deliver comprehensive information about a topic. In addition, technology devices will improve interventions through coaching and motivational messages that can be delivered between prevention sessions that are conducted in person. Technology can also be used to strengthen record keeping and data collection, as behavior can be monitored and surveys completed electronically and at convenient times. Electronic data collection may also facilitate gathering of information from individuals who are not direct recipients of a prevention intervention, such as parents and caregivers, teachers, and friends. Prevention evaluations will be improved if data from other sources, in addition to self-report data, can be collected.

Prevention research and applications are projected to increase in the future. This book provides a broad examination of the historical antecedents and current state of prevention. Theories and perspectives applicable to prevention at individual, social, and policy levels are discussed, along with examples of prevention interventions in different settings, with different age groups, and conducted by different disciplinary specialties. The book also addresses professional issues of ethics, training, and funding that are important to prevention, as well as future directions for the specialty. I hope that the book gives readers a comprehensive representation of prevention and that it motivates new and experienced professionals to consider prevention as an important component of their professional identity and professional activities.

APPENDIX A:
AMERICAN PSYCHOLOGICAL ASSOCIATION GUIDELINES FOR PREVENTION IN PSYCHOLOGY

Guideline 1. Psychologists are encouraged to select and implement preventive interventions that are theory- and evidence-based.

Guideline 2. Psychologists are encouraged to use culturally relevant prevention practices adapted to the specific context in which they are implemented.

Guideline 3. Psychologists are encouraged to develop and implement interventions that reduce risks and promote human strengths.

Guideline 4. Psychologists are encouraged to incorporate research and evaluation as integral to prevention program development and implementation, including consideration of environmental contexts that impact prevention.

Guideline 5. Psychologists are encouraged to consider ethical issues in prevention research and practice.

Guideline 6. Psychologists are encouraged to attend to contextual issues of social disparity that may inform prevention practice and research.

Guideline 7. Psychologists are encouraged to increase their awareness, knowledge, and skills essential to prevention through continuing education, training, supervision, and consultation.

Guideline 8. Psychologists are encouraged to engage in systemic and institutional interventions that strengthen the health of individuals, families, and communities, and prevent psychological and physical distress and disability.

Guideline 9. Psychologists are encouraged to inform the deliberation of public policies that promote health and well-being when relevant prevention science findings are available.

Approved by American Psychological Association Council, February 2013. From "Guidelines for Prevention in Psychology," by the American Psychological Association, 2014, *American Psychologist, 69,* p. 296. Copyright 2014 by the American Psychological Association.

APPENDIX B:
PREVENTION RESOURCES

U.S. GOVERNMENT RESOURCES

Substance Abuse and Mental Health Services Administration (SAMHSA; http://www.samhsa.gov)

This agency, within the U.S. Department of Health and Human Services, aims to strengthen the behavioral health of the nation. SAMSHA offers many resources at no cost through publications across many topics. Grant opportunities are also available through SAMSHA. Below are examples of resources SAMHSA provides.

A. *Building Blocks for a Healthy Future (http://www.bblocks.samhsa.gov)*

Information, materials, and curricula for preschool and early-school children to be used by parents, caregivers, and teachers. Site includes games, songs, and activities for this age group to promote positive child development.

B. *Center for Substance Abuse Prevention Centers for the Application of Prevention Technologies (http://www.captus.samhsa.gov)*

Provides prevention training and technical assistance to strengthen prevention systems and the behavioral health workforce. For example, the site lists suggestions for submitting a prevention program for National Registry of Evidence-Based Prevention Programs and Practices review.

C. *SAMHSA Grant Funds (http://www.beta.samhsa.gov/grants)*

Funding opportunities to support treatment and prevention programs for substance abuse and mental health initiatives. The site includes grant application process, review, and management.

D. *Safe Schools/Healthy Students (http://www.sshs.samhsa.gov)*

Awards grant funds to state departments of education and mental health through a collaboration of three U.S. federal departments to support school and community partnerships to reduce violence and substance abuse and promote school achievement and student mental health.

Adapted from *Focus on Prevention*, by Substance Abuse and Mental Health Services Administration, 2010, Rockville, MD: Author. In the public domain.

E. *Division of Workplace Programs (http://www.dwp.samhsa.gov/)*

Provides oversight to eliminate illicit drug use in the federal workforce and certifies laboratories to conduct drug testing for federal agencies. Promotes health and safety in work environments through comprehensive health and wellness programs in the workplace.

F. *Too Smart to Start (http://www.toosmarttostart.samhsa.gov/)*

Public education initiative designed to combat underage alcohol use; offers materials and strategies for youth, adolescents, educators, families, and community leaders through materials, publications, and age-appropriate online games to educate about underage alcohol use.

G. *National Survey on Drug Use and Health (http://www.oas.samhsa.gov/ nsduh.htm)*

Provides prevalence rates of alcohol and drug use and abuse and mental health status in the U.S. population, ages 12 and older (formerly called the National Household Survey). The National Survey is conducted by SAMHSA's Office of Applied Statistics. Extensive data about U.S. prevalence rates based on the National Survey are also available through SAMHSA's Data, Outcomes, and Quality website (http://www.samhsa.gov/data).

H. *National Registry of Evidence-Based Prevention Programs and Practices (http://www.nrepp.samhsa.gov)*

Resource to identify prevention interventions and practices that have been approved for dissemination after review by this registry. The National Registry is widely cited in this book.

Centers for Disease Control and Prevention (CDC; http://www.cdc.gov)

A formidable unit within the U.S. Department of Health and Human Services, the CDC promotes health and well-being to improve quality of life through prevention and control of disease, disability, and injury. The CDC website provides materials and information related to the health of the nation. Representative units within the CDC are listed below.

A. *Office on Smoking and Health (OSH; http://www.cdc.gov/tobacco)*

Established in 1965 and dedicated to reducing tobacco-related death and disability. The site includes statistical data on tobacco use, programs, tips to quit smoking, and funding opportunities.

B. *Youth Risk Behavior Surveillance System (YRBSS; http://www.cdc.gov/ HealthyYouth/yrbs/index.htm)*

Monitors six types of health risk behaviors that contribute to poor health and disabilities among youth and adults: alcohol and drug use, tobacco use, unhealthy diets, physical inactivity, sexual risk behaviors, and injuries and violence. YRBSS also measures the prevalence of obesity and asthma, and participates in the Global School-Based Student Health Survey in collaboration with the World Health Organization and the United Nations.

C. *Division of Violence Prevention (http://www.cdc.gov/violenceprevention)*

Dedicated to preventing injuries and death caused by violence, including child maltreatment, intimate partner violence, elder abuse, and suicide. The site offers publications and materials for professionals and laypersons, including research and statistical data, information about risk and protective factors, and funding opportunities.

D. *National Center for Chronic Disease Prevention and Health Promotion (http://www.cdc.gov/chronicdisease)*

Dedicated to the prevention and delay of onset of many health problems, such as cancer, diabetes, heart disease, and stroke. Offers information and materials to educate professionals and the public to strengthen community and school health through a variety of public health programs and health-monitoring activities.

National Institutes of Health (NIH; http://www.nih.gov)

As part of the U.S. Department of Health and Human Services, NIH is a U.S. medical research agency that promotes research to enhance health and reduce illness and disability. NIH comprises 27 institutes and centers, focusing on different aspects of health. Four of the institutes are annotated below.

A. *National Institute of Mental Health (NIMH; http://www.nimh.nih.gov)*

Comprises several divisions that support basic and clinical research to gain a better understanding of mental illness to improve prevention efforts and to strengthen recovery and cures of mental illness.

B. *National Cancer Institute (NCI; http://www.cancer.gov)*

Coordinates the National Cancer Program that conducts and supports cancer research, training, and dissemination of health information related to the prevention, diagnosis, and treatment of cancer.

C. *National Institute on Drug Abuse (NIDA; http://www.nida.nih.gov)*

Supports research to prevent drug abuse and addiction; also disseminates research findings to professionals, the public, and policymakers. Funding opportunities are available through NIDA.

D. *National Institute on Alcohol Abuse and Alcoholism (NIAAA; http://www.niaaa.nih.gov)*

The largest funder of alcohol research worldwide; supports and conducts research on the impact of alcohol on health and well-being. It also translates and disseminates alcohol research to professionals and to the general public.

U.S. Department of Education

A. *Office of Safe and Healthy Students (OSHS; http://www2.ed.gov/about/offices/list/oese/oshs/index.html)*

Focuses on programs and activities to improve school environments and support student learning, health, and well-being (formerly called the Office of Safe and Drug-Free Schools). OSHS emphasizes several areas, including drug and violence prevention, character and civic education, and student physical and mental health. OSHS, part of the Office of Elementary and Secondary Education, supports several grant programs.

B. *What Works Clearinghouse (WWC; http://www.whatworks.ed.gov)*

Established in 2002 as part of the Institute of Education Sciences (IES) and administered by the National Center for Education Evaluation within IES. WWC is a resource for educators, researchers, and policymakers. WWC reports research on educational topics (e.g., dropout prevention, early education, student behavior), and educational practices and policies to improve student educational outcomes.

Office of Juvenile Justice and Delinquency Prevention (OJJDP; http://www.ojjdp.gov)

As part of the U.S. Department of Justice, OJJDP offers resources to prevent and respond to juvenile delinquency and victimization. Provides publications and statistical data on topics such as child protection, risk and protective factors, and strategies to strengthen families and parenting. Grant programs are available.

Office of National Drug Control Policy
(ONDCP; http://www.whitehousedrugpolicy.gov)

ONDCP, as part of the executive branch of the U.S. government, coordinates drug control efforts and resources across the federal government. Among its activities, ONDCP provides a directory of federally funded prevention programs and supports grants to community coalitions to prevent youth drug use. ONDCP also fosters international partnerships to combat drug use, and reports on drug use internationally.

Interagency Working Group on Youth Programs: Find Youth Info
(http://www.findyouthinfo.gov)

The Interagency Working Group is composed of representatives from 18 federal agencies that support programs and services for youth. Find Youth Info provides resources and tools for organizations, schools, communities, and families on a variety of topics, such as bullying, mental health, civic engagement, and sexuality.

Federal Interagency Forum on Child and Family Statistics
(http://www.childstats.gov)

The Forum reports statistics on U.S. children and families across several domains, including family and social environments, health care, safety, behavior, and education. The Forum also fosters coordination and collaboration across federal government agencies related to child and family well-being.

PRIVATE ORGANIZATIONS

Children, Youth, and Families Education and Research Network
(http://www.cyfernet.org)

This organization provides resources for professionals and parents related to children, youth, and families. The resources are collected from all public land-grant universities in the United States. Materials include evidence-based programs and activities, curricula, and evaluation and research strategies.

Community Anti-Drug Coalitions of America (http://www.cadca.org)

This organization aims to prevent alcohol, tobacco, and drug abuse through community coalitions. The website includes community funding strategies, policy and advocacy activities, training opportunities, and interactive media presentations.

Monitoring the Future (http://www.monitoringthefuture.org)

Provides data, through publications and news releases, about the behaviors, attitudes, and values of U.S. high school and college students and young adults collected through yearly surveys of these population groups.

National Asian Pacific American Families Against Substance Abuse (http://www.napafasa.org)

Founded in 1987 to prevent and reduce alcohol and drug and related issues (e.g., mental health, gangs) in the Asian American, Native Hawaiian, and other Pacific Islander populations. The website provides information about the organization's projects and fact sheets about drug and alcohol use in the ethnic communities the organization serves.

National Center on Addiction and Substance Abuse (http://www.casacolumbia.org)

Founded in 1992 at Columbia University, the Center aims to prevent, reduce, and eliminate addiction. The website includes materials (e.g., research and publications, addiction-risk screening tools) for health care providers, policymakers, and the general public.

National Latino Tobacco Control Network (http://www.latinotobaccocontrol.org/)

This network is funded by the CDC to build community alliances and leadership in reducing health tobacco use and disparities in Latino communities. The organization produces newsletters, publications, and technical assistance for culturally competent training.

Partnership at Drugfree.org (http://www.drugfree.org/)

A drug and alcohol abuse prevention and intervention resource for parents and professionals to address abuse among teens and young adults. It includes resources such as a toll-free hotline, a guide to commonly abused drugs, and information about current topics (e.g., legalization of marijuana).

Prevention Partners (http://www.preventionpartners.com/)

This company sells materials and resources (e.g., pens, posters, apparel) for use in prevention campaigns on a variety of topics, such as alcohol and tobacco use, violence prevention, and character education. It also offers funding support to prevention programs.

Blueprints for Healthy Youth Development (http://www.blueprintsprograms.com)

This program is part of the Center for the Study and Prevention of Violence at the University of Colorado Boulder. The website identifies scientifically based prevention/intervention programs on topics related to violence prevention and other areas of healthy youth development. The site lists and rates programs, including those identified as model programs and those that show promise. Cost–benefit analysis is also provided for model programs.

Child Trends (http://www.childtrends.org)

This nonprofit research center provides information, data, and analysis on topics related to the well-being of children and youth. It provides a list of effective out-of-school prevention programs, cross-national comparisons of data about child well-being, and child well-being data for specific ages and ethnic groups.

World Health Organization (WHO; http://www.who.org)

WHO directs and coordinates global issues on health and well-being across the globe, within the United Nations. The organization conducts research on health, monitors worldwide trends, and offers technical support. WHO addresses many topics related to prevention worldwide, including the prevention of violence and sexual assault, suicide, and substance abuse.

The Campbell Collaboration: What Helps? What Harms? Based on What Evidence? (http://www.campbellcollaboration.org)

The Campbell Collaboration is an international organization with its main office in Oslo, Norway. Among the resources produced by the organization is a monograph series that produces systematic and comparative peer-reviewed research papers on various public policies and prevention and intervention topics related to education, criminal justice, international development, and social welfare.

Promising Practices Network on Children Families and Communities (http://www.promisingpractices.net)

The Network is operated by the RAND Corporation, a research organization dedicated to providing information and solutions for major problems across the globe. The Network provides resources and research-based information on interventions and programs for children and families, offering information about model programs and best practices for service providers and policymakers.

REFERENCES

Abraham, C., & Sheeran, P. (2003). Implications of goal theories of reasoned action and planned behavior. *Current Psychology, 22,* 264–280. doi:10.1007/s12144-003-1021-7

Adams, J., & Scott, J. (2000). Predicting medication adherence in severe mental disorders. *Acta Psychiatrica Scandinavica, 101,* 119–124. doi:10.1034/j.1600-0447.2000.90061.x

Administration on Aging. (n.d.). *Aging statistics.* Retrieved from http://www.aoa.gov/AoARoot/Aging_Statistics/index.aspx

Agency for Healthcare Research and Quality. (2004). *National healthcare disparities report.* Retrieved from http://www.ahrq.gov/qual/nhdr03/nhdrsum03.htm

Ajzen, I. (1991). The theory of planned behavior. *Organizational Behavior and Human Decision Processes, 50,* 179–211. doi:10.1016/0749-5978(91)90020-T

Ajzen, I., & Fishbein, M. (1980). *Understanding attitudes and predicting social behavior.* Englewood Cliffs, NJ: Prentice-Hall.

Ajzen, I., & Fishbein, M. (2004). Questions raised by a reasoned action approach: Comments on Ogden (2003). *Health Psychology, 23,* 431–434. doi:10.1037/0278-6133.23.4.431

Albarracín, D., Fishbein, M., Johnson, B. T., & Muellerleile, P. A. (2001). Theories of reasoned action and planned behavior as models of condom use: A meta-analysis. *Psychological Bulletin, 127,* 142–161. doi:10.1037/0033-2909.127.1.142

Albee, G. W. (1959). *Mental health manpower trends.* New York, NY: Basic Books.

Albee, G. W. (1970). The uncertain future of clinical psychology. *American Psychologist, 25,* 1071–1080. doi:10.1037/h0030393

Albee, G. W. (1983). Psychopathology, prevention, and the just society. *The Journal of Primary Prevention, 4,* 5–40. doi:10.1007/BF01359083

Albee, G. W. (1986). Toward a just society: Lessons from observations on the primary prevention of psychopathology. *American Psychologist, 41,* 891–898. doi:10.1037/0003-066X.41.8.891

Albee, G. W. (1996). Revolutions and counterrevolutions in prevention. *American Psychologist, 51,* 1130–1133. doi:10.1037/0003-066X.51.11.1130

Albee, G. W. (2000). Commentary on prevention and counseling psychology. *The Counseling Psychologist, 28,* 845–853. doi:10.1177/0011000000286006

Albee, G. W. (2005). Call to revolution in the prevention of emotional disorders. *Ethical Human Psychology and Psychiatry: An International Journal of Critical Inquiry, 7,* 37–44.

Albee, G. W., & Canetto, S. S. (1996). A family-focused model of prevention. In L. Bickman, & D. J. Rog (Series Eds.), & C. A. Hefflinger, & C. T. Nixon (Vol. Eds.), *Children's mental health series: Vol. 2. Families and the mental health system for children and adolescents: Policy, services, and research* (pp. 41–62). Thousand Oaks, CA: Sage.

Alexopoulos, G. S. (2005). Depression in the elderly. *The Lancet, 365*, 1961–1970. doi:10.1016/S0140-6736(05)66665-2

Alexopoulos, G. S., Katz, I. R., Bruce, M. L., Heo, M., Ten Have, T., Raue, P., . . . PROSPECT Group. (2005). Remission in depressed geriatric primary care patients: A report from the PROSPECT study. *The American Journal of Psychiatry, 162*, 718–724. doi:10.1176/appi.ajp.162.4.718

Allicock, M., Kaye, L., Johnson, L., Carr, C., Alick, C., Gelin, M., & Campbell, M. (2012). The use of motivational interviewing to promote peer-to-peer support for cancer survivors. *Clinical Journal of Oncology Nursing, 16*, E156–E163. doi:10.1188/12.CJON.E156-E163

American Psychiatric Association. (2000). *Diagnostic and statistical manual of mental disorders* (4th ed., text rev.). Arlington, VA: American Psychiatric Publishing.

American Psychological Association. (2008). *APA Task Force calls for reframing research to account for factors that contribute to resilience among African-American youth* [press release]. Retrieved from http://www.apa.org/news/press/releases/ 2008/08/reframing-research.aspx

American Psychological Association. (2010). *Ethical principles of psychologists and code of conduct (2002; Amended June 1, 2010)*. Retrieved from https://www.apa.org/ ethics/code/index.aspx

American Psychological Association. (2014). Guidelines for prevention in psychology. *American Psychologist, 69*, 285–296. doi:10.1037/a0034569

American Psychological Association. (n.d.). *Public Interest Directorate*. Retrieved from http://www.apa.org/pi/

American Psychological Association, Task Force on Resilience and Strength in Black Children and Adolescents. (2008). *Resilience in African American children and adolescents: A vision for optimal development*. Washington, DC: Author. Retrieved from http://www.apa.org/pi/cyf/resilience.html

Americans With Disabilities Act of 1990, Pub. L. No. 101-336, 104 Stat. 328 (1990).

American School Counseling Association. (2003). *American school counselor association national model: A framework for school counseling programs*. Alexandria, VA: Author.

Andresen, M. A., & Boyd, N. (2010). A cost–benefit and cost-effectiveness analysis of Vancouver's supervised injection facility. *International Journal on Drug Policy, 21*, 70–76. doi:10.1016/j.drugpo.2009.03.004

Arden, M. A., & Armitage, C. J. (2008). Predicting and explaining transtheoretical model stage transitions in relation to condom-carrying behavior. *British Journal of Health Psychology, 13*, 719–735. doi:10.1348/135910707X249589

Armitage, C. J. (2009). Is there utility in the transtheoretical model? *British Journal of Health Psychology, 14*, 195–210. doi:10.1348/135910708X368991

Armitage, C. J., & Arden, M. A. (2008). How useful are the stages of change for targeting interventions? Randomized test of a brief intervention to reduce smoking. *Health Psychology, 27,* 789–798. doi:10.1037/0278-6133.27.6.789

Armitage, C. J., & Connor, M. (2001). Efficacy of the theory of planned behavior: A meta-analytic review. *British Journal of Social Psychology, 40,* 471–499. doi:10.1348/014466601164939

Armstrong, M. J., Mottershead, T. A., Ronksley, P. E., Sigal, R. J., Campbell, T. S., & Hemmelgarn, B. R. (2011). Motivational interviewing to improve weight loss in overweight and/or obese patients: A systematic review and meta-analysis of randomized controlled trials. *Obesity Reviews, 12,* 709–723.

Aronson, E., Wilson, T. D., & Akert, R. M. (2003). *Social psychology.* Upper Saddle River, NJ: Prentice Hall.

August, G. J., Bloomquist, M. L., Lee, S. S., Realmuto, G. M., & Hektner, J. M. (2006). Can evidence-based prevention programs be sustained in community practice settings? The Early Risers' advanced-stage effectiveness trial. *Prevention Science, 7,* 151–165. doi:10.1007/s11121-005-0024-z

August, G. J., Realmuto, G. M., Hektner, J. M., & Bloomquist, M. L. (2001). An integrated components preventive intervention for aggressive elementary school children: The Early Risers program. *Journal of Consulting and Clinical Psychology, 69,* 614–626. doi:10.1037/0022-006X.69.4.614

August, G. J., Realmuto, G. M., Winters, K. C., & Hektner, J. M. (2001). Prevention of adolescent drug abuse: Targeting high-risk children with a multifaceted intervention model: The Early Risers "Skills for Success" program. *Applied & Preventive Psychology, 10,* 135–154.

Backer, T. E., & Rogers, E. M. (1998). Diffusion of innovations theory and worksite AIDS programs. *Journal of Health Communication, 3,* 17–28. doi:10.1080/108107398127481

Badr, H., Carmack, C. L., Kashy, D. A., Cristofanilli, M., & Revenson, T. A. (2010). Dyadic coping in metastatic breast cancer. *Health Psychology, 29,* 169–180. doi:10.1037/a0018165

Baer, J. S., Kivlahan, D. R., Blum, A. W., McKnight, P., & Marlatt, G. A. (2001). Brief intervention for heavy-drinking college students: A 4-year follow-up and natural history. *American Journal of Public Health, 91,* 1310–1316. doi:10.2105/AJPH.91.8.1310

Baker, S. B., & Gerler, E. R. (2004). *School counseling for the twenty-first century* (4th ed.). Upper Saddle River, NJ: Pearson.

Baker, S. B., & Shaw, M. C. (1987). *Improving counseling through primary prevention.* Columbus, OH: Merrill.

Bandura, A. (1986). *Social foundations of thought and action: A social cognitive theory.* Englewood Cliffs, NJ: Prentice Hall.

Baptiste, D., Blachman, D., Cappella, E., Dew, D., Dixon, K., Bell, C. C., . . . McKay, M. M. (2007). Transferring a university-led HIV/AIDS prevention initiative to a community agency. *Social Work in Mental Health, 5,* 269–293. doi:10.1300/J200v05n03_02

Barnett, E., Sussman, S., Smith, C., Rohrbach, L. A., & Spruijt-Metz, D. (2012). Motivational interviewing for adolescent substance use: A review of the literature. *Addictive Behaviors, 37,* 1325–1334. doi:10.1016/j.addbeh.2012.07.001

Barwick, M. A., Bennett, L. M., & Johnson, S. N. (2012). Training health and mental health professionals in motivational interviewing: A systematic review. *Children and Youth Services Review, 34,* 1786–1795. doi:10.1016/j.childyouth.2012.05.012

Beck, A. T. (1976). *Cognitive therapy and the emotional disorders.* New York, NY: International Universities Press.

Beck, A. T., Ward, C. H., Mendelson, M., Mock, J. E., & Erbaugh, J. K. (1961). An inventory for measuring depression. *Archives of General Psychiatry, 4,* 561–571. doi:10.1001/archpsyc.1961.01710120031004

Beers, C. (1908). *A mind that found itself.* Pittsburgh, PA: University of Pittsburgh Press.

Benson, P. L. (1993). *Troubled journey: A portrait of 6th–12th-grade youth.* Minneapolis, MN: Search Institute.

Benson, P. L. (2006). *All kids are our kids: What communities must do to raise caring and responsible children and adolescents* (2nd ed.). Minneapolis, MN: Search Institute.

Berg, R. C., Ross, M. W., & Tikkanen, R. (2011). The effectiveness of MI4MSM: How useful is motivational interviewing as an HIV risk prevention program for men who have sex with men? *AIDS Education and Prevention, 23,* 533–549. doi:10.1521/aeap.2011.23.6.533

Bernat, D., August, G. J., Hektner, J. M., & Bloomquist, M. L. (2007). The Early Risers preventive intervention: Six-year outcomes and mediational processes. *Journal of Abnormal Child Psychology, 35,* 605–617. doi:10.1007/s10802-007-9116-5

Bernat, D. H., Oakes, J. M., Pettingell, S. L., & Resnick, M. (2012). Risk and protective factors for youth violence: Results from the National Longitudinal Study of Adolescent Health. *American Journal of Preventive Medicine, 43*(Suppl. 1), 57–66.

Blazer, D. G. (2002). Self-efficacy and depression in late life: A primary prevention proposal. *Aging & Mental Health, 6,* 315–324. doi:10.1080/1360786021000006938

Bodenmann, G. (1997). Dyadic coping: A systemic-transactional view of stress and coping among couples: Theory and empirical findings. *European Review of Applied Psychology/Revue Européenne de Psychologie Appliqué, 47,* 137–141.

Bodenmann, G. (2005). Dyadic coping and its significance for marital functioning. In T. A. Revenson, K. Kayser, & G. Bodenmann (Eds.), *Couples coping with stress: Emerging perspectives on dyadic coping* (pp. 33–49). Washington, DC: American Psychological Association. doi:10.1037/11031-002

Bond, L. A., & Albee, G. W. (1990). Training preventionists in the ethical implications of their actions. In G. B. Levin, E. J. Trickett, & R. E. Hess (Eds.), *Ethical implications of primary prevention* (pp. 111–126). New York, NY: Hawthorne Press. doi:10.1300/J293v08n02_07

Borsari, B., & Carey, K. B. (2000). Effects of a brief motivational interview with college student drinkers. *Journal of Consulting and Clinical Psychology, 68,* 728–733. doi:10.1037/0022-006X.68.4.728

Bosworth, K., Orpinas, P., & Hein, K. (2009). Development of a positive school climate. In M. E. Kenny, A. M. Horne, P. Orpinas, & L. E. Reese (Eds.), *Realizing social justice: The challenge of preventive interventions* (pp. 229–248). Washington, DC: American Psychological Association. doi:10.1037/11870-011

Botvin, G. J. (2000). Inaugural editorial. *Prevention Science, 1,* 1–2. doi:10.1023/A:1010091031329

Botvin, G. J., Baker, E., Dunesbury, L., Botvin, E. M., & Diaz, T. (1995). Long-term follow-up results of a randomized drug abuse prevention trial in a white middle-class population. *JAMA, 273,* 1106–1112. doi:10.1001/jama.1995.03520380042033

Botvin, G. J., Griffin, K. W., & Nichols, T. R. (2006). Preventing youth violence and delinquency through a universal school-based prevention approach. *Prevention Science, 7,* 403–408. doi:10.1007/s11121-006-0057-y

Bridle, C., Riemsma, P., Pattenden, J., Sowden, A. J., Mather, L., Watt, I. S., & Walker, A. (2005). Systematic review of the effectiveness of health behavior interventions based on the transtheoretical model. *Psychology & Health, 20,* 283–301. doi:10.1080/08870440512331333997

Brown, R. T., Freeman, W. S., Brown, R. A., Belar, C., Hersch, L., Hornyak, L. M., . . . Reed, G. (2002). The role of psychology in health care delivery. *Professional Psychology: Research and Practice, 33,* 536–545. doi:10.1037/0735-7028.33.6.536

Bruce, M. L., Ten Have, T. R., Reynolds, C. F., III, Katz, I. I., Schulberg, H. C., Mulsant, B. H., . . . Alexopoulos, G. S. (2004). Reducing suicidal ideation and depressive symptoms in depressed older primary care patients: A randomized controlled trial. *JAMA, 291,* 1081–1091. doi:10.1001/jama.291.9.1081

Brunwasser, S. M., Giliham, J. E., & Kim, E. S. (2009). A meta-analytic review of the Penn's Resiliency Program's effect on depressive symptoms. *Journal of Consulting and Clinical Psychology, 77,* 1042–1054. doi:10.1037/a0017671

Burns, G. L., Taylor, T. K., & Rusby, J. C. (2001). *Child and Adolescent Disruptive Behavior Inventory 2.3.* Pullman: Washington State University, Department of Psychology.

Buss, D. M. (2000). The evolution of happiness. *American Psychologist, 55,* 15–23. doi:10.1037/0003-066X.55.1.15

Caldwell, R., Classen, C., Lagana, L., McGarvey, E., Baum, L., Duenke, S. D., & Koopman, C. (2003). Changes in sexual functioning and mood among women treated for gynecological cancer who receive group therapy: A pilot study. *Journal of Clinical Psychology in Medical Settings, 10,* 149–156. doi:10.1023/A:1025402610404

Campbell, M. K., Carr, C., DeVellis, B., Switzer, B., Biddle, A., Amamoo, A., . . . Sandler, R. (2009). A randomized trial of tailoring and motivational interviewing to promote fruit and vegetable consumption for cancer prevention and control. *Annals of Behavioral Medicine, 38,* 71–85. doi:10.1007/s12160-009-9140-5

Caplan, G. (1964). *Principles of preventive psychiatry*. New York, NY: Basic Books.

Carlbring, P., Jonsson, J., Josephson, H., & Forsberg, L. (2010). Motivational interviewing versus cognitive-behavioral group therapy in the treatment of problem and pathological gambling: A randomized controlled trial. *Cognitive Behaviour Therapy, 39*, 92–103. doi:10.1080/16506070903190245

Caskey, J. D., & Rosenthal, S. L. (2005). Conducting research on sensitive topics with adolescents: Ethical and developmental considerations. *Journal of Developmental and Behavioral Pediatrics, 26*, 61–67.

Catalano, R. F., Kosterman, R., Hawkins, J. D., Newcomb, M. D., & Abbott, R. D. (1996). Modeling the etiology of adolescent substance use: A test of the social development model. *Journal of Drug Issues, 26*, 429–455.

Centers for Disease Control and Prevention. (2012). *Suicide facts at a glance*. Retrieved from: http://www.cdc.gov/violenceprevention

Ceperich, S. D., & Ingersoll, K. S. (2011). Motivational interviewing and feedback intervention to reduce alcohol-exposed pregnancy risk among college binge drinkers: Determinants and patterns of response. *Journal of Behavioral Medicine, 34*, 381–395. doi:10.1007/s10865-010-9308-2

Cerezo, A., & McWhirter, B. T. (2012). A brief intervention designed to improve social awareness and skills to improve Latino college student retention. *College Student Journal, 46*, 867–879.

Champion, V. L., Ray, D. W., Heilman, D. K., & Springston, J. K. (2000). A tailored intervention for mammography among low-income African American women. *Journal of Psychosocial Oncology, 18*, 1–13. doi:10.1300/J077v18n04_01

Champion, V. L., & Scott, C. R. (1997). Reliability and validity of breast cancer screening belief scales in African American women. *Nursing Research, 46*, 331–337. doi:10.1097/00006199-199711000-00006

Chapman, L. (2007). Closing thoughts. *American Journal of Health Promotion, 21*, 12.

Chapman, L. S. (2005). Meta-evaluation of worksite health promotion economic return studies: 2005 update. *American Journal of Health Promotion, 19*, 1–11.

Chaput, L. A., Adams, S. H., Simon, J. A., Blumenthal, R. S., Vittinghoff, E., Lin, F., . . . Matthews, K. A. (2002). Hostility predicts recurrent events among postmenopausal women with coronary heart disease. *American Journal of Epidemiology, 156*, 1092–1099. doi:10.1093/aje/kwf158

Chiauzzi, E., Green, T. C., Lord, S., Thum, C., & Goldstein, M. (2005). MyStudentBody: A high-risk drinking prevention web site for college students. *Journal of American College Health, 53*, 263–274. doi:10.3200/JACH.53.6.263-274

Christensen, H., Pallister, E., Smale, S., Hickie, I. B., & Calear, A. L. (2010). Community-based prevention programs for anxiety and depression in youth: A systematic review. *The Journal of Primary Prevention, 31*, 139–170. doi:10.1007/s10935-010-0214-8

Civil Rights Act of 1964, Pub. L. No. 88-352, 78 Stat. 241 (1964).

Clayton, A. H., McGarvey, E. L., & Clavet, G. J. (1996). Changes in Sexual Functioning Questionnaire (CSFQ): Validation Study [abstract]. *Psychopharmacology Bulletin, 32*(3), 423.

Clifton, D. O., & Nelson, P. (1992). *Soar with your strengths.* New York, NY: Delacorte Press.

Coard, S. I., Foy-Watson, S., Zimmer, C., & Wallace, A. (2007). Considering culturally relevant parenting practices in intervention development and adaptation: A randomized control trial of the Black Parenting Strengths and Strategies (BPSS) program. *The Counseling Psychologist, 35,* 797–820. doi:10.1177/0011000007304592

Coates, T. J., & Szekeres, G. (2004). A plan for the next generation of HIV prevention research: Seven key policy investigative challenges. *American Psychologist, 59,* 747–757. doi:10.1037/0003-066X.59.8.747

Coie, J. D., Watt, N. F., West, S. G., Hawkins, J. D., Asarnow, J. R., Markman, H. J., . . . Long, B. (1993). The science of prevention: A conceptual framework and some directions for a national research program. *American Psychologist, 48,* 1013–1022. doi:10.1037/0003-066X.48.10.1013

Colby, S. M., Nargiso, J., Tervyaw, T. O., Barnett, N. P., Metrik, J., Lewander, W., . . . Monti, P. (2012). Enhanced motivational interviewing versus brief advice for adolescent smoking cessation: Results from a randomized clinical trial. *Addictive Behaviors, 37,* 817–823. doi:10.1016/j.addbeh.2012.03.011

Community Mental Health Act of 1963, Pub. L. No. 88-164 (1963).

Constantine, M. G., & Sue, D. W. (2006). Factors contributing to optimal human functioning in people of color in the United States. *The Counseling Psychologist, 34,* 228–244. doi:10.1177/0011000005281318

Conyne, R. K. (1984). Primary prevention through a campus alcohol education project. *The Personnel and Guidance Journal, 62,* 524–528. doi:10.1111/j.2164-4918.1984.tb00268.x

Conyne, R. K. (1997). Educating students in preventive counseling. *Counselor Education and Supervision, 36,* 259–269. doi:10.1002/j.1556-6978.1997.tb00394.x

Conyne, R. K. (2004). *Preventive counseling* (2nd ed.). New York, NY: Brunner-Routledge.

Conyne, R. K. (2013). A history of prevention in counseling psychology. In E. M. Vera (Ed.), *The Oxford handbook of prevention in counseling psychology* (pp. 18–35). New York, NY: Oxford University Press.

Conyne, R. K., Newmeyer, M. D., Kenny, M., Romano, J. L., & Matthews, C. R. (2008). Two key strategies for teaching prevention: Specialized course and infusion. *The Journal of Primary Prevention, 29,* 375–401. doi:10.1007/s10935-008-0146-8

Costa, P. T., & McCrae, R. R. (1992). *Revised NEO Personality Inventory and NEO Five-Factor Inventory professional manual.* Odessa, FL: Psychological Assessment Resources, Inc.

Cowen, E. L. (1983). Primary prevention in mental health: Past, present, and future. In R. D. Felner, L. A. Jason, J. N. Moritsugu, & S. S. Farber (Eds.), *Preventive psychology: Theory, research, and practice* (pp. 11–25). Elmsford, NY: Pergamon.

Cugelman, B., Thelwall, M., & Dawes, P. (2011). Online interventions for social marketing health behavior change campaigns: A meta-analysis of psychological architectures and adherence factors. *Journal of Medical Internet Research, 13*, e17. doi:10.2196/jmir.1367

Cunningham, P. J. (2009). Beyond parity: Primary care physicians' perspectives on access to mental health care. *Health Affairs, 28*, 490–501. Retrieved from http://content.healthaffairs.org/content/28/3/490.full.html

Dahir, C. A. (2008). School counseling: Moving toward standards and models. In H. L. K. Coleman & C. Yeh (Eds.), *Handbook of school counseling* (pp. 37–47). New York, NY: Routledge.

Dawson, G., Munson, J., Webb, S. J., Nalty, T., Abbott, R., & Toth, K. (2007). Rate of head growth decelerates and symptoms worsen in the second year of life in autism. *Biological Psychiatry, 61*, 458–464. doi:10.1016/j.biopsych.2006.07.016

DeLeon, P. H., Giesting, B., & Kenkel, M. B. (2003). Community health centers: Exciting opportunities for the 21st century. *Professional Psychology: Research and Practice, 34*, 579–585. doi:10.1037/0735-7028.34.6.579

DeMers, S. T., VanHorne, B. A., & Rodolfa, E. R. (2008). Changes in training and practice of psychologists: Current challenges for licensing boards. *Professional Psychology: Research and Practice, 39*, 473–479. doi:10.1037/0735-7028.39.5.473

Denham, S. A., & Burton, R. (1996). A social–emotional intervention for at-risk 4-year-olds. *Journal of School Psychology, 34*, 225–245. doi:10.1016/0022-4405(96)00013-1

de Paoli, M. M., Manongi, R., & Klepp, K.-I. (2004). Factors influencing acceptability of voluntary counseling and HIV-testing among pregnant women in Northern Tanzania. *AIDS Care, 16*, 411–425. doi:10.1080/09540120410001683358

Derksen, J. (2009). Primary care psychologists in the Netherlands: 30 years of experience. *Professional Psychology: Research and Practice, 40*, 493–501. doi:10.1037/a0015743

Dewey, J. (1938). *Experience and education.* Toronto, Ontario, Canada: Collier-MacMillan Canada Ltd.

Diabetes Prevention Program Research Group. (2002). The Diabetes Prevention Program (DPP): Description of lifestyle intervention. *Diabetes Care, 25*, 2165–2171. doi:10.2337/diacare.25.12.2165

DiClemente, C. C., & Prochaska, J. O. (1985). Processes and stages of change: Coping and competence in smoking behavior change. In S. Shiffman & T. A. Wills (Eds.), *Coping and substance abuse* (pp. 319–343). San Diego, CA: Academic Press.

Diener, E. (2000). Subjective well-being: The science of happiness and a proposal for a national index. *American Psychologist, 55*, 34–43. doi:10.1037/0003-066X.55.1.34

Dignan, M., Sharp, P., Blinson, K., Michielutte, R., Konen, J., Bell, R., & Lane, C. (1995). Development of a cervical cancer education program for Native American women in North Carolina. *Journal of Cancer Education, 9,* 235–242.

Donovan, E., Hernandez, J., Chiauzzi, E., DasMahapatra, P., Achilles, T., & Hemm, A. (2012). Results of a pilot study to investigate community college student perceptions of the value of an online health-risk reduction program. *Community College Journal of Research and Practice, 36,* 821–825. doi:10.1080/10668926. 2012.690317

Dray, J., & Wade, T. D. (2012). Is the transtheoretical model and motivational interviewing approach applicable to the treatment of eating disorders? A review. *Clinical Psychology Review, 32,* 558–565. doi:10.1016/j.cpr.2012.06.005

Dubas, J. S., Lynch, K. B., Galano, J., Geller, S., & Hunt, D. (1998). Preliminary evaluation of a resiliency-based preschool substance abuse and violence prevention project. *Journal of Drug Education, 28,* 235–255. doi:10.2190/ VBY0-RLXA-WJ05-NPRX

Duncan, D. F. (1994). The prevention of primary prevention, 1960–1994: Notes toward a case study. *The Journal of Primary Prevention, 15,* 73–79. doi:10.1007/ BF02196348

Durlak, J. A. (1995). *School-based prevention programs for children and adolescents.* Thousand Oaks, CA: Sage.

Durlak, J. A., Weissberg, R. P., Dymnicki, A. B., Taylor, R. D., & Schellinger, K. B. (2011). The impact of enhanced students' social and emotional learning: A meta-analysis of school-based universal interventions. *Child Development, 82,* 405–432. doi:10.1111/j.1467-8624.2010.01564.x

Durlak, J. A., & Wells, A. M. (1997). Primary prevention mental health programs for children and adolescents. A meta-analytic review. *American Journal of Community Psychology, 25,* 115–152. doi:10.1023/A:1024654026646

Eddy, J. M., Smith, P., Brown, C. H., & Reid, J. B. (2005). A survey of prevention science training: Implications for educating the next generation. *Prevention Science, 6,* 59–71. doi:10.1007/s11121-005-1253-x

Eggert, L. L., Herting, J. R., & Thompson, E. A. (1995). *The High School Questionnaire: A profile of experiences.* Seattle: Reconnecting At-Risk Youth Prevention Research Program, University of Washington School of Nursing.

Eggert, L. L., Thompson, E. A., Herting, J. R., & Nicholas, L. J. (1995). Reducing suicide potential among high-risk youth: Tests of a school-based prevention program. *Suicide and Life-Threatening Behavior, 25,* 276–296.

Embry, D. D. (2004). Community-based prevention using simple, low-cost, evidence-based kernels and behavior vaccines. *Journal of Community Psychology, 32,* 575–591. doi:10.1002/jcop.20020

Englard, I. (2009). *Corrective and distributive justice: From Aristotle to modern times.* Oxford, England: Oxford University Press.

Espelage, D. L., & Poteat, V. P. (2012). Counseling psychologists in schools. In N. A. Fouad, J. A. Carter, & L. M. Subich (Eds.), *APA handbook of counseling psychology* (Vol. 2, pp. 541–566). Washington, DC: American Psychological Association.

Evers, K. E., Prochaska, J. O., Johnson, J. L., Mauriello, L. M., Padula, J. A., & Prochaska, J. M. (2006). A Randomized clinical trial of a population- and trans-theoretical model-based stress-management intervention. *Health Psychology, 25,* 521–529. doi:10.1037/0278-6133.25.4.521

Fagan, A. A., Hanson, K., Hawkins, J. D., & Arthur, M. W. (2008). Implementing effective community-based prevention programs in the community youth development study. *Youth Violence and Juvenile Justice, 6,* 256–278. doi:10.1177/1541204008315937

Fishbein, M. (Ed.). (1967). *Readings in attitude theory and measurement.* New York, NY: Wiley.

Fishbein, M., & Ajzen, I. (1975). *Belief, attitude, intention, and behavior: An introduction to theory and research.* Reading, MA: Addison-Wesley.

Fiske, A., & Arbore, P. (2000/2001). Future directions in late life suicide prevention. *Omega: Journal of Death and Dying, 42,* 37–53. doi:10.2190/3T4G-T5U2-Q724-E0K8

Flores, E., Cicchetti, D., & Rogosch, F. A. (2005). Predictors of resilience in maltreated and nonmaltreated Latino children. *Developmental Psychology, 41,* 338–351. doi:10.1037/0012-1649.41.2.338

Fondacaro, M. R., & Weinberg, D. (2002). Concepts of social justice in community psychology: Toward a social ecological epistemology. *American Journal of Community Psychology, 30,* 473–492. doi:10.1023/A:1015803817117

Foubert, J. D. (2000). The longitudinal effects of a rape-prevention program on fraternity men's attitudes, behavioral intent, and behavior. *Journal of American College Health, 48,* 158–163.

Foubert, J. D., Tatum, J. L., Godin, E. E. (2010). First-year male students' perceptions of a rape prevention program seven months after their participation: Attitude and behavior changes. *Journal of College Student Development, 51,* 707–715. doi:10.1177/0886260511416480

Fraguela, J. A., Martin, A. L., & Trinanes, E. A. (2003). Drug-abuse prevention in the school: Four-year follow-up of a programme. *Psychology in Spain, 7,* 29–38.

Francis, P. C. (2003). Developing ethical institutional policies and procedures for working with suicidal students on a college campus. *Journal of College Counseling, 6,* 114–123. doi:10.1002/j.2161-1882.2003.tb00232.x

Fritz, M. S., MacKinnon, D. P., Williams, J., Goldberg, L., Moe, E. L., & Elliot, D. L. (2005). Analysis of baseline by treatment interactions in a drug prevention and health promotion program for high school male athletes. *Addictive Behaviors, 30,* 1001–1005. doi:10.1016/j.addbeh.2004.08.030

Frohlich, N. (2007). A very short history of distributive justice. *Social Justice Research, 20,* 250–262. doi:10.1007/s11211-007-0039-7

Galassi, J., & Akos, P. (2007). *Strengths-based counseling: Promoting student development and achievement*. Mahwah, NJ: Erlbaum.

Galavotti, C., Cabral, R. J., Lansky, A., Grimley, D. M., Riley, G. E., & Prochaska, J. O. (1995). Validation of measures of condom and other contraceptive use among women at high risk for HIV infection and unintended pregnancy. *Health Psychology, 14*, 570–578. doi:10.1037/0278-6133.14.6.570

Gallagher, N. L. (1999). *Breeding better Vermonters: The eugenics project in the Green Mountain State*. Hanover, NH: University Press of New England.

Garbarino, J. (1995). *Raising children in a socially toxic environment*. San Francisco, CA: Jossey-Bass.

Garbarino, J., & Bedard, C. (2001). *Parents under siege*. New York, NY: Free Press.

Garber, J., Clarke, G. N., Weersing, V. R., Beardslee, W. R., Brent, D. A., Gladstone, T. R. G., . . . Iyengar, S. (2009). Prevention of depression in at risk adolescents: A randomized controlled trial. *JAMA, 301*, 2215–2224. doi:10.1001/jama.2009.788

Garcia-Shelton, L. (2006). Meeting U.S. health care needs: A challenge to psychology. *Professional Psychology: Research and Practice, 37*, 676–682. doi:10.1037/0735-7028.37.6.676

Garrett Lee Smith Memorial Act of 2004, Pub. L. No. 108-355. 118 Stat 104. (2004).

Gensheimer, L. K., Ayers, T. S., & Roosa, M. W. (1993). School-based preventive interventions for at risk populations. *Evaluation and Program Planning, 16*, 159–167. doi:10.1016/0149-7189(93)90028-7

Gitterman, A., & Germain, C. B. (2008). *The life model of social work practice*. New York, NY: Columbia University Press.

Glider, P., Midyett, S. J., Mills-Novoa, B., Johannessen, K., & Collins, C. (2001). Challenging the collegiate rite of passage: A campus-wide social marketing media campaign to reduce binge drinking. *Journal of Drug Education, 31*, 207–220. doi:10.2190/U466-EPFG-Q76D-YHTQ

Goetzel, R. Z., & Ozminkowski, R. J. (2008). The health and cost benefits of work site health promotion programs. *Annual Review of Public Health, 29*, 303–323. doi:10.1146/annurev.publhealth.29.020907.090930

Goetzel, R. Z., Reynolds, K., Breslow, L., Roper, W. L., Shechter, D., Stapleton, D. C., . . . McGinnis, J. M. (2007). Health promotion in later life: It's never too late. *American Journal of Health Promotion, 21*, 1–5.

Goldberg, L., MacKinnon, D. P., Elliot, D. L., Moe, E. L., Clarke, G., & Cheong, J. W. (2000). The adolescent training and learning to avoid steroids program. *Archives of Pediatrics & Adolescent Medicine, 154*, 332–338. doi:10.1001/archpedi.154.4.332

Goodheart, C. D. (2011). Psychology practice: Design for tomorrow. *American Psychologist, 66*, 339–347. doi:10.1037/a0024222

Goodman, L. A., Liang, B., Helms, J. E., Latta, R. E., Sparks, E., & Weintraub, S. R. (2004). Training counseling psychologists as social justice agents: Feminist and multicultural principles in action. *The Counseling Psychologist, 32,* 793–836. doi:10.1177/0011000004268802

Gordon, R. (1987). An operational definition of disease prevention. In J. A. Sternberg & M. M. Silverman (Eds.), *Preventing mental disorders* (pp. 20–26). Rockville, MD: U.S. Department of Health and Human Services.

Greenberg, M. T., Weissberg, R. P., O'Brien, M. U., Zins, J. E., Fredericks, L., Resnik, H., & Elias, M. J. (2003). Enhancing school-based prevention and youth development through coordinated social, emotional, and academic learning. *American Psychologist, 58,* 466–474. doi:10.1037/0003-066X.58.6-7.466

Griffin, K. W., Botvin, G. J., & Nichols, T. R. (2006). Effects of a school-based drug abuse prevention program for adolescents on HIV risk behaviors in young adulthood. *Prevention Science, 7,* 103–112. doi:10.1007/s11121-006-0025-6

Griffin, K. W., Botvin, G. J., Nichols, T. R., & Doyle, M. M. (2003). Effectiveness of a universal drug abuse prevention approach for youth at high risk for substance use initiation. *Preventive Medicine, 36,* 1–7. doi:10.1006/pmed.2002.1133

Haas, A., Koestner, B., Rosenberg, J., Moore, D., Garlow, S. J., Sedway, J., . . . Nemeroff, C. B. (2008). An interactive web-based method of outreach to college students at risk for suicide. *Journal of American College Health, 57,* 15–22. doi:10.3200/JACH.57.1.15-22

Hack, M., Flannery, D. J., Schluchter, M., Cartar, L., Borawski, E., & Klein, N. (2002). Outcomes of young adulthood for very-low-birth-weight infants. *The New England Journal of Medicine, 346,* 149–157. doi:10.1056/NEJMoa010856

Hage, S. M., Barnett, S., & Schwartz, J. P. (2008). Youth development and prevention in the schools. In H. L. K. Coleman & C. Yeh (Eds.), *Handbook of school counseling* (pp. 381–396). New York, NY: Taylor & Francis.

Hage, S. M., & Kenny, M. (2009). Promoting a social justice approach to prevention: Future directions for training, practice, and research. *The Journal of Primary Prevention, 30,* 75–87. doi:10.1007/s10935-008-0165-5

Hage, S. M., Romano, J. L., Conyne, R. K., Kenny, M., Matthews, C., Schwartz, J. P., & Waldo, M. (2007). Best practice guidelines on prevention practice, research, training, and social advocacy for psychologists. *The Counseling Psychologist, 35,* 493–566. doi:10.1177/0011000006291411

Haines, D. J., Davis, L., Rancour, P., Robinson, M., Neel-Wilson, T., & Wagner, S. (2007). A pilot intervention to promote walking and wellness and to improve the health of college faculty and staff. *Journal of American College Health, 55,* 219–225. doi:10.3200/JACH.55.4.219-225

Hall, J. E., Simon, T. R., Mercy, J. A., Loeber, R., Farrington, D. P., & Lee, R. D. (2012). Centers for Disease Control and Prevention's Expert Panel on Prevention Factors for Youth Violence Perpetration: Background and overview. *American Journal of Preventive Medicine, 43*(Suppl. 1), 1–7. doi:10.1016/j.amepre.2012.04.026

Hammig, B. J., & Moranetz, C. A. (2000). Violent victimization: Perceptions and preventive behaviors among young adults. *American Journal of Health Behavior*, 24, 143–150.

Hane, A. (2013). *Prevention programs in community mental health organizations* (Unpublished master's thesis). Department of Educational Psychology, Counseling and Student Personnel Psychology Program, University of Minnesota, Minneapolis.

Harris Abadi, M. H., Shamblen, S. R., Thompson, K., Collins, D. A., & Johnson, K. (2011). Influence of risk and protective factors on substance use outcomes across developmental periods: A comparison of youth and young adults. *Substance Use & Misuse*, 46, 1604–1612. doi:10.3109/10826084.2011.598598

Harris, A. H. S., Thoresen, C. E., & Lopez, S. J. (2007). Integrating positive psychology into counseling: Why and (when appropriate) how. *Journal of Counseling & Development*, 85, 3–13. doi:10.1002/j.1556-6678.2007.tb00438.x

Harris, R., Good, R. S., & Pollack, L. (1982). Sexual behavior of oncologic cancer patients. *Archives of Sexual Behavior*, 11, 503–510. doi:10.1007/BF01542475

Harrison, J. A., Mullen, P. D., & Green, L. W. (1992). A meta-analysis of studies of the health belief model with adults. *Health Education Research*, 7, 107–116. doi:10.1093/her/7.1.107

Hausmann, L. R. M., Schofield, J. W., Woods, R. L. (2007). Sense of belonging as a predictor of intentions to persist among African American and White first-year college students. *Research in Higher Education*, 48, 803–839. doi:10.1007/s11162-007-9052-9

Hawkins, J. D., & Catalano, R. F. (1992). *Communities That Care: Action for drug abuse prevention*. San Francisco, CA: Jossey-Bass.

Hawkins, J. D., Catalano, R. F., & Miller, J. Y. (1992). Risk and protective factors for alcohol and other drug problems in adolescence and early adulthood: Implications for substance-abuse prevention. *Psychological Bulletin*, 112, 64–105. doi:10.1037/0033-2909.112.1.64

Hemingway, H., & Marmot, M. (1999). Evidence-based cardiology: Psychosocial factors in the aetiology and prognosis of coronary heart disease. Systematic review of prospective cohort studies. *BMJ*, 318, 1460–1467. doi:10.1136/bmj.318.7196.1460

Henry, D. B., Tolan, P. H., Gorman-Smith, D., & Schoeny, M. E. (2012). Risk and direct protective factors for youth violence: Results from the Centers for Disease Control and Prevention's multisite violence prevention project. *American Journal of Preventive Medicine*, 43(Suppl. 1), 67–75. doi:10.1016/j.amepre.2012.04.025

Heppner, P. P., Casas, J. M., Carter, J., & Stone, G. L. (2000). The maturation of counseling psychology: Multifaceted perspectives, 1978–1998. In S. D. Brown & R. W. Lent (Eds.), *Handbook of counseling psychology* (3rd ed., pp. 3–49). New York, NY: Wiley.

Heppner, P. P., Neal, G. W., & Larson, L. (1984). Problem-solving training as prevention with college students. *The Personnel and Guidance Journal, 62,* 514–519. doi:10.1111/j.2164-4918.1984.tb00266.x

Hermann, M. A., & Finn, A. (2002). An ethical and legal perspective on the role of school counselors in preventing violence in schools. *Professional School Counseling, 6,* 46–54.

Herzog, T. A. (2008). Analyzing the transtheoretical model using the framework of Weinstein, Rothman, and Sutton (1998): The example of smoking cessation. *Health Psychology, 27,* 548–556.

Hochbaum, G. M. (1958). *Public participation in medical screening programs: A sociopsychological study* (PHS Publication No. 572). Washington, DC: U.S. Government Printing Office.

Holden, E. W., & Black, M. M. (1999). Theory and concepts of prevention as applied to clinical psychology. *Clinical Psychology Review, 19,* 391–401. doi:10.1016/S0272-7358(98)00090-7

Holmes, C. L. (2009). An intergenerational program with benefits. *Early Childhood Education Journal, 37,* 113–119. doi:10.1007/s10643-009-0329-9

Honeycutt, A. A., Clayton, L. L., Khavjou, O., Finkelstein, E. A., Prabhu, M., Blitstein, J. L., . . . & Renaud, J. M. (2006). *Guide to analyzing the cost-effectiveness of community public health prevention approaches* (RTI Project No. 0208827.001). Research Triangle Park, NC: RTI International.

Hopko, D. R., Bell, J. L., Armento, M., Robertson, S., Mullane, C., Wolf, N., & Lejuez, C. W. (2008). Cognitive-behavior therapy for depressed cancer patients in a medical care setting. *Behavior Therapy, 39,* 126–136. doi:10.1016/j.beth.2007.05.007

Horowitz, M., Wilner, N., & Alvarez, W. (1979). Impact of Event Scale: A measure of subjective stress. *Psychosomatic Medicine, 41,* 209–218.

Hotz, V. J., & Scholz, J. K. (2001). *The earned income tax credit* (NBER Working Paper No. 807). Cambridge, MA: National Bureau of Economic Research. Retrieved from http://www.nber.org/papers/w8078

Humphries, M. L., & Keenan, K. E. (2006). Theoretical, developmental, and cultural orientations of school-based prevention programs for preschoolers. *Clinical Child and Family Psychology Review, 9,* 135–148. doi:10.1007/s10567-006-0005-1

Hunsley, J., Best, M., Lefebvre, M., & Vito, D. (2001). The seven-item short form of the dyadic adjustment scale: Further evidence for the construct validity. *The American Journal of Family Therapy, 29,* 325–335.

Individuals With Disabilities Act of 2004, Pub. L. No. 108-146, 118 Stat. 2647 (2004).

Ivey, A. E., Ivey, M. B., & Zalaquett, C. P. (2009). *Intentional interviewing and counseling: Facilitating client development in a multicultural society* (7th ed.). Belmont, CA: Brooks/Cole.

James, A. S., Campbell, M. K., & Hudson, M. A. (2002). Perceived barriers and bene-fits to colon cancer screening among African Americans in North Carolina: How does perception relate to screening behavior? *Cancer Epidemiology, Biomarkers & Prevention, 11*, 529–534.

James, S., Montgomery, S. B., Leslie, L. K., & Zhang, J. (2009). Sexual risk behaviors among youth in the child welfare system. *Children and Youth Services Review, 31*, 990–1000. doi:10.1016/j.childyouth.2009.04.014

Janz, N. K., & Becker, M. H. (1984). The health belief model: A decade later. *Health Education Quarterly, 11*, 1–47. doi:10.1177/109019818401100101

Janz, N. K., Champion, V. L., & Strecher, V. J. (2002). The health belief model. In K. Glanz, B. K. Rimer, & F. M. Lewis (Eds.), *Health behavior and health educa-tion: Theory, research, and practice* (pp. 45–66). San Francisco, CA: Jossey-Bass.

Janz, N. K., Wren, P. A., Schottenfeld, D., & Guire, K. E. (2003). Colorectal cancer screening attitudes and behavior: A population-based study. *Preventive Medicine, 37*, 627–634. doi:10.1016/j.ypmed.2003.09.016

Jason, L. A. (2012). Small wins matter in advocacy movements: Giving voice to patients. *American Journal of Community Psychology, 49*, 307–316. doi:10.1007/s10464-011-9457-7

Jensen, C. D., Cushing, C., Aylward, B. S., Craig, J. T., Sorell, D. M., & Steele, R. G. (2011). Effectiveness of Motivational Interviewing interventions for adolescent substance use behavior change: A meta-analytic review. *Journal of Consulting and Clinical Psychology, 79*, 433–440. doi:10.1037/a0023992

Jessor, R., Van Den Bos, J., Vanderryn, J., Costa, F. M., & Turbin, M. S. (1995). Protective factors in adolescent problem behavior: Moderator effects and developmental change. *Developmental Psychology, 31*, 923–933. doi:10.1037/0012-1649.31.6.923

Johannessen, K., Glider, P., Collins, C., Hueston, H., & DeJong, W. (2001). Pre-venting alcohol related problems at the University of Arizona's homecoming: An environmental management case study. *The American Journal of Drug and Alcohol Abuse, 27*, 587–597. doi:10.1081/ADA-100104520

Johnson, P., Nichols, C. N., Buboltz, C., & Riedesel, B. (2002). Assessing a holistic trait and factor approach to career development of college students. *Journal of College Counseling, 5*, 4–14. doi:10.1002/j.2161-1882.2002.tb00202.x

Johnson, S. B., & Millstein, S. G. (2003). Prevention opportunities in health care settings. *American Psychologist, 58*, 475–481. doi:10.1037/0003-066X.58.6-7.475

Julian, D. A., Ross, M., & Partridge, C. (2008). Challenges in supporting community implementation of science-based programs: A critical review of local partner-ships for success plans. *American Journal of Community Psychology, 41*, 351–360. doi:10.1007/s10464-008-9166-z

Juniper, K. C., Oman, R. F., Hamm, R. M., & Kerby, D. S. (2004). The relationships among constructs in the health belief model and the transtheoretical model among African American college women for physical activity. *American Journal of Health Promotion, 18,* 354–357. doi:10.4278/0890-1171-18.5.354

Jurkovic, G. J., Kuperminc, G., Perilla, J., Murphy, A., Ibáñez, G., & Casey, S. (2004). Ecological and ethical perspectives on filial responsibility: Implications for primary prevention with immigrant Latino adolescents. *The Journal of Primary Prevention, 25,* 81–104. doi:10.1023/B:JOPP.0000039940.99463.eb

Kanekar, A., & Sharma, M. (2010). Interventions for safer sex behaviors among college students. *American Journal of Health Studies, 25,* 138–148.

Kangas, M., Bovbjerg, D. H., & Montgomery, G. H. (2008). Cancer-related fatigue: A systematic and meta-analytic review of nonpharmacological therapies for cancer patients. *Psychological Bulletin, 134,* 700–741. doi:10.1037/a0012825

Kaponda, C. P. N., Dancy, B. L., Norr, K. F., Kachingwe, S. I., Mbeba, M. M., & Jere, D. L. (2007). Research brief: Community consultation to develop an acceptable and effective adolescent HIV prevention intervention. *Journal of the Association of Nurses in AIDS Care, 18,* 72–77. doi:10.1016/j.jana.2007.01.001

Kenny, M. E., & Hage, S. M. (2009). The next frontier: Prevention as an instrument of social justice. *The Journal of Primary Prevention, 30,* 1–10.

Kenny, M. E., Horne, A. M., Orpinas, P., & Reese, L. E. (Eds.). (2009a). *Realizing social justice: The challenge of preventive interventions.* Washington, DC: American Psychological Association. doi:10.1037/11870-000

Kenny, M. E., Horne, A. M., Orpinas, P., & Reese, L. E. (2009b). Social justice and the challenge of preventive interventions: An introduction. In M. E. Kenny, A. M. Horne, P. Orpinas, & L. E. Reese (Eds.), *Realizing social justice: The challenge of preventive interventions* (pp. 3–14). Washington, DC: American Psychological Association. doi:10.1037/11870-000

Kenny, M. E., & Medvide, M. B. (2013). Prevention in pursuit of social justice. In E. M. Vera (Ed.), *The Oxford handbook of prevention in counseling psychology* (pp. 125–140). New York, NY: Oxford University Press.

Kenny, M. E., & Romano, J. L. (2009). Promoting positive development and social justice: through prevention: A legacy for the future. In M. E. Kenny, A. M. Horne, P. Orpinas, & Reese, L. E. (Eds.), *Realizing social justice: The challenge of preventive interventions* (pp. 17–35). Washington, DC: American Psychological Association.

Kenny, M. E., Sparks, E., & Jackson, J. (2007). Striving for social justice through interprofessional university school collaboration. In E. Aldarondo (Ed.), *Advancing social justice through clinical practice* (pp. 313–335). Mahwah, NJ: Erlbaum.

Kessler, R. C., Demler, O., Frank, R. G., Olfson, M. D., Pincus, H. A., Walters, E. E., & Zaslavsky, A. M. (2005). Prevalence and treatment of mental disorders, 1990–2003. *The New England Journal of Medicine, 352,* 2515–2523. doi:10.1056/NEJMsa043266

Kiselica, M. S. (2004). When duty calls: The implications of social justice work for policy, education, and practice in the mental health professions. *The Counseling Psychologist, 32,* 838–854. doi:10.1177/0011000004269272

Klein, J. (2011, July 7). Time to ax public programs that don't yield results. *Time Magazine*. Retrieved from http://content.time.com/time/nation/article/0,8599,2081778,00.html

Kleist, D. M., & White, L. J. (1997). The values of counseling: A disparity between a philosophy of prevention in counseling and counselor practice and training. *Counseling and Values, 41*, 128–140. doi:10.1002/j.2161-007X.1997.tb00395.x

Kloeblen, A. S. (1999). Folate knowledge, intake from fortified grain products, and periconceptional supplementation patterns of a sample of low-income pregnant women according to the health belief model. *Journal of the American Dietetic Association, 99*, 33–38. doi:10.1016/S0002-8223(99)00011-5

Komro, K. A., Kelder, S. H., Perry, C. L., & Klepp, K.-I. (1993). Effects of a saliva pipeline procedure on adolescent self-reported smoking behavior and youth smoking prevention outcomes. *Preventive Medicine, 22*, 857–865.

Komro, K. A., Perry, C. L., Veblen-Mortenson, S., Bosma, L. M., Dudovitz, B. S., Williams, C. L., . . . Toomey, T. L. (2004). The adaptation of Project Northland for urban youth. *Journal of Pediatric Psychology, 29*, 457–466. doi:10.1093/jpepsy/jsh049

Komro, K. A., Perry, C. L., Williams, C. L., Stigler, M. H., Farbakhsh, K., & Veblen-Mortenson, S. (2001). How did Project Northland reduce alcohol use among young adolescents? Analysis of mediating variable. *Health Education Research, 16*, 59–70. doi:10.1093/her/16.1.59

Koniak-Griffin, D., Lesser, J., Nyamathi, A., Uman, G., Stein, J. A., & Cumberland, W. G. (2003). Project CHARM: An HIV prevention program for adolescent mothers. *Family & Community Health, 26*, 94–107. doi:10.1097/00003727-200304000-00003

Konnert, C., Gatz, M., & Hertzsprung Meyen, E. A. (1999). Preventive interventions for older adults. In M. Duffy (Ed.), *Handbook of counseling and psychotherapy with older adults* (pp. 314–334). New York, NY: Wiley.

Koocher, G. P. (2005). Following the money: Economic inhibitions of change affecting graduate education in clinical psychology. *Journal of Clinical Psychology, 61*, 1171–1174. doi:10.1002/jclp.20159

Kraaij, V., Arensman, E., & Spinhoven, P. (2002). Negative life events and depression in elderly persons: A meta-analysis. *Journal of Gerontology: Series B. Psychological Sciences and Social Sciences, 57*, 87–94. doi:10.1093/geronb/57.1.P87

Kraemer, K. L. (2007). The cost effectiveness and cost–benefit of screening and brief intervention for unhealthy alcohol use in medical settings. *Substance Abuse, 28*, 67–77. doi:10.1300/J465v28n03_07

Kuper, H., Marmot, M., & Hemingway, H. (2002). Systematic review of prospective cohort studies of psychosocial factors in the etiology and prognosis of coronary heart disease. *Seminars in Vascular Medicine, 2*, 267–314. doi:10.1055/s-2002-35401

LaBrie, J. W., Lamb, T. F., Pederson, E. R., & Quinlan, T. (2006). A group motivational interviewing intervention reduces drinking and alcohol-related consequences in adjudicated college students. *Journal of College Student Development, 47*, 267–280. doi:10.1353/csd.2006.0031

LaBrie, J. W., Pedersen, E., Lamb, T., & Quinlan, T. (2007). A campus-based motivational enhancement group intervention reduces problematic drinking in freshmen male college students. *Addictive Behaviors, 32*, 889–901. doi:10.1016/j.addbeh.2007.05.014

LaFromboise, T. (2006). American Indian youth suicide prevention. *Prevention Researcher, 13*, 16–18.

LaFromboise, T., & Howard-Pitney, B. (1995). The Zuni Life Skills Development curriculum: Description and evaluation of a suicide prevention program. *Journal of Counseling Psychology, 42*, 479–486.

LaFromboise, T., & Lewis, H. A. (2008). The Zuni Life Skills Development program: A school/community-based suicide prevention intervention. *Suicide and Life-Threatening Behavior, 38*, 343–353. doi:10.1521/suli.2008.38.3.343

LaFromboise, T. D., Medoff, L., Lee, C. C., & Harris, A. (2007). Psychosocial and cultural correlates of suicidal ideation among American Indian early adolescents on a Northern Plains reservation. *Research in Human Development, 4*, 119–143. doi:10.1080/15427600701481020

Lantz, P. M., Jacobson, P. D., Warner, K. E., Wasserman, J., Pollack, H. A., Berson, J., & Ahlstrom, A. (2000). Investing in youth tobacco control: A review of smoking prevention and control strategies. *Tobacco Control, 9*, 47–63. doi:10.1136/tc.9.1.47

Last, J. M., & Wallace, R. B. (Eds.). (1992). *Maxcy–Rosenau–Last public health and preventive medicine* (13th ed.). Norwalk, CT: Appleton and Lange.

Lazarus, R. S., & Folkman, S. (1984). *Stress appraisal and coping.* New York, NY: Springer.

LBJ Presidential Library. (2012). *The 1965 Medicare Amendment to the Social Security Act.* Retrieved from http://www.lbjlibrary.org/press/the-1965-medicare-amendment-to-the-social-security-act

Lead Contamination Control Act of 1988, Pub. L. No. 100-572, 102 Stat. 2884 (1988).

Lee, E. O. (2007). Mind–body–spirit practice and perceived self-efficacy for mental health promotion: An exploratory study. *International Journal of Mental Health Promotion, 9*, 35–47. doi:10.1080/14623730.2007.9721841

Lee, R. M. (2005). Resilience against discrimination: Ethnic identity and other-group orientation as protective factors for Korean Americans. *Journal of Counseling Psychology, 52*, 36–44. doi:10.1037/0022-0167.52.1.36

Lee, V. E., & Loeb, S. (1995). Where do Head Start attendees end up? One reason why preschool effects fade out. *Educational Evaluation and Policy Analysis, 17*, 62–82.

Levant, R. F., Tolan, P., & Dodgen, D. (2002). New directions in children's mental health: Psychology's role. *Professional Psychology: Research and Practice, 33*, 115–124. doi:10.1037/0735-7028.33.2.115

Lewis, M., & Lewis, J. (1981). Educating counselors for primary prevention. *Counselor Education and Supervision, 20*, 172–181. doi:10.1002/j.1556-6978.1981.tb01645.x

Li, C., Unger, J. B., Schuster, D., Rohrbach, L. A., Howard-Pitney, B., & Norman, G. (2003). Youths' exposure to environmental tobacco smoke (ETS): Associations with health beliefs and social pressure. *Addictive Behaviors, 28*, 39–53. doi:10.1016/S0306-4603(01)00215-5

Long, B. B. (1989). The Mental Health Association and prevention: A history. *Prevention in Human Services, 6*, 5–44.

Lonsway, K. A. (1996). Preventing acquaintance rape through education: What do we know? *Psychology of Women Quarterly, 20*, 229–265. doi:10.1111/j.1471-6402.1996.tb00469.x

Lopez, S. J., Hodges, T. D., & Harter, J. K. (2005). *Clifton StrengthsFinder technical report: Development and validation*. Omaha, NE: Gallup Organization.

Lopez, S. J., Magyar-Moe, J. L., Petersen, S. E., Ryder, J. A., Krieshok, T. S., O'Byrne, K. K., . . . Fry, N. A. (2006). Counseling psychology's focus on positive aspects of human functioning. *The Counseling Psychologist, 34*, 205–227. doi:10.1177/0011000005283393

Lopez, S. J., & Snyder, C. R. (Eds.). (2009). *Oxford handbook of positive psychology* (2nd ed.). New York, NY: Oxford University Press. doi:10.1093/oxfordhb/9780195187243.001.0001

Lösel, F., & Farrington, D. P. (2012). Direct protective and buffering protective factors in the development of youth violence. *American Journal of Preventive Medicine, 43*(Suppl. 1), 8–23. doi:10.1016/j.amepre.2012.04.029

Lothen-Kline, C., Howard, D. E., Hamburger, E. K., Worrell, K. D., & Boekeloo, B. O. (2003). Truth and consequences: Ethics, confidentiality, and disclosure in adolescent longitudinal prevention research. *Journal of Adolescent Health, 33*, 385–394. doi:10.1016/S1054-139X(03)00184-8

Lundahl, B., & Burke, B. L. (2009). The effectiveness and applicability of motivational interviewing: A practice-friendly review of four meta-analyses. *Journal of Clinical Psychology, 65*, 1232–1245. doi:10.1002/jclp.20638

Luthar, S. S., Cicchetti, D., & Becker, B. (2000). The construct of resilience: A critical evaluation and guidelines for future work. *Child Development, 71*, 543–562. doi:10.1111/1467-8624.00164

MacQueen, K. M., Karim, Q. A., & Sugarman, J. (2003). Ethics guidance for HIV prevention trials. *BMJ, 327*, 340. doi:10.1136/bmj.327.7410.340

Maguen, S., Armistead, L. P., & Kalichman, S. (2000). Predictors of HIV antibody testing among gay, lesbian, and bisexual youth. *Journal of Adolescent Health, 26*, 252–257. doi:10.1016/S1054-139X(99)00078-6

Marshall, J. W., Ruth, B. J., Sisco, S., Bethke, C., Piper, T. M., Cohen, M., & Bachman, S. (2011). Social work interest in prevention: A content analysis of the professional literature. *Social Work, 56*, 201–211. doi:10.1093/sw/56.3.201

Martins, R. K., & McNeil, D. W. (2009). Review of motivational interviewing in promoting health behavior. *Clinical Psychology Review, 29*, 283–293. doi:10.1016/j.cpr.2009.02.001

Matthews, C. R. (2012). Teaching prevention: Preparing the next generation of psychologists. In E. M. Vera (Ed.), *The Oxford handbook of prevention in counseling psychology* (pp. 76–90). New York, NY: Oxford University Press.

Matthews, C. R., & Skowron, E. A. (2004). Incorporating prevention in mental health counselor training. *Journal of Mental Health Counseling, 26*, 349–359.

McCullough, M. E., & Snyder, C. R. (2000). Classical sources of human strengths: Revisiting an old home and building a new one. *Journal of Social and Clinical Psychology, 19*, 1–10. doi:10.1521/jscp.2000.19.1.1

McDaniel, S. H., & Fogarty, C. T. (2009). What primary care has to offer the patient-centered medical home. *Professional Psychology: Research and Practice, 40*, 483–492. doi:10.1037/a0016751

McIntosh, J. M., Jason, L. A., Robinson, W. L., & Brzezinski, L. (2004). Mulitculturalism and primary prevention: Toward a new primary prevention culture. *The Journal of Primary Prevention, 25*, 1–15. doi:10.1023/B:JOPP.0000039936.64367.99

McNair, D. M., Lorr, M., & Droppleman, L. F. (1992). *POMS manual.* San Diego, CA: San Diego Education and Industrial Testing Services.

McPherson, T. L., Cook, R. F., Back, A. S., Hersch, R. K., & Hendrickson, A. (2006). A field test of a web-based substance abuse prevention training program for health promotion professionals. *American Journal of Health Promotion, 20*, 396–400. doi:10.4278/0890-1171-20.6.396

McWhirter, J. J., McWhirter, B. T., McWhirter, E. H., & McWhirter, R. J. (2007). *At-risk youth: A comprehensive response for counselors, teachers, psychologists, and human service professionals.* Belmont, CA: Thomson Brooks/Cole.

Mental Health Parity Act of 1996, Pub. L. No. 104-204, 110 Stat. 2874 (1997).

Mental Health Parity and Addiction Equity Act of 2008, Pub. L. No. 110-343, 122 Stat. 3765 (2008).

Michielsen, H. J., Van der Steeg, A. F., Roukema, J. A., & De Vries, J. (2007). Personality and fatigue in patients with benign or malignant breast disease. *Supportive Care in Cancer, 15*, 1067–1073. doi:10.1007/s00520-007-0222-2

Miller, A. M., & Champion, V. L. (1997). Attitudes about breast cancer and mammography: Racial, income, and educational differences. *Women & Health, 26*, 41–63. doi:10.1300/J013v26n01_04

Miller, T., & Hendrie, D. (2008). *Substance abuse prevention dollars and cents: A cost–benefit analysis* (DHHS Publication No. [SMA] 07-4298). Rockville, MD: Center for Substance Abuse Prevention, Substance Abuse and Mental Health Services Administration.

Miller, W. R., & Rollnick, S. (2002). *Motivational Interviewing* (2nd ed.). New York, NY: Guilford Press.

Miller, W. R., & Rose, G. S. (2009). Toward a theory of motivational interviewing. *American Psychologist, 64*, 527–537. doi:10.1037/a0016830

Mishara, B. L., & Weisstub, D. N. (2005). Ethical and legal issues in suicide research. *International Journal of Law and Psychiatry, 28*, 23–41. doi:10.1016/j.ijlp.2004.12.006

Mokdad, A. H., Bowman, B. A., Ford, E. S., Vinicor, F., Marks, J. S., & Koplan, J. P. (2001). The continuing epidemics of obesity and diabetes in the United States. *JAMA, 286*, 1195–1200. doi:10.1001/jama.286.10.1195

Montaño, D. E., & Kasprzyk, D. (2002). The theory of reasoned action and the theory of planned behavior. In K. Glanz, B. K. Rimer, & F. M. Lewis (Eds.), *Health behavior and health education: Theory, research, and practice* (pp. 67–98). San Francisco, CA: Jossey-Bass.

Montgomery, G. H., & Bovbjerg, D. H. (2001). Specific response expectancies predict anticipatory nausea during chemotherapy for breast cancer. *Journal of Consulting and Clinical Psychology, 69*, 831–835. doi:10.1037/0022-006X.69.5.831

Montgomery, G. H., Bovbjerg, D. H., Schnur, J. B., David, D., Goldfarb, A., Weltz, C. R., . . . Silverstein, J. H. (2007). A randomized clinical trial of a brief hypnosis intervention to control side effects in breast surgery patients. *Journal of the National Cancer Institute, 99*, 1304–1312. doi:10.1093/jnci/djm106

Montgomery, G. H., Kangas, M., David, D., Hallquist, M. N., Green, S., Bovbjerg, D. H., . . . Silverstein, J. H. (2009). Fatigue during breast cancer radiotherapy: An initial randomized study of cognitive–behavioral therapy plus hypnosis. *Health Psychology, 28*, 317–322. doi:10.1037/a0013582

Morrill, W. H., & Hurst, J. C. (1971). A preventative and developmental role for the college counselor. *The Counseling Psychologist, 2*, 90–95. doi:10.1177/001100007100200405

Morrill, W. H., Oetting, E. R., & Hurst, J. C. (1974). Dimensions of counselor functioning. *The Personnel and Guidance Journal, 52*, 354–359. doi:10.1002/j.2164-4918.1974.tb04041.x

Morrow, J. A., & Ackermann, M. E. (2012). Intention to persist and retention of first-year students: The importance of motivation and sense of belonging. *College Student Journal, 46*, 483–491.

Mosher, R. L., & Sprinthall, N. A. (1970). Psychological education in secondary schools: A program to promote individual and human development. *American Psychologist, 25*, 911–924. doi:10.1037/h0029914

Mrazek, P. J., & Haggerty, R. J. (Eds.). (1994). *Reducing risks for mental disorders: Frontiers for preventive intervention research.* Washington, DC: National Academy Press.

Murdaugh, C. L., & Insel, K. (2009). Problems with adherence in the elderly. In S. A. Shumaker, J. K. Ockene, & K. A. Riekert (Eds.), *The handbook of health behavior change* (pp. 499–518). New York, NY: Springer.

Murphy, C., Linehan, E., Reyner, J., Musser, P., & Taft, C. (2012). Moderators of response to motivational interviewing for partner-violent men. *Journal of Family Violence, 27,* 671–680. doi:10.1007/s10896-012-9460-2

Murphy, J. G., Dennhart, A. A., Skidmore, J. R., Borsari, B., Barnett, N. P., Colby, S. M., & Martens, M. P. (2012). A randomized controlled trial of a behavioral economic supplement to brief motivational interventions for college drinking. *Journal of Consulting and Clinical Psychology, 80,* 876–886. doi:10.1037/a0028763

Murray, C. E. (2005). Prevention work: A professional responsibility for marriage and family counselors. *The Family Journal, 13,* 27–34. doi:10.1177/1066480704269179

Myers, D. G. (2000). The funds, friends, and faith of happy people. *American Psychologist, 55,* 56–67. doi:10.1037/0003-066X.55.1.56

Naar-King, S., & Suarez, M. (2010). *Motivational interviewing with adolescents and young adults.* New York, NY: Guilford Press.

Nation, M., Crusto, C., Wandersman, A., Kumpfer, K. L., Seybolt, D., Morrissey-Kane, E., & Davino, K. (2003). What works in prevention: Principles of effective prevention programs. *American Psychologist, 58,* 449–456. doi:10.1037/0003-066X.58.6-7.449

National Commission for the Protection of Human Subjects of Biomedical and Behavioral Research. (1979). *The Belmont Report.* Retrieved from http://archive.hhs.gov/ohrp/humansubjects/guidance/belmont.htm

National Institute of Mental Health. (2007). *Suicide in the U.S.: Statistics and prevention* (NIH Publication No. 06-4504). Retrieved from http://www.nimh.nih.gov/health/publications/suicide-in-the-us-statistics-and-prevention/index.shtml#adults

National Prevention Council. (2011). *National prevention strategy,* Washington, DC: U.S. Department of Health and Human Services, Office of the Surgeon General. Retrieved from http://www.surgeongeneral.gov/initiatives/prevention/strategy/report.pdf

National Research Council and Institute of Medicine. (2009). *Preventing mental, emotional, and behavioral disorders among young people: Progress and possibilities.* Washington, DC: National Academies Press.

Nelson, G., & Prilleltensky, I. (2005). *Community psychology: In pursuit of liberation and well-being.* New York, NY: Palgrave Macmillan.

O'Byrne, K. K., Brammer, S. K., Davidson, M. M., & Poston, W. S. C. (2002). Primary prevention in counseling psychology: Back to the future. *The Counseling Psychologist, 30,* 330–344. doi:10.1177/0011000002302010

O'Connor, R. C., & Armitage, C. J. (2003). Theory of planned behavior and parasuicide: An exploratory study. *Current Psychology, 22,* 196–205. doi:10.1007/s12144-003-1016-4

Oswalt, S. B., Shutt, M. D., English, E., & Little, S. D. (2007). Did it work? Examining the impact of an alcohol intervention on sanctioned college students. *Journal of College Student Development, 48,* 543–557. doi:10.1353/csd.2007.0056

Out, J. W., & Lafreniere, K. D. (2001). Baby think it over: Using role-play to prevent teen pregnancy. *Adolescence, 36*, 571–582.

Oyama, H., Koida, J., & Kudo, K. (2004). Community-based prevention for suicide in elderly by depression screening and follow-up. *Community Mental Health Journal, 40*, 249–263. doi:10.1023/B:COMH.0000026998.29212.17

Pagoto, S. L., Kantor, L., Bodenlos, J. S., Gitkind, M., & Ma, Y. (2008). Translating the diabetes prevention program into a hospital-based weight loss program. *Health Psychology, 27* (Suppl. 1), 91–98. doi:10.1037/0278-6133.27.1.S91

Painter, J. E., Borba, C., Hynes, M., Mays, D., & Glanz, K. (2008). The use of theory in health behavior research from 2000–2005: A systematic review. *Annals of Behavioral Medicine, 35*, 358–362. doi:10.1007/s12160-008-9042-y

Park, N., & Peterson, C. (2005). The Values in Action Inventory of Character Strengths for Youth. In K. A. Moore & L. H. Lippman (Eds.), *What do children need to flourish? Conceptualizing and measuring indicators of positive development* (pp. 13–23). New York, NY: Springer. doi:10.1007/0-387-23823-9_2

Parker, G., Hawkins, J., Weigel, C., Fanning, L., Round, T., & Reyna, K. (2009). Adolescent suicide prevention: The Oklahoma community reaches out. *Journal of Continuing Education in Nursing, 40*, 177–180. doi:10.3928/00220124-20090401-08

Parsons, F. (1909). *Choosing a vocation.* Boston, MA: Houghton-Mifflin.

Pasco, S., Wallack, C., Sartin, R. M., & Dayton, R. (2012). The impact of experiential exercises on communication and relational skills in a suicide prevention gatekeeper-training program for college resident advisers. *Journal of American College Health, 60*, 134–140. doi:10.1080/07448481.2011.623489

Patient Protection and Affordable Care Act of 2010, Pub. L. No. 111-148, 124 Stat. 119 (2010).

Pearson, J. L. (2000/2001). Preventing late life suicide: National Institutes for Health initiatives. *Omega: Journal of Death and Dying, 42*, 9–20. doi:10.2190/FMRG-87W0-YXDK-6EFY

Pearson, J. L., & Brown, G. K. (2000). Suicide prevention in late life: Directions for science and practice. *Clinical Psychology Review, 20*, 685–705. doi:10.1016/S0272-7358(99)00066-5

Perry, C. L., Williams, C. L., Veblen-Mortenson, S., Toomey, T. L., Komro, K. A., Anstine, P. S., . . . Wolfson, M. (1996). Project Northland: Outcomes of a community wide alcohol use prevention program during early adolescence. *American Journal of Public Health, 86*, 956–965. doi:10.2105/AJPH.86.7.956

Perry, M. J., Albee, G. W., Bloom, M., & Gullotta, T. P. (1996). Training and career paths in primary prevention. *The Journal of Primary Prevention, 16*, 357–371. doi:10.1007/BF02411741

Peters, R. D., Bradshaw, A. J., Petrunka, K., Nelson, G., Herry, Y., Craig, W. M., . . . Rossiter, M. D. (2010). The "Better Beginnings, Better Futures" ecological, community-based early childhood prevention project: Findings from grade 3 to grade 9. *Monographs of the Society for Research in Child Development, 75*, 1–174.

Peters, R. D., Petrunka, K., & Arnold, R. (2003). The Better Beginnings, Better Futures Project: A universal, comprehensive, community-based prevention approach for primary school children and their families. *Journal of Clinical Child and Adolescent Psychology, 32,* 215–227. doi:10.1207/S15374424JCCP3202_6

Peterson, C., & Park, N. (2009). Classifying and measuring strengths of character. In C. R. Snyder & S. J. Lopez (Eds.), *Oxford handbook of positive psychology* (2nd ed., pp. 25–33). New York, NY: Oxford University Press.

Peterson, C., Park, N., & Seligman, M. E. P. (2005). Orientation to happiness and life satisfaction: The full life versus the empty life. *Journal of Happiness Studies, 6,* 25–41. doi:10.1007/s10902-004-1278-z

Peterson, C., & Seligman, M. E. P. (2004). *Character strengths and virtues: A handbook and classification.* Washington, DC: American Psychological Association.

Piaget, J., & Inhelder, B. (1969). *The psychology of the child.* New York, NY: Basic Books.

Pierce, K., Carter, C., Weinfeld, M., Desmond, J., Hazin, R., Bjork, R., & Gallagher, N. (2011). Detecting, studying, and treating autism early: The one-year well-baby check-up approach. *Journal of Pediatrics, 159,* 458–465.e6.

Pieterse, A. L., Hanus, A. E., & Gale, M. M. (2013). Advocacy and prevention: Dismantling systems of oppression. In E. M. Vera (Ed.), *The Oxford handbook of prevention in counseling psychology* (pp. 109–124). New York, NY: Oxford University Press.

Pischke, C. R., Scherwitz, L., Weidner, G., & Ornish, D. (2008). Long-term effects of lifestyle changes on well-being and cardiac variables among coronary heart disease patients. *Health Psychology, 27,* 584–592. doi:10.1037/0278-6133.27.5.584

Pope, K. S. (1990). Identifying and implementing ethical standards for primary prevention. *Prevention in Human Services, 8,* 43–64. doi:10.1300/J293v08n02_04

Poss, J. E. (2001). Developing a new model for cross-cultural research: Synthesizing the health belief model and the theory of reasoned action. *ANS: Advances in Nursing Science, 23,* 1–15. doi:10.1097/00012272-200106000-00002

Price-Evans, K., & Treasure, J. (2011). The use of motivational interviewing in anorexia nervosa. *Child and Adolescent Mental Health, 16,* 65–70. doi:10.1111/j.1475-3588.2011.00595.x

Prilleltensky, I. (2001). Value-based praxis in community psychology: Moving toward social justice and social action. *American Journal of Community Psychology, 29,* 747–778. doi:10.1023/A:1010417201918

Prilleltensky, I., & Nelson, G. (2013). Critical psychology, prevention, and social justice. In E. M. Vera (Ed.), *The Oxford handbook of prevention in counseling psychology* (pp. 141–159). New York, NY: Oxford University Press.

Prochaska, J. O., DiClemente, C. C., & Norcross, J. C. (1992). In search of how people change: Applications to addictive behaviors. *American Psychologist, 47,* 1102–1114. doi:10.1037/0003-066X.47.9.1102

Prochaska, J. O., Evers, K. E., Prochaska, J. M., Van Marter, D., & Johnson, J. L. (2007). Efficacy and effectiveness trials: Examples from smoking cessation and bullying prevention. *Journal of Health Psychology, 12*, 170–178. doi:10.1177/1359105307071751

Prochaska, J. O., Johnson, S., & Lee, P. (2009). The transtheoretical model of behavior change. In S. A. Shumaker, J. K. Ockene, & K. A. Riekert (Eds.), *The handbook of behavior change* (3rd ed., pp. 59–83). New York, NY: Springer.

Quigley, D. (2006). A review of improved ethical practices in environmental and public health research: Case examples from Native communities. *Health Education & Behavior, 33*, 130–147. doi:10.1177/1090198104272053

Ramirez, A., Bravo, J. M., & Katsikas, S. (2005). Infant feeding decisions and practices in the U.S. and Colombia. *Journal of Prenatal & Perinatal Psychology & Health, 19*, 237–249.

Randell, B. P., Eggert, L. L., & Pike, K. C. (2001). Immediate postintervention effects of two brief suicide prevention interventions. *Suicide and Life-Threatening Behavior, 31*, 41–61. doi:10.1521/suli.31.1.41.21308

Rawls, J. (1971). *A theory of justice.* Cambridge, MA: Harvard University Press.

Redd, W. H., Montgomery, G. H., & DuHamel, K. N. (2001). Behavioral intervention for cancer treatment side effects. *Journal of the National Cancer Institute, 93*, 810–823. doi:10.1093/jnci/93.11.810

Reese, L. E., & Vera, E. M. (2007). Culturally relevant prevention: The scientific and practical considerations of community-based programs. *The Counseling Psychologist, 35*, 763–778. doi:10.1177/0011000007304588

Reid, M. J., Webster-Stratton, C., & Baydar, N. (2004). Halting the development of conduct problems in Head Start children: The effects of parent training. *Journal of Clinical & Adolescent Psychology, 33*, 279–291. doi:10.1207/s15374424 jccp3302_10

Reid, M. J., Webster-Stratton, C., & Hammond, M. (2007). Enhancing a classroom social competence and problem-solving curriculum by offering parent training to families of moderate to high-risk elementary school children. *Journal of Clinical Child and Adolescent Psychology, 36*, 605–620. doi:10.1080/15374410701662741

Reijneveld, S. A., Westhoff, M. H., & Hopman-Rock, M. (2003). Promotion of health and physical activity improves the mental health of elderly immigrants: Results of a group randomized controlled trial among Turkish immigrants in the Netherlands aged 45 and over. *Journal of Epidemiology and Community Health, 57*, 405–411. doi:10.1136/jech.57.6.405

Reisch, M., & Andrews, J. (2002). *The road not taken: A history of radical social work in the United States.* New York, NY: Brunner-Routledge.

Reivich, K. J., Seligman, M. E. P., & McBride, S. (2011). Master resiliency training in the U.S. Army. *American Psychologist, 66*, 25–34. doi:10.1037/a0021897

Resnick, B., Galik, E., Nahm, E. S., Shaughnessy, M., & Michael, K. (2009). Optimizing adherence in older adults with cognitive impairment. In S. A. Shumaker, J. K. Ockene, & K. A. Riekert (Eds.), *The handbook of health behavior change* (pp. 519–544). New York, NY: Springer.

Reynolds, A. J. (1994). Effects of a preschool plus follow-on intervention for children at risk. *Developmental Psychology, 30,* 787–804. doi:10.1037/0012-1649.30.6.787

Reynolds, A. J., Rolnick, A. J., Englund, M. M., & Temple, J. A. (Eds.). (2010). *Childhood programs and practices in the first decade of life: A human capital integration.* New York, NY: Cambridge University Press. doi:10.1017/CBO9780511762666

Reynolds, A. J., Temple, J. A., White, B. A. B., Ou, S., & Robertson, D. L. (2011). Age 26 cost–benefit analysis of the Child–Parent Center Early Education Program. *Child Development, 82,* 379–404. doi:10.1111/j.1467-8624.2010.01563.x

Reynolds, C. F. (2009). Prevention of depressive disorders: A brave new world. *Depression and Anxiety, 26,* 1062–1065. doi:10.1002/da.20644

Reynolds, C. F., Cuijpers, P., Patel, V., Cohen, A., Dias, A., Chowdhary, N., . . . Albert, S. M. (2012). Early intervention to reduce the global health and economic burden of major depression in older adults. *Annual Review of Public Health, 33,* 123–135. doi:10.1146/annurev-publhealth-031811-124544

Rickards, A. L., Kelly, E. A., Doyle, L. W., & Callanan, C. (2001). Cognitive, academic progress, behavior, and self-concept at 14 years of very low birth weight children. *Journal of Developmental and Behavioral Pediatrics, 22,* 11–18. doi:10.1097/00004703-200102000-00002

Rickel, A. U. (1987). The 1965 Swampscott Conference and future topics for community psychology. *American Journal of Community Psychology, 15,* 511–513. doi:10.1007/BF00929903

Ripple, C. H., & Zigler, E. (2003). Research, policy, and the federal role in prevention initiatives for children. *American Psychologist, 58,* 482–490. doi:10.1037/0003-066X.58.6-7.482

Rivera-Mosquera, E., Phillips, J. C., Castelino, P., Martin, J. K., & Dobran, E. S. M. (2007). Design and implementation of a grassroots precollege program for Latino youth. *The Counseling Psychologist, 35,* 821–839. doi:10.1177/0011000007304593

Robitschek, C., & Woodson, S. J. (2006). Vocational psychology: Using one of counseling psychology's strengths to foster human strength. *The Counseling Psychologist, 34,* 260–275. doi:10.1177/0011000005281321

Rogers, C. R. (1951). *Client-centered therapy.* Boston, MA: Houghton-Mifflin.

Rogers, E. M. (2003). *Diffusion of innovations* (5th ed.). New York, NY: Free Press.

Romano, J. L. (1984). Stress management and wellness: Reaching beyond the counselor's office. *The Personnel and Guidance Journal, 62,* 533–537. doi:10.1111/j.2164-4918.1984.tb00270.x

Romano, J. L. (1996). School personnel prevention training: A measure of self-efficacy. *Journal of Educational Research, 90,* 57–63.

Romano, J. L. (1997). School personnel training for the prevention of tobacco, alcohol, and other drug use: Issues and outcomes. *Journal of Drug Education, 27,* 245–258. doi:10.2190/HYEW-1EEJ-74PD-P1E3

Romano, J. L., & Hage, S. M. (2000a). Prevention: A call to action. *The Counseling Psychologist, 28,* 854–856. doi:10.1177/0011000000286007

Romano, J. L., & Hage, S. M. (2000b). Prevention and counseling psychology: Revitalizing commitments for the 21st century. *The Counseling Psychologist, 28,* 733–763. doi:10.1177/0011000000286001

Romano, J. L., & Netland, J. D. (2008). The application of the theory of reasoned action and planned behavior to prevention science in counseling psychology. *The Counseling Psychologist, 36,* 777–806. doi:10.1177/0011000007301670

Rosenstock, I. M. (1974). Historical origins of the health belief model. *Health Education Monographs, 2,* 328–335.

Rosenstock, I. M., Strecher, V. J., & Becker, M. H. (1988). Social learning theory and the health belief model. *Health Education Quarterly, 15,* 175–183. doi:10.1177/109019818801500203

Rosenthal, M. S., Ross, J. S., Bilodeau, R., Richter, R. S., Palley, J. E., & Bradley, E. H. (2009). Economic evaluation of a comprehensive teenage pregnancy prevention program. *American Journal of Preventive Medicine, 37,* S280–S287. doi:10.1016/j.amepre.2009.08.014

Rothman, E., & Silverman, J. (2007). The effect of a college sexual assault prevention program on first-year students' victimization rates. *Journal of American College Health, 55,* 283–290. doi:10.1177/0886260510362884

Ruger, J. P., & Emmons, K. M. (2008). Economic evaluations of smoking cessation and relapse prevention programs for pregnant women: A systematic review. *Value in Health, 11,* 180–190. doi:10.1111/j.1524-4733.2007.00239.x

Saltz, R. F. (2011). Environmental approaches to prevention in college settings. *Alcohol Research & Health, 34,* 204–209.

Sandler, I., & Chassin, L. (1993). From research to implementation in the teaching of prevention: A postdoctoral training program. *Teaching of Psychology, 20,* 144–148. doi:10.1207/s15328023top2003_3

Sandy, S. V., & Boardman, S. K. (2000). The peaceful kids conflict resolution program. *International Journal of Conflict Management, 11,* 337–357. doi:10.1108/eb022845

Sari, N., de Castro, S., Newman, F. L., & Mills, G. (2008). Should we invest in suicide prevention programs? *Journal of Socio-Economics, 37,* 262–275. doi:10.1016/j.socec.2006.12.029

Saxe, L., Kadushin, C., Tighe, E., Beveridge, A. A., Livert, D., Brodsky, A., & Rindskopf, D. (2006). Community-based prevention programs in the war on drugs: Findings from the "Fighting Back" demonstration. *Journal of Drug Issues, 36,* 263–294. doi:10.1177/002204260603600202

Schinke, S. P. (1994). Prevention science and practice: An agenda for action. *The Journal of Primary Prevention, 15,* 45–57. doi:10.1007/BF02196346

Schmidt, J. J. (2008). History of school counseling. In H. L. K. Coleman & C. Yeh (Eds.), *Handbook of school counseling* (pp. 3–13). New York, NY: Routledge.

Schwartz, J. P., & Hage, S. M. (2009). Prevention: Ethics, responsibility, and commitment to public well-being. In M. E. Kenny, A. M. Horne, P. Orpinas, & L. E. Reese (Eds.), *Realizing social justice: The challenge of preventive interventions* (pp. 123–140). Washington, DC: American Psychological Association. doi:10.1037/11870-006

Schwartz, J. P., Hage, S. M., & González, D. M. (2013). Ethical principles for the practice of prevention. In E. M. Vera (Ed.), *The Oxford handbook of prevention in counseling psychology* (pp. 65–75). New York, NY: Oxford University Press.

Schweinhart, L. J., & Weikart, D. P. (1997). The High/Scope preschool curriculum comparison study through age 23. *Early Childhood Research Quarterly, 12,* 117–143. doi:10.1016/S0885-2006(97)90009-0

Schweinhart, L. J., & Weikart, D. P. (1999). The advantages of High/Scope: Helping children lead successful lives. *Educational Leadership, 57,* 76, 78.

Seal, K. H., Abadjian, L., McCamish, N., Shi, Y., Tarasovsky, G., & Weingardt, K. (2012). A randomized controlled trial of telephone motivational interviewing to enhance mental health treatment engagement in Iraq and Afghanistan veterans. *General Hospital Psychiatry, 34,* 450–459. doi:10.1016/j.genhosppsych.2012.04.007

Search Institute. (n.d.). *About Search Institute.* Retrieved from http://www.search-institute.org/about

Seligman, M. E. P., & Csikszentmihalyi, M. (2000). Positive psychology: An introduction. *American Psychologist, 55,* 5–14. doi:10.1037/0003-066X.55.1.5

Seligman, M. E. P., Schulman, P., DeRubeis, R. J., & Hollon, S. D. (1999). The prevention of depression and anxiety. *Prevention and Treatment, 2.* doi:10.1037/1522-3736.2.1.28a

Seligman, M. E. P., Schulman, P., & Tryon, A. M. (2007). Group prevention of depression and anxiety symptoms. *Behaviour Research and Therapy, 45,* 1111–1126. doi:10.1016/j.brat.2006.09.010

Seligman, M. E. P., Steen, T. A., Park, N., & Peterson, C. (2005). Positive psychology progress: Empirical validation of interventions. *American Psychologist, 60,* 410–421. doi:10.1037/0003-066X.60.5.410

Sheridan, S. M., & D'Amato, R. C. (2004). Partnering to chart our futures: *School Psychology Review* and *School Psychology Quarterly* combined issue on the multisite conference on the future of school psychology. *School Psychology Review, 33,* 7–11. doi:10.1002/pits.10134

Shin, R. Q., & Kendall, M. A. (2013). Dropout prevention: A (re)conceptualization through the lens of social justice. In E. M. Vera (Ed.), *The Oxford handbook of prevention in counseling psychology* (pp. 213–225). New York, NY: Oxford University Press.

Shore, N. (2006). Re-conceptualizing *The Belmont Report*: A community-based participatory research perspective. *Journal of Community Practice, 14*, 5–26. doi:10.1300/J125v14n04_02

Simonton, D. K. (2000). Creativity: Cognitive, personal, development, and social aspects. *American Psychologist, 55*, 151–158. doi:10.1037/0003-066X.55.1.151

Sims, J. M. (2010). A brief review of *The Belmont Report. Dimensions of Critical Care, 29*, 173–174.

Smit, F., Ederveen, A., Cuijpers, P., Deeg, D., & Beekman, A. (2006). Opportunities for cost-effective prevention of late-life depression. *Archives of General Psychiatry, 63*, 290–296. doi:10.1001/archpsyc.63.3.290

Smith, E. J. (2006). The strength-based counseling model. *The Counseling Psychologist, 34*, 13–79. doi:10.1177/0011000005277018

Snyder, C. R., & Elliott, T. R. (2005). Twenty-first century graduate education in clinical psychology: A four level matrix model. *Journal of Clinical Psychology, 61*, 1033–1054. doi:10.1002/jclp.20164

Snyder, C. R., & Lopez, S. J. (2007). *Positive psychology: The scientific and practical explorations of human strengths.* Thousand Oaks, CA: Sage.

Society for Community Research and Action. (n.d.). *About SCRA*. Retrieved from http://www.scra27.org/about

Spaulding, J., & Balch, P. (1983). A brief history of primary prevention in the twentieth century: 1908–1980. *American Journal of Community Psychology, 11*, 59–80. doi:10.1007/BF00898419

Spoth, R. L., Guyll, M., & Day, S. X. (2002). Universal family-focused interventions in alcohol-use disorder prevention: Cost-effectiveness and cost–benefit analyses of two interventions. *Journal of Studies on Alcohol, 63*, 219–228.

Spoth, R. L., Kavanagh, K. A., & Dishion, T. J. (2002). Family-centered preventive intervention science: Toward benefits to larger populations of children, youth, and families. *Prevention Science, 3*, 145–152. doi:10.1023/A:1019924615322

Spoth, R. L., Randall, G., Trudeau, L., Shin, C., & Redmond, C. (2008). Substance use outcome 5½ years past baseline for partnership-based, family–school preventive interventions. *Drug and Alcohol Dependence, 96*, 57–68. doi:10.1016/j.drugalcdep.2008.01.023

Spoth, R., & Redmond, C. (1995). Parent motivation to enroll in parenting skills programs: A model of family context and health belief predictors. *Journal of Family Psychology, 9*, 294–310. doi:10.1037/0893-3200.9.3.294

Stark, J. (2013, February 7). For mental health risks, depts. work together. *Minnesota Daily*, 1, 4.

State Charities Aid Association. (1910, December). Proceedings of a meeting on the prevention of insanity.

Stetson, B. A., Carrico, A. R., Beacham, A. O., Ziegler, C. H., & Mokshagundam, S. P. (2006). Feasibility of a pilot intervention targeting self-care behaviors in adults with diabetes mellitus. *Journal of Clinical Psychology in Medical Settings, 13*, 239–249. doi:10.1007/s10880-006-9034-7

Stice, E., Rohde, P., Shaw, H., & Marti, C. N. (2013). Efficacy trial of a selective prevention program targeting both eating disorders and obesity among female college students: 1- and 2-year follow-up effects. *Journal of Consulting and Clinical Psychology, 81*, 183–189. doi:10.1037/a0031235

Stice, E., Shaw, H., & Marti, C. N. (2007). A meta-analytic review of eating disorder prevention programs: Encouraging findings. *Annual Review of Clinical Psychology, 3*, 207–231. doi:10.1146/annurev.clinpsy.3.022806.091447

Stone, A. L., Becker, L. G., Huber, A. M., & Catalano, R. F. (2012). Review of risk and protective factors of substance use and problem use in emerging adulthood. *Addictive Behaviors, 37*, 747–775. doi:10.1016/j.addbeh.2012.02.014

Stone, D. M., Barber, C. W., & Potter, L. (2005). Public health training on-line: The National Center for Suicide Prevention Training. *American Journal of Preventive Medicine, 29*, 247–251. doi:10.1016/j.amepre.2005.08.019

Strait, G. G., Smith, B. H., McQuillin, S., Terry, J., Swan, S., & Malone, P. S. (2012). A Randomized trial of motivational interviewing to improve middle school students' academic performance. *Journal of Community Psychology, 40*, 1032–1039. doi:10.1002/jcop.21511

Styfco, S., & Zigler, E. (2003). Early childhood programs for a new century. In A. Reynolds & M. Wang (Eds.), *The federal commitment to preschool education: Lessons from and for Head Start* (pp. 3–33). Washington, DC: Child Welfare League of America, Inc.

Substance Abuse and Mental Health Services Administration. (2010). *Focus on prevention* (DHHS Publication No. [SMA] 10-4120). Rockville, MD: Author.

Substance Abuse and Mental Health Services Administration. (2011). *Leading change: A plan for SAMHSA's roles and actions 2011–2014 Executive summary and introduction* (DHHS Publication No. [SMA] 11-4629 Summary). Rockville, MD: Author.

Sue, D. W., Arredondo, P., & McDavis, R. J. (1992). Multicultural counseling competencies and standards: A call to the profession. *Journal of Counseling & Development, 70*, 477–486. doi:10.1002/j.1556-6676.1992.tb01642.x

Sutton, S., McVey, D., & Glarz, A. (1999). A comparative test of the theory of reasoned action and the theory of planned behavior in the prediction of condom use intentions in a national sample of English young people. *Health Psychology, 18*, 72–81. doi:10.1037/0278-6133.18.1.72

Swisher, J. D., Scherer, J., & Yin, R. K. (2004). Cost–benefit estimates in prevention research. *The Journal of Primary Prevention, 25*, 137–148. doi:10.1023/B:JOPP.0000042386.32377.c0

Takahashi, L. M., Candelario, J., Young, T., & Mediano, E. (2007). Building capacity for HIV/AIDS prevention among Asian Pacific Islander organizations: The experience of a culturally appropriate capacity-building program in Southern California. *Journal of Public Health Management Practice* (Suppl. 1), 55–63.

Taleff, M. J., & Neal, A. (2000). An ethical code for AOD faculty: A proposed set of guidelines. *Journal of Drug Education, 30*, 157–170. doi:10.2190/63JV-YYVK-3PFR-ML0M

Taveras, E. M., Sobol, A. M., Hannon, C., Finkelstein, D., Wiecha, J., & Gortmaker, S. L. (2007). Youths' perceptions of overweight-related prevention counseling at a primary care visit. *Obesity*, *15*, 831–836. doi:10.1038/oby.2007.594

Taylor, T. K., Webster-Stratton, C., Feil, E. G., Broadbent, B., Widdop, C. S., & Severson, H. H. (2008). Computer-based intervention with coaching: An example using the Incredible Years program. *Cognitive Behaviour Therapy*, *37*, 233–246. doi:10.1080/16506070802364511

Tebes, J. K., Kaufman, J. S., & Chinman, M. J. (2002). Teaching about prevention in mental health professions. In L. A. Jason & D. S. Glenwick (Eds.), *Innovative strategies for promoting health and mental health across the life span* (pp. 37–60). New York, NY: Springer.

Thato, S., Charron-Prochownik, D., Dorn, L. D., Albrecht, S. A., & Stone, C. A. (2003). Predictors of condom use among adolescent Thai vocational students. *Journal of Nursing Scholarship*, *35*, 157–163. doi:10.1111/j.1547-5069.2003.00157.x

Thompson, D. R., Chair, S. Y., Chan, S. W., Astin, F., Davidson, P. M., & Ski, C. F. (2011). Motivational interviewing: A useful approach to improving cardiovascular health. *Journal of Clinical Nursing*, *20*, 1236–1244. doi:10.1111/j.1365-2702.2010.03558.x

Thompson, E. A., & Eggert, L. L. (1999). Using the suicide risk screen to identify suicidal adolescents among potential high school dropouts. *Journal of the American Academy of Child & Adolescent Psychiatry*, *38*, 1506–1514. doi:10.1097/00004583-199912000-00011

Thompson, E. A., Eggert, L. L., Randell, B. P., & Pike, K. C. (2001). Evaluation of indicated suicide risk prevention approaches for potential high school dropouts. *American Journal of Public Health*, *91*, 742–752. doi:10.2105/AJPH.91.5.742

Thompson, E. A., Mazza, J. J., Herting, J. R., Randell, B. P., & Eggert, L. L. (2005). The mediating roles of anxiety, depression, and hopelessness on adolescent suicide behaviors. *Suicide and Life-Threatening Behavior*, *35*, 14–34. doi:10.1521/suli.35.1.14.59266

Thompson, E. A., Moody, K., & Eggert, L. L. (1994). Discriminating suicide ideation among high-risk youth. *The Journal of School Health*, *64*, 361–367. doi:10.1111/j.1746-1561.1994.tb06205.x

Thompson, M. N., & Phillips, J. C. (2013). Promoting college retention in first-generation college students. In E. M. Vera (Ed.), *The Oxford handbook of prevention in counseling psychology* (pp. 330–346). New York, NY: Oxford University Press.

Title IX of the Education Amendments of 1972, Pub. L. No. 92-318, 86 Stat. 373 (1972).

Tovian, S. M. (2004). Health services and health care economics: The health psychology marketplace. *Health Psychology*, *23*, 138–141. doi:10.1037/0278-6133.23.2.138

Townsend, S. M., & Campbell, R. (2008). Identifying common practices in community-based rape prevention programs. *Journal of Prevention & Intervention in the Community, 36,* 121–135. doi:10.1080/10852350802022399

Traube, D. E., James, S., Zhang, J., & Landsverk, J. (2012). A national study of risk and protective factors for substance use among youth in the child welfare system. *Addictive Behaviors, 37,* 641–650. doi:10.1016/j.addbeh.2012.01.015

Trickett, E. J. (1992). Prevention ethics: Explicating the context of prevention activities. *Ethics and Behavior, 2,* 91–100. doi:10.1207/s15327019eb0202_2

Trickett, E. J. (2007). George Albee and the nurturing spirit of primary prevention. *The Journal of Primary Prevention, 28,* 61–64. doi:10.1007/s10935-006-0072-6

Tucker, C. M., Ferdinand, L. A., Mirsu-Paun, A., Herman, K. C., Delgado-Romero, E., van den Berg, J. J., & Jones, J. D. (2007). The role of counseling psychologists in reducing health disparities. *The Counseling Psychologist, 35,* 650–678. doi:10.1177/0011000007301687

Umemoto, K., Baker, C. K., Helm, S., Miao, T., Goebert, D. A., & Hishinuma, E. S. (2009). Moving toward comprehensiveness and sustainability in a social ecological approach to youth violence prevention: Lessons from the Asian/Pacific Islander Youth Violence Prevention Center. *American Journal of Community Psychology, 44,* 221–232. doi:10.1007/s10464-009-9271-7

University of Minnesota. (2007, November 16). Report on health and habits of college students released. *ScienceDaily.* Retrieved from http://www.sciencedaily.com/releases/2007/11/071115125827.htm

Upshur, C., & Barreto-Cortez, E. (1995). What is participatory evaluation? What are its roots? *The Evaluation Exchange, 1,* 7–9.

U.S. Department of Education, National Center for Education Statistics. (2012). *Table 126. Number and percentage of 9th- to 12th-graders who dropped out of public schools, by race/ethnicity, grade, and state or jurisdiction: 2009–10.* Retrieved from http://nces.ed.gov/programs/digest/d12/tables/dt12_126.asp

U.S. Department of Health and Human Services. (1999). *Mental health: A report of the Surgeon General.* Rockville, MD: National Institute of Mental Health.

U.S. Department of Health and Human Services. (2001). *Mental health: Culture, race, and ethnicity—A supplement to mental health: A report of the Surgeon General.* Rockville, MD: National Institute of Mental Health.

U.S. Department of Health and Human Services. (2003a). *The power of prevention: Reducing the health and economic burdens of chronic disease.* Atlanta, GA: Centers for Disease Control and Prevention, National Center for Chronic Disease Prevention and Health Promotion.

U.S. Department of Health and Human Services. (2003b). *Prevention makes common "cents."* Retrieved from http://aspe.hhs.gov/health/prevention/prevention.pdf

U.S. Department of Health and Human Services. (2010a). *Head Start impact study: Final report.* Washington, DC: Administration for Children and Families Office of Planning, Research and Evaluation.

U.S. Department of Health and Human Services. (2010b). *Healthy People 2020*. Washington, DC: Author. Retrieved from http://www.cdc.gov/nchs/healthy_people/hp2020.htm

U.S. Department of Health and Human Services. (2011). *History and development of Healthy People*. Retrieved from http://www.healthypeople.gov/2020/about/history.aspx

U.S. Department of Health and Human Services. (2012). *Preventing tobacco use among youth and young adults: A report of the Surgeon General*. Rockville, MD: Public Health Service, Office of the Surgeon General.

U.S. Department of Health and Human Services. (2014). *The health consequences of smoking: 50 years of progress. A report of the Surgeon General*. Atlanta, GA: Centers of Disease Control and Prevention, National Center for Chronic Disease and Health Promotion, Office of Smoking and Health. Retrieved from http://www.surgeongeneral.gov/library/reports/50-years-of-progress/index.html

U.S. Public Health Service. (1964). *Smoking and health: Report of the Advisory Committee to the Surgeon General of the Public Health Service* (PHS Publication No. 1103). Atlanta, GA: U.S. Department of Health, Education, and Welfare, Public Health Service, Centers for Disease Control.

Vacha-Haase, T. (2012). Clinical practice with older adults. In N. A. Fouad, J. A. Carter, & L. M. Subich (Eds.), *APA handbook of counseling psychology* (Vol. 2, pp. 497–513). Washington, DC: American Psychological Association.

Valentine, A. D., & Meyers, C. A. (2001). Cognitive and mood disturbance as causes and symptoms of fatigue in cancer patients. *Cancer, 92,* 1694–1698. doi:10.1002/1097-0142(20010915)92:6+<1694:AID-CNCR1499>3.0.CO;2-S

Van Sluijs, E. M. F., Van Poppel, M. N. M., & Van Mechelen, W. (2004). Stage-based lifestyle interventions in primary care: Are they effective? *American Journal of Preventive Medicine, 26,* 330–343. doi:10.1016/j.amepre.2003.12.010

Vera, E. M., Caldwell, J., Clarke, M., Gonzales, R., Morgan, M., & West, M. (2007). The Choices Program: Multisystemic interventions for enhancing the personal and academic effectiveness of urban adolescents of color. *The Counseling Psychologist, 35,* 779–796. doi:10.1177/0011000007304590

Vera, E. M., & Kenny, M. E. (2013). *Social justice and culturally relevant prevention*. Thousand Oaks, CA: Sage.

Vera, E. M., & Shin, R. Q. (2006). Promoting strengths in a socially toxic world: Supporting resiliency with systematic interventions. *The Counseling Psychologist, 34,* 80–89. doi:10.1177/0011000005282365

Vera, E. M., & Speight, S. L. (2003). Multicultural competence, social justice, and counseling psychology: Expanding our roles. *The Counseling Psychologist, 31,* 253–272. doi:10.1177/0011000003031003001

Vincus, A. A., Ringwalt, C., Harris, M. S., & Shamblen, S. R. (2010). A short-term, quasi-experimental evaluation of D.A.R.E.'s revised elementary school curriculum. *Journal of Drug Education, 40,* 37–49. doi:10.2190/DE.40.1.c

Viner, R. M., Ozer, E. M., Denny, S., Marmot, M., Resnick, M., Fatusi, A., & Currie, C. (2012, April). Adolescence and the social determinants of health. *The Lancet, 379*, 1641–1652.

Violence Against Women Reauthorization Act of 2013, Pub. L. No. 113-114, 127 Stat. 54 (2013).

Waern, M., Rubenowitz, E., & Wilhelmson, K. (2003). Predictors of suicide in the old elderly. *Gerontology, 49*, 328–334. doi:10.1159/000071715

Waldo, M., Kaczmarek, M., & Romano, J. L. (2004, August). Ethical dilemmas in prevention in prevention research and practice. In S. Hage & J. Schwartz (Co-Chairs), *Ethics of prevention: Diverse perspectives within counseling psychology.* Symposium conducted at the meeting of the American Psychological Association, Honolulu, HI.

Webster-Stratton, C., & Reid, M. J. (2003). The Incredible Years parents, teachers and child training series: A multifaceted treatment approach for young children with conduct problems. In A. E. Kazdin & J. R. Weisz (Eds.), *Evidence-based psychotherapies for children and adolescents* (pp. 224–240). New York, NY: Guilford Press.

Webster-Stratton, C., Reid, M. J., & Hammond, M. (2001). Preventing conduct problems, promoting social competence: A parent and teacher training partnership in Head Start. *Journal of Clinical Child Psychology, 30*, 283–302. doi:10.1207/S15374424JCCP3003_2

Webster-Stratton, C., Rinaldi, J., & Reid, J. M. (2011). Long-term outcomes of Incredible Years parenting program: Predictors of adolescent adjustment. *Child and Adolescent Mental Health, 16*, 38–46. doi:10.1111/j.1475-3588.2010.00576.x

Weinstein, N. D. (1993). Testing four competing theories of health-protective behavior. *Health Psychology, 12*, 324–333. doi:10.1037/0278-6133.12.4.324

Weinstein, N. D., Rothman, A. J., & Sutton, S. R. (1998). Stage theories of health behavior: Conceptual and methodological issues. *Health Psychology, 17*, 290–299. doi:10.1037/0278-6133.17.3.290

Welsh, B. C., & Farrington, D. P. (2000). Correctional intervention programs and cost-benefit analysis. *Criminal Justice and Behavior, 27*, 115–133. doi:10.1177/0093854800027001007

Wenzel, L. B., Donnelly, J. P., Fowler, J. M., Habbal, R., Taylor, T. H., Aziz, N., & Cella, D. (2002). Resilience, reflection, and residual stress in ovarian cancer survivorship: A gynecological oncology group study. *Psycho-Oncology, 11*, 142–153. doi:10.1002/pon.567

Werch, C. E., Moore, M. J., Bian, H., DiClemente, C. C., Ames, S. C., Weiler, R. M., . . . Pokorny, S. B. (2008). Efficacy of a brief image-based multibehavior intervention for college students. *Annals of Behavioral Medicine, 36*, 149–157. doi:10.1007/s12160-008-9055-6.

Werner, E. E., Bierman, J. M., & French, F. E. (1971). *The children of Kauai Honolulu.* Honolulu: University of Hawaii Press.

West, S. L., & Graham, C. W. (2005). A survey of substance abuse prevention efforts at Virginia's colleges and universities. *Journal of American College Health, 54,* 185–191. doi:10.3200/JACH.54.3.185-192

Westefeld, J. S., Homaifar, B., Spotts, J., Furr, S., Range, L., & Werth, J. L. (2005). Perceptions concerning college student suicide: Data from four universities. *Suicide and Life Threatening Behavior, 35,* 640–645. doi:10.1521/suli.2005.35.6.640

Wetherby, A. M., Brosnan-Maddox, S., Peace, V., & Newton, L. (2008). Validation of disorders from 9 to 24 months of age. *Autism: The International Journal of Research and Practise, 12,* 487–511. doi:10.1177/1362361308094501

Williams, S. L., DiMatteo, M. R., & Haskard, K. B. (2009). Psychosocial barriers to adherence and lifestyle change. In S. A. Shumaker, J. K. Ockene, & K. A. Riekert (Eds.), *The handbook of health behavior change* (3rd ed., pp. 445–461). New York, NY: Springer.

World Health Organization. (2013, July). *Questions and answers on electronic cigarettes or electronic nicotine delivery systems (ENDS).* Retrieved from http://www.who.int/tobacco/communications/statements/electronic_cigarettes/en/index.html

Yick, A. G., & Oomen-Early, J. (2009). Using the PEN-3 model to plan culturally competent domestic violence intervention and prevention services in Chinese American and immigrant communities. *Health Education, 109,* 125–139. doi:10.1108/09654280910936585

Zak-Place, J., & Stern, M. (2004). Health belief factors and dispositional optimism as predictors of STD and HIV preventive behavior. *Journal of American College Health, 52,* 229–236. doi:10.3200/JACH.52.5.229-236

Zeldin, S. (2004). Preventing youth violence through the promotion of community engagement and membership. *Journal of Community Psychology, 32,* 623–641. doi:10.1002/jcop.20023

Zollinger, T. W., Saywell, R. M., Muegge, C. M., Wooldridge, J. S., Cummings, S. F., & Caine, V. A. (2003). Impact of the Life Skills Training curriculum on middle school students tobacco use in Marion County, Indiana 1997–2000. *The Journal of School Health, 73,* 338–346. doi:10.1111/j.1746-1561.2003.tb04190.x

INDEX

Abraham, C., 34
ACA (American Counseling Association), 18–19, 80
Academic achievement, 43, 70–71
Action stage (transtheoretical model), 26
Active consent, 147
Addams, Jane, 19–20
Addictive behaviors, 24–25, 41–42
Adler, Alfred, 13
Administration for Community Living, 112
Adolescent problem behavior, 51–52
Adolescents. *See* Youth
Adolescents Training and Learning to Avoid Steroids (ATLAS), 98–99
Advisory groups, 132
Affordable Health Care Act of 2010, 69, 79–80, 151, 154–155
African American youth, 56–57
Aggressive behaviors, 91–92, 94
Ajzen, I., 30–32, 34
Albarracín, B., 32
Albee, George, 59–60, 67–72
Alcohol use and abuse
    ATLAS to prevent, 98–99
    CCAA to prevent, 100–101
    LST to prevent, 93–94
    MI interventions to reduce college, 43
    Project Northland to prevent, 92–93
Alexopoulos, G. S., 113, 125
American Counseling Association (ACA), 18–19, 80
American Indians. *See* Native Americans
American Journal of Community Psychology, 18
American Journal of Prevention Medicine, 52
American Psychiatric Association, 80
American Psychological Association (APA)
    Division 17 of, 13, 19
    Division 27 of, 18
    prevention guidelines by, 8, 131, 144, 161
    on public policy, 80

on resilience in minority youth, 56
    and social justice, 65–66
American Psychologist, 60
American School Counseling Association (ASCA), 19
Americans With Disabilities Act of 1990, 17
Anxiety
    and cancer, 117
    studies on, reviewed, 110–112
    and suicide, 96
APA. *See* American Psychological Association
APA Task Force on Resilience and Strength in Black Children and Adolescents report, 56–57
Arensman, E., 113
Armitage, C. J., 29, 32, 34
ASCA (American School Counseling Association), 19
ASD (autism spectrum disorders), 123–124
ATLAS (Adolescents Training and Learning to Avoid Steroids), 98–99
Attitudes, 30–32
Autism spectrum disorders (ASD), 123–124

Badr, H., 117, 118
Baker, S. B., 84
Bandura, A., 28, 41
Baptiste, D., 138–140
Barnett, E., 42
BBBF (Better Beginnings, Better Futures) program, 108–110
Becker, L. G., 54
Becker, M. H., 36, 37, 39
Beers, Clifford, 12–13
Behavioral change, 25, 140
Behaviors
    addictive, 24–25, 41–42
    adolescent problem, 51–52
    aggressive, 91–92, 94
    lifestyle, 120–121, 140

The Belmont Report (National Commission for the Protection of Human Subjects of Biomedical and Behavioral Research), 144
Berg, R. C., 42
Bernat, D. H., 52
Better Beginnings, Better Futures (BBBF) program, 108–110
Biological factors, 49
Blueprints for Healthy Youth Development, 169
Bodenlos, J. S., 121–122
Boekeloo, B. O., 145
Borba, C., 23
Boston College, 149–150
Botvin, G. J., 94
Bravo, J. M., 33
Breast cancer, 117–119
Breeding Better Vermonters (Gallagher), 14
Bridle, C., 29
Brown, G. K., 114
Bruce, M. L., 125
Brunwasser, S. M., 103
Buffering protective factors, 49
Burke, B. L., 42
Bush, George W., 17

Caldwell, R., 120
The Campbell Collaboration, 169
Campus prevention programs. *See* Postsecondary school prevention interventions
Cancer
    depression and anxiety with, 116–117
    gynecological, and sexual functioning, 120
    studies of patients with breast, 117–120
Canetto, S. S., 69
Caplan, G., 5–7
Cardiovascular disease, 153
Care, Assess, Respond, Empower (CARE), 95–96
Caregivers, 52
Carmack, C. L., 117
Case management approach, 125
Caskey, J. D., 145
CAST (Coping and Support Training), 95–96

Catalano, R. F., 54
Causal factors, 12
CBPR (community-based participatory research), 146
CBT (cognitive behavioral therapy), 44, 119
CBTH (cognitive behavioral therapy and hypnosis), 119–120
CD (conduct disorder), 91–92
Centers for Disease Control and Prevention (CDC), 14–15, 103, 152–153, 164–165
Challenging College Alcohol Abuse (CCAA), 100–101
CHAMP (Collaborative HIV/AIDS Adolescent Mental Health Project), 138–140
Champion, V. L., 40
Change
    processes of, in transtheoretical model, 27–28
    stages of, in transtheoretical model, 25–27
Character Strengths and Virtues (CSV) classification, 60
Charity Organization Societies, 20
CHD (coronary heart disease), 120–121
Chiauzzi, E., 43
Child–Parent Centers, 154
Children. *See* Youth
Children, Youth, and Families Education and Research Network, 167
Children First, 62–63
Child Trends, 169
Choosing a Vocation (Parsons), 13
Christensen, H., 110, 111
Civil Rights Act of 1964, 17, 78
Civil rights movement, 17
Clifton, Donald, 61
Clifton StrengthsFinder classification, 61–62
Clinical trials, 144
Cognitive behavioral approaches, 111, 116–117
Cognitive behavioral skills, 101
Cognitive behavioral therapy (CBT), 44, 119
Cognitive behavioral therapy and hypnosis (CBTH), 119–120

Cognitive development, 57
Coie, J. D., 50
Colby, S. M., 42–43
Collaborative HIV/AIDS Adolescent Mental Health Project (CHAMP), 138–140
Collective wellness, 72–73
College prevention programs. *See* Post-secondary school prevention interventions
Colleges. *See also specific institutions*
   prevention interventions designed for, 85–87
   and suicide prevention, 103–104
   transferring prevention interventions to community settings from, 138–140
Committee on Prevention of Mental Disorders, 6
Committee on the Prevention of Mental Disorders and Substance Abuse Among Children, Youth, and Young Adults, 7, 48
Communicable Disease Center, 14
Communication and Symbolic Behavior Scales Developmental Profile Infant–Toddler Checklist, 124
Communities, assessing needs of, 133
Communities That Care (CTC), 137–138
Community Anti-Drug Coalitions of America, 167–168
Community-based participatory research (CBPR), 146
Community-based prevention interventions
   cost-effectiveness of, 153
   for older adults, 112–114
   for youth, 110–112
Community Mental Health Act of 1963, 17
Community protective factors, 50, 133
Community psychology, 18
Community settings, 107–114
   BBBF program, 108–110
   community-based prevention for older adults in, 112–114
   community-based prevention for youth in, 110–112

resources for, 127–128
   transferring prevention interventions from university to, 138–140
Community Youth Development Study, 137
Competence, 70–71, 89
Condom use, 34
Conduct disorder (CD), 91–92
Conference on Primary Prevention of Psychopathology, 18
Confidentiality, 145
Connor, M., 32
Consciousness raising (as process of change), 27
Contemplation stage (transtheoretical model), 26
Contingency management (as process of change), 27
Conyne, R. K., 6, 149
Coping, 117–118
Coping and Support Training (CAST), 95–96
Coronary heart disease (CHD), 120–121
Costa, F. M., 51
Cost-effectiveness
   of community-based prevention, 153
   of prevention, 152–154
   of school-based prevention, 153–154
   of workplace health promotion programs, 153
Council for Accreditation of Counseling and Related Educational Programs, 151
Counseling, prevention in, 18–19
The Counseling Psychologist, 60
Counter-conditioning (as process of change), 27
Cowen, E. L., 5
Crisis intervention model, 68, 148
Cristofanilli, M., 117
Csikszentmihalyi, M., 59–60
CSV (Character Strengths and Virtues) classification, 60
CTC (Communities That Care), 137–138
Cues to action (health belief model), 36
Cugelman, B., 126

D.A.R.E. (Drug Abuse Resistance Education), 79
Data collection, 136, 160
Dawes, P., 126
Dayton, R., 103
De Castro, S., 103
Decisional balance construct (transtheoretical model), 28
Decision-making stage (transtheoretical model), 26
Depression
    comorbid with serious medical conditions, 116–117
    in older adulthood, 55–56
    and older adults, 125–126
    prevention of, in older adults, 113–114
    PRTCS as prevention intervention for, 101–103
    studies on, reviewed, 110–112
    and suicide, 96
DeRubeis, R. J., 102
Developmental assets, 62–63
Developmental disorders, 124
Developmental–ecological framework, 91
Developmental stage, 55, 145
Developmental theory, 89
Diabetes mellitus, 123, 153
Diabetes Prevention Program (DPP), 122–123
DiClemente, C. C., 24, 26
Difference principle, 67
Diffusion of innovations theory (DIT), 121–123
Direct protective factors, 49
Discrepancy, in motivational interviewing, 41
Distress, psychological, 120–121
Distributive justice, 67
DIT (diffusion of innovations theory), 121–123
Division 17 (of APA), 13, 19
Division 27 (of APA), 18
DPP (Diabetes Prevention Program), 122–123
Dramatic relief (as process of change), 27
Dray, J., 44

Drug Abuse Resistance Education (D.A.R.E.), 79
Durlak, J. A., 84
Dyadic coping, 117–118
Dyadic stress, 117

Early Risers program, 91–92
Earned Income tax credit, 79
Eating disorders, 44
Economics, of prevention interventions, 151–155
Eddy, J. M., 148
Education
    in motivational interviewing, 45
    on prevention, 148–152
    of psychologists, prevention in, 21
Educational settings, 83–105
    elementary school prevention interventions, 89–92
    high school prevention interventions, 95–99
    history of prevention in, 84–87
    middle school prevention interventions, 92–94
    postsecondary school prevention interventions, 99–104
    preschool prevention interventions, 87–88
Eggert, L. L., 95, 96
Electronic data collection, 160
Elementary school prevention interventions, 89–92
Elicitation research
    to address ethical issues, 146–147
    and ethnicity, 33, 34
    in TRA and TPB, 33
Elliott, T. R., 149
Emotional development, 57
Empathy, in motivational interviewing, 41
Environmental factors
    as ethical issue, 146
    as protective factors, 50, 58
    and psychopathology, 68
    as stress, 70
    and substance use, 55
Environmental reevaluation (as process of change), 27
Equality, legislation promoting, 17

"Ethical Principles of Psychologists and Code of Conduct" (APA), 144
Ethics, prevention, 143–147
Ethnicity
    educational and health disparities related to, 69
    and elicitation research, 33, 34
    ethical issues related to, 146–147
    and identification of protective/risk factors, 53
    and resilience in youth and young adults, 56
    in ZLSD, 96–97
Eugenics movement, 13–14
Evaluation
    conducting, of prevention interventions, 136–137
    importance of improving, 160
    selecting criteria for, of prevention interventions, 135
Exploitation, 70
External assets, 62

Fagan, A. A., 137, 138
Family considerations, 49, 96
Farrington, D. P., 49, 50
Fatigue, 119–120
Federal Interagency Forum on Child and Family Statistics, 167
Finn, A., 145–146
Fishbein, M., 30–32, 34
Flores, E., 57
Focus on Prevention (SAMHSA), 127–128, 133–135
Fogarty, C. T., 115
Frameworks, for prevention interventions, 135
Fritz, M. S., 99
Funding, prevention, 152

Gallagher, N. L., 14
Garbarino, J., 58
Garrett Lee Smith Memorial Act of 2004, 79, 99
Gitkind, M., 121–122
Glanz, K., 23
Glider, P., 101
Goetzel, R. Z., 153
Goldstein, M., 43
Goodheart, Carol, 115

Gordon, R., 5–7
Gorman-Smith, D., 53
Graham, C. W., 101
Green, L. W., 36
Green, T. C., 43
"Guidelines for Prevention in Psychology" (APA), 8, 131–132, 161
Guide to Analyzing the Cost-Effectiveness of Community Public Health Prevention Approaches (U.S. Department of Health and Human Services), 154
Gullotta, Tom, 18
Gun control, 79–80

Habilitative Systems Incorporated (HSI), 139
Hage, S. M., 7, 66, 148
Haggerty, R. J., 13
Hamburger, E. K., 145
Harrison, J. A., 36–37, 39
Hawkins, J. D., 54
HBM. *See* Health belief model
Head Start program, 17, 78–79
Health-based prevention interventions, for youth, 127
Health belief model (HBM), 35–40
    cues to action in, 36
    and social cognitive theory, 36–38
    strengths and limitations of, 38–40
Health disparities, 15–16
Health information technology, 160
Health promotion
    motivational interviewing and, 44
    for older adults, 113
    in workplace programs, 153
Health reform, 159
Healthy People (Surgeon General's Office), 15–16
Helping relationships (as process of change), 27–28
Henry, D. B., 53
Hermann, M. A., 145–146
Herting, J. R., 96
Herzog, T. A., 29
High school prevention interventions, 95–99
The High School Questionnaire (HSQ), 96

HighScope, 88
HIV prevention programs, 33–34
Hollon, S. D., 102
Hopelessness
    decreased, in ZLSD, 97
    and suicide, 96
Hopko, D. R., 116
Howard, D. E., 145
Howard-Pitney, B., 97
HSI (Habilitative Systems Incorporated), 139
HSQ (The High School Questionnaire), 96
Huber, A. M., 54
Humphries, M. L., 87–88
Hurst, J. C., 85
Hynes, M., 23
Hypnosis, 119

Identity development, 57
Incredible Years, 89–91
Indicated prevention
    defined, 6
    ethical issues in, 147
    and transtheoretical model, 30
Individual characteristics, 50
Individuals with Disabilities Act of 2004, 79
Informed consent, 147
InShape, 100
Institute of Medicine, 6, 7, 48
Insurance companies, 151, 154–155
Interagency Working Group on Youth Programs, 167
Internal assets, 62
Internet public health campaigns, 126–127

Janz, N. K., 36, 37, 39
Jessor, R., 51
Johnson, B. T., 32
Johnson, Lyndon B., 17, 78
Johnson, S., 24
Johnson, S. B., 115
Journal of Clinical Psychology, 149
Journal of Community Psychology, 18
Journal of Primary Prevention, 18, 72, 74
Journal of Social and Clinical Psychology, 60
Juniper, K. C., 38

Jurkovic, G. J., 146
Just society, 67

Kantor, L., 121–122
Kashy, D. A., 117
Kasprzyk, D., 32, 34
Katsikas, S., 33
Keenan, K. E., 87–88
Kendall, M. A., 74
Kennedy, John F., 17
Kenny, M. E., 11, 66, 75–76
Koocher, G. P., 151
Korean Americans, 58
Kraaij, V., 113

LaFromboise, T., 97
Latino youth
    ethical issues related to, 146
    high school retention rate of, 75–76
    HIV prevention program for, 33–34
    resilience in, 57–58
Lead Contamination Control Act of 1988, 79
Lee, P., 24
Lee, R. M., 58
Legislation, 17. See also specific acts
Life Skills Training (LST), 93–94
Lifestyle behaviors, 120–121, 140
Linehan, E., 44
Long, B. B., 12
Lopez, S. J., 59, 61
Lord, S, 43
Lösel, F., 49, 50
Lothen-Kline, C., 145
LST (Life Skills Training), 93–94
Lundahl, B., 42

Ma, Y., 121–122
Maintenance stage (transtheoretical model), 26–27
Martins, R. K., 44
Mays, D., 23
Mazza, J. J., 96
McDaniel, S. H., 115
McIntosh, J. M., 75
McNeil, D. W., 44
Medical costs, 152–153
Medical model, 68–69

Medical settings, 114–127
    depressed geriatric patients, 125–126
    and DIT, 121–123
    health-based prevention for youth,
        127
    importance of prevention in,
        114–116
    opportunities in, 128–129
    prevention interventions for, 140–141
    prevention interventions with
        medically referred patients,
        116–121
    public health campaigns, 126–127
    screening for ASD, 123–124
Medicare and Medicaid program, 79
Mental health, 16
Mental Health America, 12
Mental health disorders, 69–70
Mental Health Manpower Trends
    (Albee), 67
Mental Health Parity Act of 1996, 17
Mental Health Parity and Addiction
    Equity Act of 2008, 17, 79
Mental health professionals
    and cost of prevention interventions,
        154–155
    in medical settings, 115–116,
        128–129, 140–141
    prevention in education of, 21
    referrals to, 141
Mental health promotion, 12, 16
Mental Hygiene (journal), 12
Mental hygiene movement, 12–13
Mental illness, 16
Meyer, Adolf, 13
MI. *See* Motivational interviewing
Middle school prevention interven-
    tions, 92–94
Military families, supports for, 159
Miller, A. M., 40
Miller, J. Y., 54
Miller, W. R., 40, 41
Mills, G., 103
Millstein, S. G., 115
A Mind That Found Itself (Beers), 12
Minority young adults, 56–58
Mishara, B. L., 146
Monitoring the Future, 168
Montaño, D. E., 32, 34

Montgomery, G. H., 119
Moody, K., 95
Morrill, W. H., 85
Mosher, R. L., 84
Motivational interviewing (MI), 40–45
    in InShape, 100
    research on, 41–44
    strengths and limitations of, 44–45
Mrazek, P. J., 13
Muellerleile, P. A., 32
Mullen, P. D., 36
Multiculturalism
    and health belief model, 38–39
    and social justice, 74–76
Murphy, C., 44
Murphy, J. G., 43
Murray, C. E., 146
Musser, P., 44

National Asian Pacific American Fami-
    lies Against Substance Abuse, 168
National Association of Social Work-
    ers, 80
National Center for Education Statis-
    tics, 69
National Center on Addiction and Sub-
    stance Abuse, 168
National Commission for the Protection
    of Human Subjects of Biomedical
    and Behavioral Research, 144
National Committee for Mental
    Hygiene, 12–13
National Communicable Disease
    Center, 14
National Institute of Mental Health
    (NIMH), 14, 113
National Institutes of Health (NIH),
    165–166
National Latino Tobacco Control
    Network, 168
National Longitudinal Study of Adoles-
    cent Health, 52
National Mental Health Act of 1946, 14
National Prevention Conference, 50
National Prevention Council, 152
National Prevention Strategy, 8, 9, 80
National Registry of Evidence Based
    Programs and Practices (NREPP),
    87, 133

National Research Council, 7, 48
National Vocational Guidance Association, 13
Native Americans, 97, 146
Needs assessments, 133
Netherlands, 116
Netland, J. D., 33, 34
Newman, F. L., 103
NIH (National Institutes of Health), 165–166
NIMH (National Institute of Mental Health), 14, 113
Norcross, J. C., 24, 26
NREPP (National Registry of Evidence Based Programs and Practices), 87, 133

Oakes, J. M., 52
Obesity, 153
O'Connor, R. C., 34
ODD (oppositional defiant disorder), 91–92
Oetting, E. R., 85
Office of Juvenile Justice and Delinquency Prevention (OJJDP), 166
Office of National Drug Control Policy (ONDCP), 167
OJJDP (Office of Juvenile Justice and Delinquency Prevention), 166
Older adulthood
    community-based prevention for, 112–114
    and depression, 125–126
    prevention interventions for, 80
    protective factors for depression in, 55–56
ONDCP (Office of National Drug Control Policy), 167
Online prevention training, 152
Online public health campaigns, 126–127
Oppositional defiant disorder (ODD), 91–92
Organic factors, 70
Organizations, as resources, 134, 135, 167–170
Ornish, D., 120
Ou, S., 154
Ozminkowski, R. J., 153

Pagoto, S. L., 121–122
Painter, J. E., 23
Parent training
    in Incredible Years, 90
    intentions to participate in, 37–38
Park, N., 59, 60–61
Parsons, Frank, 13
Partnership at Drugfree.org, 168
Partner violence, 44
Pasco, S., 103
Passive consent, 147
Patient-Centered Medical Home (PCMH), 115–116
Patient Protection and Affordable Care Act of 2010, 8, 69, 79, 80, 151, 154–155
PCMH (Patient-Centered Medical Home), 115–116
Pearson, J. L., 114
Pediatricians, 124
Peer relationships, 49–50
Penn Resilience Training for College Students (PRTCS), 101–103
Perceived barriers (health belief model), 35, 37
Perceived behavioral control (PCB), 31–32
Perceived benefits (health belief model), 35
Perceived severity (health belief model), 35, 37
Perceived susceptibility (health belief model), 35
Perceived threat (health belief model), 35
Perry, C. L., 93
Personality characteristics, 49
Person-centered theory, 40
Peters, R. D., 108
Peterson, C., 59–61
Pettingell, S. L., 52
Physical health
    and development, for African American youth, 57
    and health belief model, 37
    integration of, with mental health, 16, 115–116
    and motivational interviewing for behavior change, 42

prevention classifications designed for, 6–7
problems, comorbidity with depression, 116–117
promotion of, by InShape, 100
Pierce, K., 123–124
Pike, K. C., 95
Pischke, C. R., 120, 121
Pope, K. S., 144
Positive psychology, 59–63
Postsecondary school prevention interventions, 99–104
Praxis, in collective wellness, 73
Precontemplation stage (transtheoretical model), 25–26
Preparation stage (transtheoretical model), 26
Preschool prevention interventions, 87–88
Preventing Mental, Emotional, and Behavioral Disorders Among Young People (National Research Council and Institute of Medicine), 48
Prevention
    defined, 5–8
    in medical settings, 114–116
    in psychologists' education, 21
Prevention classifications, 5–7
Prevention ethics, 143–147
Prevention funding, 152–155
Prevention Guidelines (APA), 8, 10, 131, 144, 161
Prevention history, 11–22
    in early 20th century, 12–14
    in educational settings, 84–87
    in mid- to late 20th century, 17–20
    prevention theories in, 20–21
    U.S. government's role in, 14–17
Prevention interventions, 131–142. *See also specific types*
    considering multiculturalism in, 74–75
    developing, 132–135
    evaluating, 136–137
    fidelity of, 137–138
    implementing, 136
    with medically referred patients, 116–121
    for medical settings, 140–141

provision for, in Patient Protection and Affordable Care Act, 80
targeted, with elicitation research, 33
transferring, from university to community settings, 138–140
transtheoretical model as framework for, 29
"Prevention Makes Common 'Cents'" (U.S. Department of Health and Human Services), 153
Prevention model, 68–69
Prevention of Suicide in Primary Care Elderly: Collaborative Trial (PROSPECT), 125
Prevention Partners, 169
Prevention psychology, 4, 157–160
Prevention resources, 163–170
    accessing, during development of prevention intervention, 133–135
    for community settings, 127–128
    private organizations, 167–170
    U.S. government resources, 163–167
Prevention Science (journal), 20
Prevention specialists
    collaboration with, 151
    national priorities tracked by, 159
    role of, in prevention interventions, 133–137
Prevention theories, 23–45
    health belief model (HBM), 35–40
    motivational interviewing (MI), 40–45
    role of, in history of prevention, 20–21
    theory of planned behavior (TPB), 31–34
    theory of reasoned action (TRA), 30–34
    transtheoretical model (TTM), 24–30
Prilleltensky, Isaac, 72–73
Primary prevention, 5
Prochaska, J. O., 24–29
Project CHARM, 33–34
Project Northland, 92–93
Promising Practices Network on Children Families and Communities, 170
PROSPECT (Prevention of Suicide in Primary Care Elderly: Collaborative Trial), 125

Protective factors, 47–63
    in adolescent problem behavior,
        51–52
    buffering, 49
    community, 50, 133
    defined by Committee on the Pre-
        vention of Mental Disorders
        and Substance Abuse Among
        Children, Youth, and Young
        Adults, 48
    for depression in older adulthood,
        55–56
    direct, 49
    enhancing systemic, 58
    and positive psychology, 59–63
    promoting, in schools, 53–54
    resilience as, 56–58
    and risk factors, 48–55
    for substance use in adolescence and
        young adulthood, 54–55
    for youth violence, 52–53
PRTCS (Penn Resilience Training for
    College Students), 101–103
Psychoeducational interventions, 55
Psychological distress, 120–121
Psychological interventions, 55
Psychologist(s). See Mental health
    professionals
Psychopathology, 68
Psychopharmaceutical interventions, 55
Public health approach, 16, 160
Public health campaigns, 126–127
Public Interest Directorate (APA), 80
Public policy advocacy
    economic feasibility of policies, 77
    as prevention, 7–8
    and social justice, 77–81
    as systemic protective factors, 58

Quigley, D., 146

Racial equality, 17
Radiation therapy, 119
Ramirez, A., 33
Randell, B. P., 95, 96
Rawls, John, 67
Recovery support, 159
Redmond, C., 37, 38
Reese, L. E., 74

Relaxation training, 43
Research Triangle Institute Interna-
    tional, 154
Resilience, as protective factor, 56–58
Resistance, in motivational interview-
    ing, 41
Resnick, M., 52
Revenson, T. A., 117
Reyner, J., 44
Reynolds, A. J., 154
Reynolds, C. F., 55
Richmond, Mary, 20
Rickel, A. U., 18
Ripple, C. H., 79
Risk factors
    in adolescent problem behavior,
        51–52
    defined by Committee on the Pre-
        vention of Mental Disorders
        and Substance Abuse Among
        Children, Youth, and Young
        Adults, 48
    and protective factors, 48–55
    for substance use in adolescence and
        young adulthood, 54–55
    for youth violence, 52–53
Robertson, D. L., 154
Rogers, C. R., 40
Rohrbach, L. A., 42
Rollnick, S., 40, 41
Romano, J. L., 7, 11, 33, 34, 53, 148
Rosenstock, I. M., 36
Rosenthal, M. S., 153
Rosenthal, S. L., 145
Ross, M. W., 42

SAMHSA. See Substance Abuse
    and Mental Health Services
    Administration
Sari, N., 103
Sartin, R. M., 103
Scherer, J., 153
Scherwitz, L., 120
Schoeny, M. E., 53
School-based prevention interventions
    continuing efficacy of, 79
    cost-effectiveness of, 153–154
    ethical issues with, 147
    lack of consistency in, 84–85

School dropout prevention
 interventions
 and social justice, 74
 and suicide prevention programs, 95
Schools
 promoting protective factors in,
  53–54
 as protective or risk factors, 49
Schulman, P., 102
Schwartz, J. P., 144
Schweinhart, J. L., 88
SCRA (Society for Community Research
  and Action)—Community
  Psychology, 65–66
SCT (social cognitive theory), 36–38
Seal, K. H., 43
Search Institute, 62–63, 133
Search Institute Developmental Assets,
  62–63
Secondary prevention, 5
Selective prevention
 defined, 6
 ethical issues in, 147
 and transtheoretical model, 30
Self-efficacy
 in health belief model, 36
 in motivational interviewing, 41
 in transtheoretical model, 28
Self-esteem, 71
Self-liberation (as process of change),
  27
Self-reevaluation (as process of change),
  27
Self-report measures, 93
Seligman, M. E. P., 59–61, 102
Settlement Movement, 19–20
Sexual functioning, 120
SFAS (substance-free activity session),
  43
Shaw, M. C., 84
Sheeran, P., 34
Shin, R. Q., 58, 74
Smith, C., 42
Smoking
 attitudes and social norms about,
  31
 cessation of, and transtheoretical
  model, 24
 LST to prevent, 93–94

motivational interviewing interven-
  tion for cessation of, 42–43
national cost of, 152
public policies on, 77–78
Surgeon General's report on, 15
Snyder, C. R., 59, 61, 149
Social cognitive theory (SCT), 36–38
Social development, 57
Social development model, 52
Social justice, 65–82
 George Albee's work in, 67–72
 and multiculturalism, 74–76
 as prevention, 7–8
 Isaac Prilleltensky's work in, 72–73
 and public policy advocacy, 77–81
 John Rawls' work in, 67
Social liberation (as process of change),
  27
Social norms, 31, 32
Social toxins, 58
Social work, 19–20
Society for Community Research and
  Action (SCRA)—Community
  Psychology, 65–66
Society for Prevention Research (SPR),
  20
Society for Community Research and
  Action (Division 27 of APA), 18
Society of Counseling Psychology (Divi-
  sion 17 of APA), 13, 19, 68
Spinhoven, P., 113
Spoth, R., 37, 38
SPR (Society for Prevention Research),
  20
Sprinthall, N. A., 84
Spruijt-Metz, D., 42
Steen, T. A., 59
Stern, M., 36
Steroids, 98–99
Stetson, B. A., 123
Stigma, 16–17
Stimulus control (as process of change),
  27
STM (systemic-transactional model),
  117–118
Stone, A. L., 54
Strait, G. G., 43
Strecher, V. J., 36
Strength-based psychology, 61

Strengthening Families Program, 94

Stress
as causal factor for mental illness, 12
dyadic, 117
and mental health disorders, 70

Stroke, 153

Student well-being (SWB), 53

Subjective norms, 31, 32

Substance Abuse and Mental Health Services Administration (SAMHSA),
87, 127–128, 133–135, 159–160,
163–164

Substance-free activity session (SFAS),
43

Substance use and abuse
in adolescence and young adulthood,
54–55
ATLAS to prevent, 98–99
interventions for reducing, 159
LST to prevent, 93–94
online prevention training about, 152
study on protective and risk factors
for, 51–52
and suicide, 96

Suicide
factors related to, 96
prevention of, in older adults,
113–114

Suicide prevention intervention(s)
CAST and CARE as, 95–96
and college campuses, 103–104
funding of, by Garrett Lee Smith
Memorial Act, 99–100
online prevention training about, 152
ZLSD as, 96–98

Suicide Prevention Resource Center
Best Practices Registry, 95

Support groups, 141

Support networks, 71

Surgeon General, 15–16

Sussman, S., 42

Sustainability, of prevention interventions, 135

Swampscott Conference, 18

SWB (student well-being), 53

Swisher, J. D., 153

Systemic protective factors, 58

Systemic-transactional model (STM),
117–118

Taft, C., 44

Taveras, E. M., 127

Taylor, T. K., 90

Technology
online prevention training, 152
online public health campaigns,
126–127
use of, in prevention, 160

Temple, J. A., 154

Temptation construct (transtheoretical
model), 28–29

Termination stage (transtheoretical
model), 27

Tertiary prevention, 5

Thelwall, M., 126

A Theory of Justice (Rawls), 67

Theory of planned behavior (TPB)
elicitation research on, 33
strengths and limitations of, 33–34
and TRA, 31–32

Theory of reasoned action (TRA),
30–34
attitudes and subjective norms in,
30–31
elicitation research on, 33
strengths and limitations of, 33–34
and TPB, 31–32

Thompson, D. R., 42

Thompson, E. A., 95, 96

Thum, C., 43

Tikkanen, R., 42

Title IX Education Amendments of
1972, 17

Tobacco use. See Smoking

Tolan, P. H., 53

Tovian, S. M., 114

TPB. See Theory of planned behavior

TRA. See Theory of reasoned action

Transtheoretical model (TTM), 24–30
decisional balance in, 28
and health belief model, 38
processes of change in, 27–28
self-efficacy in, 28
stages of change in, 25–27
strengths and limitations of, 29–30
temptation in, 28–29

Trauma, 159

Treatment seeking, 43–44

Trickett, E. J., 72

Troubled Journey: A Portrait of 6th–12th Grade Youth (Search Institute), 62
TTM. *See* Transtheoretical model
Turbin, M. S., 51

Universal prevention
    BBBF as, 108
    CCAA as, 100–101
    defined, 5
    ethical issues in, 147
    online public health campaigns as, 126
    suicide prevention programs as, 104
    and transtheoretical model, 29
University of Cincinnati, 149
University of Minnesota, 85, 149, 150
University of Oregon, 150
University of Wisconsin, 150
Upward Bound program, 17
U.S. Administration on Aging, 112
U.S. Department of Education, 166
U.S. Department of Education, National Center for Education Statistics, 69
U.S. Department of Health and Human Services, 16, 69, 112, 153, 154
U.S. government
    as prevention resource, 163–167
    role of, in prevention history, 14–17
U.S. Patient Protection and Affordable Health Care Act of 2010, 8, 69, 79–80
U.S. Public Health Service
    health belief model developed by, 35
    prevention addressed by, 15

"Value-based praxis," 72
Values, in collective wellness, 72–73
Values in Action Survey of Character, 61
Van Den Bos, J., 51
Vanderryn, J., 51
Van Sluijs, E. M. F., 29
Vera, E. M., 58, 74–76
VIA (Virtues in Action) classification, 60–61
VIA Inventory of Strengths, 61
Violence Against Women Reauthorization Act of 2013, 80
Virtues in Action (VIA) classification, 60–61

Vocational guidance, 13, 18–19
Vocational Guidance Bureau, 13
Volitional control, 32

Wade, T. D., 44
Wallack, C., 103
War on Poverty, 17, 78
Weidner, G., 120
Weight loss programs, 122–123
Weikart, D. P., 88
Weinstein, N. D., 39
Weisstub, D. N., 146
Wells, A. M., 84
Werch, C. E., 100
West, S. L., 101
White, B. A. B., 154
White House Conference on Child Health and Protection, 13
WHO (World Health Organization), 78, 169
Women's movement, 17
Workplace health and wellness programs, 153
World Health Organization (WHO), 78, 169
Worrell, K. D., 145

Yin, R. K., 153
Young adults, minority, 56–58
Youth
    African American, 56–57
    community-based prevention for, 110–112
    ethical issues in working with, 145
    health-based prevention for, 127
    Latino. *See* Latino youth
    minority, and resilience, 56–58
    Penn Resiliency Training used with, 103
    prevention interventions for, 80
    use of motivational interviewing with, 45
Youth violence, 52–53

Zak-Place, J., 36
Zigler, E., 79
Zuni Life Skills Development (ZLSD), 96–98
Zuni Pueblo, 96

ABOUT THE AUTHOR

John L. Romano, PhD, is a professor of educational psychology in the Counseling and Student Personnel Psychology Program at the University of Minnesota. He is also a licensed psychologist, and served two terms on the Minnesota Board of Psychology. Dr. Romano received his undergraduate, master's, and doctoral degrees from LeMoyne College (Syracuse, NY), Pennsylvania State University, and Arizona State University, respectively. He is cofounder of the Prevention Section of the American Psychological Association (APA) Society of Counseling Psychology, and he was the recipient of the Prevention Section's inaugural Lifetime Achievement Award in 2005. Dr. Romano has also been recognized for Distinguished Contributions to Counseling Psychology by the Society of Counseling Psychology (2010). He holds APA Fellow status in Divisions 17 (Society of Counseling Psychology) and 52 (International Psychology). Dr. Romano was chairperson of the work group that produced the APA *Guidelines for Prevention in Psychology*. He has been principal investigator on several U.S. Department of Education school personnel training grants to promote safe and drug-free schools. Dr. Romano has received research awards from the American Counseling Association, and he has authored numerous publications on prevention. He has served on several journal editorial boards in the United States and abroad. As a former Peace Corps volunteer, Dr. Romano has maintained an international focus throughout his career, teaching and consulting abroad, and serving as assistant vice president for international scholarship at the University of Minnesota.